THE
SECRET AGENT

INSIDE THE WORLD OF THE FOOTBALL AGENT

This edition first published in Great Britain in 2016 by
ARENA SPORT
An imprint of Birlinn Limited
West Newington House
10 Newington Road
Edinburgh
EH9 1QS

www.arenasportbooks.co.uk

ISBN: 9781909715431
eBook ISBN: 9780857908155

British Library Cataloguing-in-Publication Data
A catalogue record for this book is available on request from the
British Library.

Designed and typeset by Polaris Publishing, Edinburgh

Printed and bound by Grafica Veneta, Italy

CONTENTS

PROLOGUE

I HAVE DIVIDED my life in my mind between the before and after. The before is the time that preceded me standing, trembling, in the dock while a judge decided my future; and the after is what I did with my life with a criminal record. This is the story of the before.

I was a football agent. Once. But then there are many of us who can say that because the role, technically, no longer exists. In April 2015, FIFA decided that the best way forward for a business riddled with a cancer of underhand and unlicensed transactions across the world was to deregulate it. They handed the responsibility of supervising agents to each national association and the term 'agent' was abolished, to be replaced by 'intermediary'.

And the result? The wild bloody west. Under the new rules virtually anybody can be an intermediary. You no longer have to pass an exam to qualify to represent a footballer; all you have to do is have the literacy to complete an application form online, £500 to pay for the application and (unfortunately for me) have a clean criminal record, and there you go. That. Is. It. The world is your oyster.

But how does that all affect me now that I fail the one criteria they are firm on? I tried, of course, applying to be an intermediary on the off-chance that the FA's bureaucratic incompetence might miss my record, but no dice. And the cheeky bastards even had the temerity to hold onto my five hundred quid.

'Well fuck them,' I thought. 'I'll get that back and I'll get it back in spades.' Because what they hadn't realised was that the whole new stupid system had, in fact, made it possible for people like me (so-called outlaws in the game) to flourish and prosper.

All the pariahs of world football who had been the secret deal-makers and puppet-masters for years could now safely crawl out from their bunkers and operate in the open. Just a few years ago there were around 400 or so licensed agents operating just in England alone. Now there are over *1400* intermediaries and the number is rising all the time as the lure of money draws them in from all walks of life. And it is these guys who are now my public face. I've got my pick of all the barmen, second-hand car salesmen, ex-professional footballers, insurance salesmen, estate agents and the whole raggle taggle bunch of gypsies who want a slice of the dream that I once had. The dream that turned into a nightmare.

But I will never allow that to happen again. I've learned my lessons and now I am fully awake to what I can do – which is basically everything that the FA and everybody else in charge of football says I can't. All the things that are going to make me wealthy all over again.

But what of my life before the fall? What were the lessons that I learned? Let me enlighten you.

ONE

THE SEED

I ALWAYS KNEW I wanted to do something in football, just like I always knew I wanted to be rich. The trouble was that, as a kid, I was pretty crap on the pitch, and when you come from an East London council estate with parents who both have to work for a living, then the odds are really stacked against you.

So, ruling out being the next David Beckham, or buying my own club, that left me with fairly limited choices. I was great with stats. But Jeff Stelling had the prime job in that area all tied up, and not being blonde, female and with great tits, I couldn't see a future for myself on Sky Sports. I thought about coaching, but that was a long and rocky road, and I knew that not having played the game at the highest level, or any level at all when it came to that (other than my school class Second XI – and given that there were only twenty boys in my class that was no real achievement), I was at some disadvantage from the start.

But then I watched a programme that changed my life. Or at least made me make a life-changing decision. It was one of those fly-on-the-wall documentaries that was meant to uncover the dirt and corruption that lay beneath the world of football agents. You know the sort of thing, paying bungs to managers to make a deal happen, fitting up a rival to steal a player, lying through their teeth to parents to get the first run on looking after little Tommy and, worst of all (at least as far as the programme makers were concerned), making serious money.

Now, I know that to most people that would be a turn-off. Who wants to be a part of what seemed to be one of the most reviled groups of operators in the world? I was going to call it a profession, but clearly nobody on screen (apart from the agents protesting their innocence after having been caught fairly red-handed) actually used that word to describe the trade they plied. Yet, at twenty years of age, in my final year of a degree in media studies (well, I had to pick *something* or else face going out to work straight from school) it seemed more of an opportunity than a turn-off.

The main thing that the agents on show had in common, apart from greed and duplicity, was stupidity. They had all the contacts in the world (well, two of them were ex-pros so they ought to have) but they didn't have a brain cell between them. The fact that they'd all fallen for the TV network's sting proved it. So that was when I decided that I could do better than them.

It was an odd decision for me to make. I'd never done anything dishonest in my life, and in a way it felt like suddenly deciding to embark on a life of crime. I was never going to be one for armed robbery or even Bernie Madoff-type fraud (although I confess to having had a sneaking admiration for Bernie which was balanced by disappointment when he got caught), but the opportunity for taking on what seemed to be nothing other than a career for chancers did appeal to me. It didn't seem to be very different from what bankers and share dealers were doing, and a lot more fun.

There were, of course, some drawbacks to my plan. I didn't know any footballers personally, although I knew an awful lot about them as I obsessively compiled profiles and statistics of every single player in the UK. I had them all nailed down: from the English Premier League to the Football Conference, and taking in all the Scottish Divisions on the way. It's amazing what you can pull together using Google, YouTube, Twitter and Facebook coupled with the sports papers and magazines.

My first decision was to create a fairly inventive CV. I wasn't really looking for paid employment at one of the big accountancy or law firms, so I reckoned I was pretty safe from a close inspection and I was certain I'd impress if I could only get in front of somebody for an interview. That, in itself, was much harder than I thought it would be.

Times have changed now, of course. In those days every agent in England had to register with the Football Association (FA) who provided a list online of what they call 'Authorised Licensed Agents'. FIFA has now done away with the term 'football agent' and instead created the role of the 'intermediary'. 'And why?' you may ask. Basically FIFA decided that they couldn't be bothered to regulate agents any more and so the simplest way to deal with that was to get rid of the whole bunch of them. Not just get rid of them but get rid of their profession as well. Nothing like a bit of ethnic cleansing.

But let me digress; when I was starting out it was in the good old days of proper, dirty FA-approved football agents. I spent a whole day trawling through the names. Some I'd heard of through the media, some were part of the big agencies and others were clearly just one-man bands operating from their front rooms. It hadn't occurred to me up to that point that I'd need to pass an exam to pursue my chosen career, but there were details of the next FA Agents' Exam posted on the website together with how to get the details of the syllabus. I'd never had any problem in passing exams so I figured that wasn't much of an obstacle, but again, at that point, I didn't have a clue as to how hard the authorities might make the exam. There were a lot of things I didn't have a clue about then, but over the next five years I unravelled them all, and more. (Although I have to say that any situation involving Latvian twins born either side of midnight to parents who were South American was not a practical problem I ever had to face in real life. I kid you not, that really was one a part of one of the exam questions.)

As I wrote my letters of application or fired off emails where I could, I felt this enormous sense of excitement. I could do this, I knew it. And I'd be good at it, of that I was certain. I just needed somebody to give me a chance.

TWO

GETTING STARTED

I T WAS MUCH harder than I thought. I wrote to all the mega agencies like WMG, Stellar, SEM, First Artist and James Grant, and although for the most part I got polite letters back saying they had no vacancies at the moment but wishing me luck for the future, I never got a sniff of an interview.

The breakthrough came when one of the guys, whose name I'd read about often in the paper, actually replied to my email and offered to meet me for a coffee. If I thought I was about to be invited to one of London's exclusive members' clubs then I was disappointed because the venue was a Starbucks not far from Oxford Circus.

I recognised him immediately. I knew he was over fifty, but he looked a good ten years younger. Smart casual clothing, hair impeccably groomed, dark glasses even though it was January and we were meeting indoors. That was one of my first lessons. The right image was important. If you were meeting a young player for the first time, there was no point in turning up in a suit and a shirt with a collar and a tie. He had to be able to gauge the value of what you were wearing to be able to decide if you were cool and sharp enough to represent him. Players are judged by their agents. They talk about them in the dressing room as if they're trophies.

'My man reps . . .' and then he lists a series of England internationals. No good saying you're somebody's only client.

No street cred in that at all, and don't even think about turning up at the training ground in any vehicle worth less than £40k.

I extended my hand and – I'm going to call him 'R' – R nodded in the direction of the counter and said, 'Mine's an Americano. And a skinny muffin while you're at it.' Which was when I understood that an invitation to coffee did not extend to the actual purchase.

It didn't take me long in the industry to discover that most agents are intuitively tight-fisted. They're happy (well, not exactly happy, but certainly prepared) to shower gifts and freebies on their players because they're investing in them, but when it comes to anything else, then their wallets remain firmly folded, opening only to receive and not to give.

I brought the drinks over to the table and waited for him to open the conversation, but when nothing was forthcoming it dawned on me that he was waiting for me to try and impress him.

'Thanks for seeing me,' I said, an opening gambit that merely made him yawn and glance at his diamond-encrusted Rolex. I noted that he made sure that I saw it too and I automatically tugged down my sleeve to conceal the watch that I'd worn ever since my bar mitzvah.

'I see everybody that contacts me,' R said.

'That's good of you,' I replied.

He grunted, took a sip of his coffee and said, 'It's just to tell you that if you want to become an agent you're fucking delusional. Are you a gambler, son?'

'Not really,' I said.

'OK. Let me show you the odds then. There are ninety-two clubs in the League. Let's say they each have thirty or so professionals. That's two thousand, seven hundred players. And there are about four hundred agents not to mention all the others working the same patch – lawyers, close relations, foreign agents registered elsewhere. Then there are the unlicensed guys who do the same job and hide behind either a lawyer or a real agent. I couldn't begin to tell you how many of them there are but it probably runs into the hundreds. The top half-a-dozen agencies have about a hundred players each, including the pick of the crop. So that leaves about two thousand players divided amongst about five or six hundred agents, about three or four players each. Now, even if you're lucky and you manage to sign up your quota, let's say those players aren't the best. Let's say they only earn an average of thirty to fifty grand a year. You charge five per cent. So for a deal you might make fifteen hundred to two-and-a-half grand a year. Multiply that by the number of players you have and build in the probability that not every one of them will get a deal each year and what have you got? Eight, ten grand a year coming in? And I'm being optimistic here. You might be representing League Two or Football Conference players or even Scottish fuckers earning less than five hundred quid a week – so do the arithmetic. Still think it's worth it?'

'Yes,' I said. 'But I'm thinking you don't do deals for that level. And I'm also thinking from the value of that watch you're wearing and the cost alone of those shades that you don't just charge five per cent.'

For the first time I'd piqued his interest. He pushed back his glasses and I saw his eyes – so dark brown they were almost black – and I felt them drilling into me, seeming to reach right down into my deepest thoughts, and I wondered how anybody ever won any negotiations when he was sitting on the other side of a desk.

'So,' he said, almost to himself, 'the kid thinks. That's good because I have to tell you that most people in this game don't think at all. They're so busy chasing after deals that they don't even think about tying up their shoelaces, which means the minute they try to run they fall over. This,' he lifted my CV, 'it's a load of shit, isn't it?'

I nodded, thinking that the meeting was coming to an end, but suddenly there was a little smile on his face.

'You know what, you've got chutzpah at least, I'll give you that; and in this game, you need that in barrow loads. It's a bit like selling double glazing or telesales. You knock on a hundred doors, you make a thousand calls but you only need one old lady to invite you in or ask you to visit and you know your day has been worthwhile. Substitute footballers for old ladies and there you are. We trawl for them, we pick up what we can and we hope for the best. If they're no good we throw them back in the sea. But the ones we catch, the ones we want to keep, that's where the money is. It's hard to pick them, hard to reel them in and even harder to keep them. Don't suppose you're licensed, are you?'

'No, but I reckon I can pass that exam easily enough.'

R laughed out loud. 'That's what they all say, but the pass rate is less than twenty per cent. I've known blokes with first-class honours degrees fail a couple of times. What they ask you is totally obscure and if you really want to do this then it's also fucking useless. I tell you what. I like you. If you work with me then you won't need a licence anyway. So this is what I'll offer you. I'm going to give you three months to sign six players for me. I'm not going to pay you but if I earn anything out of those players I'll make sure you're looked after. I'll pay you your expenses as long as you clear them with me first, and whether you make the grade with me or not I promise you that at the end of those three months you'll have learned a fucking sight more than you ever got out of books at college or what you'd have stuffed into your head working for that FA exam.'

'Do I get anything in writing?' I asked.

'Listen, son, you've heard the old saying that a verbal contract isn't worth the paper it's written on?'

I nodded. That one was down to one of the old movie moguls.

'Well, in this sweet world of football the effort of chopping down the tree to make the paper to write a contract is also a total fucking waste of time. Now, do you want to do this or not? 'Cos if you do you can buy me another coffee, you can tell me the players you're going to target and I'm going to explain to you exactly how you're going to go about getting them.'

I reached towards him and extended my hand and, as somebody told me far too late, I should've counted my fingers when his grip relaxed.

THREE

PLAYER RECRUITMENT LESSON ONE: KNOW YOUR ENEMY

I T DIDN'T TAKE me too long to discover what I was in for working alongside R. To be fair to him, he did exactly what he'd promised. He even got me some business cards printed with his company name and logo and my name with the word 'Scout' beneath it.

That word covered a multitude of sins. The guys operating below the radar in the industry were either scouts or consultants. They seemed to fall into two distinct categories. There were wannabe agents like myself, all bright-eyed and bushy-tailed, getting to as many matches as we could during a week at all levels; and there were the seasoned ex-pros who'd never bothered to pass the exams but were still, to all intents and purposes, carrying on the business of a football agent.

As I realised from the off, the enemy was the FA. It's a bit better now as they seem to have given up the ghost after the demise of the agent and with so many intermediaries now in the game it's getting harder and harder for them to police it all. Not that they don't try but let's be honest they're not the CIA or MI5 or even PC Plod. The challenge then was to bypass their dreaded Agents' Regulations (now you need to get round the far more relaxed Working with Intermediaries Rules),but the Agents' Regs had been introduced some years previously to try to bring some order into what had been pretty much the Wild West. I've been to meetings of the Association of Football Agents (AFA) since and heard speakers say that they didn't want to return to the bad old days of 'the Wild West', but my experience is that those days never went away and for the people who made fortunes they were anything but the 'bad old days'. And now that I know what I do those speakers are quite often the ones who only pay lip service to any rule that might stand in the way of them earning a few more bob.

The way the system was supposed to work was a civil servant's dream and a businessman's nightmare. Only 'Licensed Agents' could carry out what was described as 'Agency Activity' in the regs. That just about covered everything from making the first phone call to get the player, meeting him, signing him up and then finding him a club and negotiating his contract. What the FA had done was create a *War and Peace*-scale document for every step of the process. You got the player to sign the contract and you had to get it signed in triplicate. You had to tell the player to get independent advice. You sent it off to the FA who got one of their bean counters to check it and send it back if a comma was out of place. Then when they registered it, the result was that only the agent named in the contract could deal with the club, and the club was supposedly obliged only to deal with that agent.

It simply didn't work like that, as I'll explain later when I get down to some of the sleazier deals I got involved with. The lodged contract also meant that if you did get to the point of agreeing terms with a club then all the forms that had to be signed were also multi-copied and signed by everybody: club, player and you. And when your payment was due, the club paid the FA, the FA eventually released the money to you and that was where it got interesting.

Only the actual agent involved was allowed to be paid and he was supposed to tell the FA if he was paying anybody else. Yeah, right. I suppose R could've got away with telling the FA he was paying his scouts some bonuses but I couldn't see him telling them about the payments that went to the managers and the parents (particularly the fathers) of the player concerned and sometimes the players themselves. Or, indeed, all sorts of dubious individuals both in this country and abroad who had helped to oil the wheels of any of his equally dubious transactions.

I made it my business to find out how a transaction was supposed to work as far as the FA was concerned. The reality when I finally got to meet a potential player was very different.

I'd been to see a few academy matches on my own. I flattered myself that I could tell a decent player from the dross, but the problem was that so could everybody else who was watching. It wasn't easy getting into some of the grounds to watch the games, as you either needed to be accredited from a club or else be a close relation. I soon learned to recognise the parents of the boys who were playing and realised that if I chatted them up outside the match venue and carried on my conversation as we went in, the stewards on the gate automatically assumed I was also related. It was a bit tricky with some of the black lads, so I tended to latch on to the white parents and pretend to be an older brother.

If you praised the kid during the match then it wasn't hard to keep the dialogue going. It was obvious, at whatever level I watched, that most of the parents thought their sons were only marking time before they joined Manchester United or Barcelona. If the kid had a stinker of a match then that was down to the coach playing him out of position. It was never the boy's fault, and I found that if I encouraged the parent by telling him that we had a real inside run at a major club then they'd be more than willing to supply their phone number to set up a meeting. In those days (and I know I sound like an octogenarian talking about the good old pre-war days) there weren't that many agents chasing the kids. Now it's got so bad that many clubs won't allow agents in to watch the kids, or they insist that they go through yet another registration process whereby, if they step out of line by pestering kids or parents, their right to attend can be withdrawn.

There was a tiny problem in respect of kids in those days. The good old FA said that you couldn't sign a player up before his sixteenth birthday and, in fact, you couldn't even legally approach him before that. Now there is another problem whereby under the Intermediaries Regulations even if you do a first professional contract for a seventeen year old you can't get paid until he is eighteen. Go figure. But if you decide to wait until then, believing that the whole hassle, expense and investment of time is simply not worth risking on a young player, then he will, by the time he looks a safer bet, have almost certainly been snapped up by another agency.

There are players as young as ten or eleven who, if you ask them, will say they've got an 'agent'. Grooming on the net is nothing compared to the way agencies groom young players and their parents, so my ruse of getting the numbers and arranging a meeting was nothing compared to what was going on elsewhere – as I was to discover in spades at my first sit-down with a fifteen-year-old and his mum and dad.

FOUR

PLAYER RECRUITMENT LESSON TWO: THIS IS WHAT WE WANT

IN EVERY GENERATION there are young footballers known as 'talking players'. Everybody knew about Joe Cole and Wayne Rooney, Gareth Bale and Raheem Sterling from when they were about ten years old, and the agents who secured them when they were teenagers knew what they were doing. And they talked about them. Not that it did the poor agent who got Sterling young a lot of good because by the time he did his major move he'd already switched to another representative. Pretty par for the course in our industry which is why we are all so driven to strike while the iron is hot and maximise our income from any deal that passes our way. Tomorrow may be too late. In fact the afternoon may be too late if you don't do the deal in the morning.

Nowadays there are far more intermediaries than there were ever agents, which means there's much more competition for those precious signatures. There are two problems. As I said, one is that they can't sign until they're sixteen and the other is that a parent has to sign off as their guardian. So, you have to get the parents to like and trust you, and you have to get the kid to buy into your style of representation.

I'd spotted a target at an academy match at a London Championship side. His dad was there, and I soon found out he'd been laid off from his job a few months back and that the mother had two jobs and was the sole breadwinner of the family.

It didn't take long to figure out that his son – let's call him Ryan – was the guy's intended meal ticket for the rest of his life.

I could see the lad was a decent player. He was tall for his age and had a football brain on him, and playing in midfield he reminded me of a young Frank Lampard. He just had something about him. I went to watch him three or four times and then, when I could see other agents were also homing in on the father, I decided the time was right to make a move – and to my delight I managed to get the dad to agree to see R and me at his home one night.

I thought R was going to be delighted, but he was fairly cynical about the whole thing. 'Don't get too excited until you see what he wants,' he said, and in those early days I confess I didn't really understand what he meant.

I must have visited dozens of that type of house since then, and they're all remarkably alike. Terraced, a small front room dominated by a giant TV always locked on to Sky Sports, a wife stuck in the kitchen who is friendly but nervous, offering tea and biscuits from their best china, and a few younger siblings poking their heads around the door. The ones where there are single mums are a bit different, but more of that later.

You have to relate to them all. Conversation with the boy's mother has to reassure her that you'll look after the apple of her eye and treat him as your own. Questions to the younger ones as to what they're up to. If there's a little girl you need to know something about the latest bands; if it's a boy then does he also want to be a footballer. It's all about making a good impression and leaving a positive memory behind. The thing is, though, there are others who will be leaving something more substantial behind.

Ryan's dad eased himself into his favourite chair. I looked at the TV, R looked at the TV, and we waited for the dad to turn it off or down. No chance. He was looking at it too and continued to do so for the whole of our meeting even when talking to us.

'OK,' he said, 'so what have you lot got to offer that the others haven't?'

R began to tell him about the players he'd represented, about all the club contacts he had, about his own career as a player, and how he had kids himself and would treat Ryan as if he were his own son.

I could see that the dad wasn't impressed or really interested.

'Well,' the dad said, 'that's all very well and good, but we've spoken to a few agents already. One of them sent a Roller to pick us up and take Ryan to his office, and when we left, my boy found a brand new Xbox and iPad on the seat. Good set-up. They had (he named a current England international) there to meet us and he really likes the way Ryan plays. Thinks he's going to be a real star.'

I have to say R handled it really well.

'They're a good agency. You can tell that from the number of players they have. But that's also the downside. They act for too many to give your Ryan the individual attention he deserves. We'd be hands-on all the time.' He pointed to me. 'My assistant will be like a brother to him, I promise you.'

The dad paused for a moment and took his eyes of the screen. He appraised me. 'I get that,' he said. 'It's a good point. But what about me?'

'You'll always be involved,' R said. 'Nothing will ever happen without us speaking to you first and getting your views.'

'Yeah, well that goes without saying,' the dad replied. 'But what are you going to do to help me out? I've not worked for months and I'm the one who ferries Ryan back and forwards to the club, to training, to matches. I'm the one who has to get him all the stuff he needs . . .'

I could see this bloke raiding his wife's purse for her hard-earned cash to do just that, but I kept my counsel.

'Boots won't be a problem. And I'm sure we can help you out with petrol and so on.'

I could see it was the 'and so on' which was going to be the thing for the father.

'The other lot offered that. And they also said that when I was watching Ryan I could do some scouting for them.'

R wasn't giving up. 'You can tip us off as well. We sign anybody, we'll pay you something and we'll look after you when we do a deal for the kid.'

'The thing is,' the dad continued, warming to his task, 'I need the money now.'

The gloves were off, the sparring was over. The mother had closed the door to the kitchen as if she knew exactly when the conversation would get to this point. The younger children were up in their bedrooms. This was man's talk now.

'How much did they offer you?' R asked.

'Twenty-five grand in cash and then a scouting deal for thirty grand a year.'

R looked long and hard as if assessing whether or not the man was telling the truth.

'And if we give you this as well, will Ryan sign? We'd have to leave the date blank in the contract and fill it in when he gets to sixteen.'

'Well, we like you, and Ryan likes your lad here, so I'm thinking we might well do that. The other lot were a bit flash, a bit up themselves, if you know what I mean?'

R nodded. Yes, he knew exactly what he meant. It was a gamble on R's part. The lad's career might come to nothing. He'd sign effectively at sixteen and by the time he was eighteen when the maximum two years of the contract had run out he might not even have got a meaningful contract that could recoup the investment. But R knew that the bigger risk was letting the opportunity pass. And so the deal was done.

As it happened it was a good move. The lad was playing in the first team just a few months after his sixteenth birthday. On his seventeenth birthday the club offered him a professional contract and R managed to get the club to pay him a juicy fee. He made no mention of that to the lad or his dad and simply made a merit out of telling the kid he was doing it for nothing. A year later the kid was moving to a Premiership Club. R's fee was in the region of three hundred grand for the two deals and even after looking after the dad it wasn't a bad return for what was by then the eighty-five grand that he'd paid the dad to get the kid in the first place.

But there was a sting in the tail. When the two years were up and the boy needed to re-sign with R, the dad had become a lot more streetwise and said he'd only allow it if R paid him half of all future fees. R had no choice but to agree. If he hadn't, then others would've, and half of something was better than one hundred per cent of nothing. If I learned nothing else from R then it was to be pragmatic.

FIVE

GOT TO KEEP THE CUSTOMER SATISFIED

I NEVER ASKED where R got his cash from but it always seemed to be around. I knew he'd done a few favours for one or two managers when he'd effectively laundered some cash they'd made from a deal via another agent, but more about managers later. His other ploy was to charge a couple of per cent less than the normal five per cent, get more money into a player's contract to compensate for it and then get the player to give him one per cent back in cash. He reckoned everybody earned from that little scheme, but I doubted that HMRC would've seen it that way.

He wasn't the only one being a bag man for managers. There was an agent based abroad who kept huge stashes of cash for various managers and had an understanding with the local police who felt the need to make routine raids on his house just to appease their bosses. They'd call him an hour or so before they were coming and there would be a frantic packing-up operation. A car loaded with cash would then be taken to a lock-up garage and exchanged for another vehicle kept there just for that purpose, and the police would report back that nothing had been found.

There were always uses for cash. Players needed to be looked after in more ways than one. When one player came down from up north he asked for a guaranteed entry into a club of his choice and a hotel room booked for afterwards so he could take the girl (or girls) of his choice back there. That service paled into insignificance compared to one agent who actually maintained a flat in Central London with hookers on tap to accommodate the players' every needs as and when they were in town. I heard that he liked to test-drive the girls himself – so good clean healthy fun all round.

It wasn't just girls the players wanted their agents to provide. It was drugs as well. Obviously they were terrified of testing positive in a random post-match drug test, but when there was a good long gap between matches and they had a few days of R & R they were really into the substances, including the hard stuff.

I knew R's dealer because I used to have to collect from him occasionally, and once when we got chatting I was surprised to learn that he'd been a player himself at one time. He'd worked out that he could earn more off the pitch by supplying his teammates using the contacts he'd grown up with, and now he had a thriving business which was almost exclusively player-based.

Most of the players I met or represented came from really tough backgrounds and as schoolboys had been faced with few career opportunities. If you couldn't make it at football then a life of crime was a real alternative; and if you weren't into physical things like armed robbery or burglary, then drug dealing was an attractive career path. It offered not only big bucks but the chance of a base in somewhere like Spain, Portugal or Greece. R used to joke that you could tell the dealers by their perma-tans and the players by their dodgy knees. You could carry on dealing after you were in your mid-thirties, which was another plus, and a few players we knew went over to the dark side once their careers were over. Most players seemed to like to stick with their old buddies even though in many cases they were there for the ride. The problem about that for an agent is that the buddies come into the equation when it comes to paying for things for the player. Clothing? Great but can't you get some for the guys? A holiday? Yeah, that's good but what about taking a villa so the gang and I can have a party? You're getting a sponsored car for me, how much more difficult can it be to get a couple of cheaper models for the lads? Or my brother? Or my dad? Or my sister? It's never-ending and the one thing that should never be said to a lucrative client is 'no'. Well, to be honest, even if you did say it they wouldn't understand it.

Footballers are naturally takers rather than givers, and any agent has to be prepared to invest money in them all the time. Most boot companies won't give boots for free any more to anybody apart from the top-flight players. Although they'll nearly always give an agent a discount, they still run a pretty price from a hundred quid right up to two-fifty. If you have more than a dozen players and they run through four pairs a year on average it's a sizeable hit on your income. It's not even tax deductible. Nor can you claim back the VAT as the Revenue don't regard it as an allowable expense and the FA look on it as a potential inducement to get a player to enter into a contract. But more about boots later, and the guys at the company who dish them out. They're both a commodity just like any other. The FA's attitude to their supply is a real joke. If you want to talk about inducements, then apart from the sex and drugs I've mentioned above, I've known agents give gifts such as cars, expensive holidays, Rolex watches, and even houses for the players' families. Agents are desperate not to miss out on an opportunity and once they've done one or two massive dodgy deals and amassed a slush fund then the sky is the limit to ensure they position themselves in a transaction.

If there's a deal in the offing and there's a six- or even a seven-figure commission to earn, then it's relatively small change to pay an inducement to a player's father or mother to get him or her to persuade their son to get the payer of the bribe involved in the transaction. And the fact that the player may already have had representation is no real barrier. Not if you're richer and more powerful and more persuasive than the old agent.

Now, I know what you're thinking. Doesn't the player have to have had a contract with his previous rep? And you're right. But it often happens that, as far as the player's old agent is concerned, his client just goes AWOL. Every player has the right to represent himself even if he has a contract (welcome to the wild and wacky world of football). He tells the buying club he isn't using his agent but wants the club to use the agent who has looked after his dad (and probably him as well in a material way). The club wants to sign the player and aren't really bothered as long as they only pay one lot of fees. The new agent represents the club and recoups his 'gift' to the player's dad and the player (and any other individual who may have had to be looked after) in spades. And the added bonus is that the player doesn't have to pay any tax as he hasn't incurred any agents' fees for himself, which would normally have been paid for by the club and incurred a tax liability for the player as a benefit in kind. Sorted. Everybody's happy except the poor old agent who's been left out in the cold and, yet again our good friends at HMRC. I'm thinking this book should be essential reading for the tax inspectors and collectors though I doubt they'd get anywhere near the real practitioners who cut the Revenue out of a deal. You can forget all about those mega size corporations who plan their tax affairs so they pay little or no tax where they conduct their businesses. They've a lot to learn from football agents who take tax evasion to a whole new, stratospheric, level.

In the real world, rather than the parallel universe of football and agents, the wronged party would just sue his player-client.

But it doesn't work like that. Reputation is everything, as I'll go on to explain. Also one 'participant' in football can't sue another and that term includes players, agents and clubs and now, albeit belatedly, includes intermediaries as well. Although in my Brave New World I am none of those; I'm just another guy who helps make the wheels go around and watches the money roll in. But these guys (who did include me for a good long while) have to proceed by way of what is called a Rule K Arbitration under FA Rules. That's like a mini court case where both parties appoint and arbitrator and have to agree on a third one as well unless it can be agreed that just one guy sits as the judge. The FA are so anal about keeping everything in-house that they won't even let outside justice in through the door, nor let us out to play in the courts. It's just another example of how agents are treated as a school class with rules and punishments to match. Although I know for a fact that the FA have access to everything that's said and every piece of paper produced at one of these Rule K's, so it should come as no surprise when some charges arise to take the shine off actually winning a claim. Every time I've been called in to see the guys at the FA I've been made to feel like a naughty schoolboy who has been found smoking behind the toilets. As for the Revenue, well, they move in mysterious ways. And they don't like agents. But then who does? We might just as well adopt the old Millwall song as our theme:

We are agents, super agents,
No one likes us,
We don't care.

Perhaps we should've printed up some T-shirts bearing that legend. No one likes us: not the clubs, the FA, the Leagues, the media and certainly not the PFA, the Professional Footballers'

Association.

And to be perfectly honest, when we can make as much money as we can on any single transaction why should we give a flying fuck?

SIX

THE TRUTH, THE WHOLE TRUTH AND NOTHING BUT THE TRUTH

EVERY JOURNALIST LIKES to think he has one or more agent in his front pocket, whereas the truth is that every agent has a pet journalist in his back pocket. Not that the truth has anything to do with journalism of course. When I was at university I conducted a small experiment for a thesis I was writing. I took all the headlines from three tabloids for three months – November, December and January – those leading up to the transfer window and the window itself. Of all the headlines predicting this signing and that signing, less than twenty per cent turned out to be true. So let me tell you why that is.

Agents get called by their 'friendly' journos almost every day as the window gets near to closing. They want their cards marked in advance of an event happening. But a shrewd agent will ensure that's a two-way street. Let's assume Player X wants to leave his current club but the club is having none of it. It can be necessary to stir the waters a little and plant a story – and that has to be done very carefully.

You might say that Clubs Y and Z have expressed an interest in X, or that the manager of his current club is shopping for a player in exactly the same position (perhaps a bit younger) and that's because he doesn't fancy X much any more. Now, the club may well issue all sorts of denials, but the seeds are sown and one fact that's incontrovertible in football is that when a player wants to leave a club, he leaves. The only issue becomes how much the club gets for him. A brilliant operator like Daniel Levy at Spurs got the maximum figure for Gareth Bale because he knew exactly how to play the game. There was never ever any doubt that Bale was on his way out to Real Madrid, but Levy played it cool right to the very last moment. You have to admire clubs like Spurs for maximising income for players. Irving Scholar, one of Levy's predecessors, had the same talent. Newcastle got a crazy fee for Andy Carroll from Liverpool with similar tactics. But in each and every case the relevant agent also played a very clever hand with no little help from the media. There's nothing wrong with that whatsoever, and as I gained more experience I realised that the manipulation of the press was all part of the game.

There has to be care as to how you get the stories written. Most players will have signing-on fees payable in their contracts. That's a lump sum that the club pays when the player joins or his contract is renegotiated. Even though it's not paid in one hit, but spread over the term of the contract in equal instalments, agents like to have that in, not only because players are impressed by large capital sums even more than weekly salaries, but because it's guaranteed income and as such they're allowed to charge commission on it within the FA Rules. These say that commission can only be charged on guaranteed income and that is limited to salaries and signing-on fees. So things like appearance money, bonuses and loyalty payments (loyalty – such an inappropriate word when it comes to players and clubs) don't qualify for commissions. And we do so love our commissions.

The only problem with signing-on fees is that if a player *asks* for a transfer, then the club is entitled not to pay any outstanding signing-on fees. If they decided to sell him then the whole of the unpaid balance of the signing-on fee becomes due. As you can imagine, that can be a huge sum, so once a club realises it's going to lose a player it not only seeks to maximise the amount it gets from the buying club, but also to minimise anything it has to pay to the player and his agent.

Now, a written transfer request is one thing. That truly is a document of last resort. Once that's in, the die is cast and your player can forget all about whatever you (or your predecessor) may have negotiated for him by way of a signing-on fee. However, without anything in writing, the club may still try to prove that the player has, in effect, really asked for a transfer – and one excellent method of proof are quotes from his agent in a paper saying how unhappy his client is and how he's desperate to further his career at a club with European football guaranteed. The fact that the more successful club may well be doubling the player's salary (not to mention the agent's commission) is something that you really don't want mentioned. Anyway, once a club sees anything like that in a paper or hears words to that effect in an interview, they'll be on it like a dog with a bone saying that the player is asking for a transfer even though he hasn't put anything in writing. And you know what, they're right.

The challenge is finding a trustworthy journalist – and those words don't often go together. Now, I'm not suggesting that most journalists are dishonest. If you go to a bar with them you can safely leave your wallet on the table. I'm not so sure you can leave your girlfriend with them, but if they've got such crap taste as to be prepared to shag a journo would you really want to be with them anyway? It's not that sort of dishonesty that worries me or other agents. It's breaching trust. The magic words are 'off the record'. If you have a conversation with a journo and say it's off the record and find the next day he's written it up as a banner exclusive, then that's the last time you ever speak to him. But the damage has been done, and it may have meant the end of the relationship between you and your player, or you and a particular club.

It's a very short-term policy for journos to write up what you've told them in confidence but it's amazing how many of them do it. They have to fill a paper, they're under pressure from their editors; even their jobs can be on the line unless they deliver something sensational. The really experienced ones may try to pressurise you to go on the record but as long as you have the willpower to resist what can be daily (or even hourly) calls they'll keep schtum.

So why tell them anything confidential at all? Well, they need to feel loved for one thing. Maybe, more importantly, they want to be able to blow the story wide open as soon as you give them the go-ahead, and if they've written it up already then they get the jump on their rivals. The world of newspapers and sports media journalism is even more cut-throat than that of football agents, and that's really saying something.

You may also need a trade-off with a journalist. You give him a story and he kills another (damaging) story about your client. Believe me, that doesn't just happen in the world of Max Clifford, the once undisputed master of PR and press manipulation. A journalist may call you to tell you that he has a story and a photo of one of your star players stumbling out of a nightclub blind drunk with a wannabe footballer's wife on his arm who isn't actually his wife. It's going to take a big one to keep that out of the paper, but that biggie may be there in the shape of the player's proposed transfer which, until then, only you and the two clubs involved know about. You have to make the judgement call, because if you don't hush up the incident it may well affect the transfer itself. I told you being an agent isn't as easy as it looks. The rewards may be great, but so is the stress and effort.

Planting a story, whether in return for a favour or just because you need to plant it, is always a delicate operation. First, you don't want it traced back to you, and you want to be in a position to deny it even when you know full well it's true or is about to be true. The journalist concerned won't mind the denial and certainly not when he's proved to be one hundred per cent correct. Agreeing that he'll quote 'an unnamed source' or 'somebody close to' or 'a friend' is standard procedure for anonymity.

Sometimes an article goes beyond the line. One bloke recently called all agents 'dodgy and slimy and treacherous' (though he did back down a bit after talking to a bunch of them). Now, that description may apply to a few. You may think those few include me. But it is a bit sweeping and unfair. Maybe the writer should have done a bit more digging before he went off on one. As he now seems to accept, they aren't all like me or R. In fact most of them probably aren't. But I suppose I should be grateful because if anything will sell my story it will be articles like that. I think I'll send him a copy of this book (he's never met me so it may be educational). I know a lot of agents are thinking that 'dodgy, slimy and treacherous' applies more to journalists than agents, but as the article came out after I got banned I think I can safely say it doesn't apply to me anyway.

It's not difficult to get column inches when you have a star asset to sell in whom there's genuine interest. It gets more tricky when your player wants to move but you don't have a queue of suitors stretching around the block. Here you may have to move into a world of wishful thinking rather than reality. Pick a club that you'd like your player to join, preferably one where you think the club could do with somebody like him in his position. Get the story planted that the club is interested. That not only gives you a reason for calling the club you've named but may also get another club calling you who is suddenly reminded of the existence of the player.

And if nothing comes of it then all that's happened is that a paper has carried yet another article which turns out to be untrue and unfounded. And untruth is second nature to most journalists. That's probably how my statistic of twenty per cent true and eighty per cent false came about – and now here I am contributing to it. Not just watching fiction but playing a role in creating the script. Welcome to the dream factory.

SEVEN

THE BABY SITTER

IF ANYBODY HAS ever babysat for a niece of nephew and been told by the doting parent that he or she never wakes up – only to find that the little bugger just wants to play all night – then you kind of get the idea of what it's like to look after a footballer.

There are the odd ones who have married their childhood sweethearts, had their two or three kids by the time they reach their early twenties and never look at another woman. But they're the odd ones. Not just numerically odd but regarded as odd by their teammates. If a player doesn't shag around then all sorts of rumours get put about regarding his sexuality.

So, the control of these red-blooded young men becomes a challenge. Agents fall into two camps here. There are the ones who are only too happy to go out clubbing with their lads and partake in whatever frolics may follow. There is a girls' club who want to sleep with as many footballers as possible, notching up the bed-posts and exchanging notes. Sadly there isn't actually a similar fan club for agents. But if you're young and not too bad-looking and out on the town with your client then the odds are that you won't have to stay up all night to get lucky, as the song puts it.

Then there are the ones, usually a bit older and wiser and less rash, who have to clean up all the shit after it's hit the fan. That can come in all shades and thicknesses of brown, sometimes bordering on black.

I know one agent who has a slush fund dedicated to paying off predatory girls who either threaten to sell a story to a newspaper (often with pictures in which the pissed footballer has been a willing and laughing participant) or else want to be paid for an abortion or far worse – and this is when the picture turns really dark – belatedly cry rape.

In each and every case the player is faced with exposure not just to the media but a very angry and possibly vengeful wife or partner at home who will become a financial nemesis far worse than any one-night stand. You might be thinking, this is just blackmail so why not go straight to the police? The fact of the matter is that the police are no friends of footballers or agents, although sometimes there can be an uneasy alliance when they've also been dropped a few quid (not to mention a few tickets) to turn a blind eye to a speeding, drink-driving or minor drug offence. Generally speaking, footballers and their agents make more money in a week (sometimes a day) than some police officers earn in a year and, from the police perspective, this is the time to level the playing field a little.

So, when these girls come calling it's just easier to pay. They seem to know their value and their price and I've come to the conclusion that they may actually talk to each other to see which players are the easiest marks. But it's never the players who have to meet them in hotels or cafés. That's the agent's lot, and although he'll have had some kind of confidentiality agreement drawn up by a lawyer you can never be a hundred per cent certain that they won't come knocking on the door again for another handout when the first one is spent.

I never cease to be surprised at the stupidity of even quite intelligent players. I had one of my brighter ones on the phone saying, 'I think I may have made a big mistake.'

'Tell me,' I said in that tone of voice which indicated that I'd heard everything before.

'Me and the lads were in the hotel before the game and we were sort of bored like. So I went online . . .'

Here we go, I thought, you summoned up a hooker to your room. But I was wrong,

'So they all go to bed and I'm even more bored and as we were an odd number I've got a room to myself.' Players usually share a room for all sorts of good reason. Camaraderie and, I guess, to influence each other to stay out of trouble.

'And I get into this video chat room and there's this girl and I thought she was really nice and as it was online I didn't think there was anything wrong and it wasn't really cheating on the missus . . .'

'What wasn't?' I asked with some trepidation now.

'Well, it all got a bit heated and she was touching herself so I started doing it too and she came and it didn't seem right for me to leave her like that so I jerked myself off as well . . .'

'Let me get this right,' I said, 'all of this was on camera?'

He didn't say anything but I could sense him nodding.

'And now?' I asked.

'Now she's sold the story to one of the Sundays, pictures of all and they want my take on it . . .'

'Your fucking take?' I replied. 'And what would that be?'

'My missus will kill me if they publish it.'

I roared into action and phoned the most expensive PR company I knew. They were more used to dealing with movie and rock stars than naughty footballers, but they did a good job. It cost a fortune but eventually the paper ran the story that the girl was just a chancer and she'd honey-trapped my player into it all and, best of all, they binned the pictures. He still had a hard time with his wife, but she knew a cushy number when she saw it and just used the situation to have a major shopping expedition with his credit cards – so, what with the cost of the

PR company and his wife's extravagance, it was an expensive exercise for an hour's 'fun' online.

Sometimes it's not money. Sometimes your client has another souvenir from a liaison in the shape of an STD, and so the agent always has to have a friendly doctor on hand who is prepared to write out private prescriptions to solve the problem. Meanwhile, the player is left to find a way to explain to his spouse why he's suddenly gone off sex for a while. Oh, the hardships of wealth, success and fame.

It's not just the problem of predatory women that agents have to deal with. Gambling is a huge problem. One very famous player couldn't walk past a betting office without going in to have a bet, and it got so bad that that the agent actually had the player's salary paid into his account each week and then doled it out to the player and his family as he needed it. He was the lucky one. He had a good agent who became his friend. Sometimes an agent only finds out there's a problem when it's too late.

After working with R for about a year I finally got my FA licence and had gathered together my own roster of about ten players, most of them youngsters with real potential. One young lad called me at two in the morning to tell me he'd had a visit from masked men wielding baseball bats and iron bars threatening to break both his legs (his most valuable assets) unless he paid them the gambling debts he'd incurred. I rolled out of bed and called R who gave me the authority to make the payment. I felt that the player owed me and R forever, but I was wrong. The player started gambling again and found another agent willing to lend him money to bail him out and signed with him when his contract with me ran out. I was really upset, but R just shrugged. 'I've seen it all before, son. And so will you in due course.'

I think he felt it was all part of his investment in my learning curve.

We both had a good laugh when this same player had to be smuggled out of the back door of his club because a couple of loan sharks were waiting outside in a car with sawn-off shotguns.

It's one small step from racking up huge gambling debts to agreeing to throw a match or assist with spot or spread betting. When bookmakers pay out on all sorts of things – times of goals, the next throw-in, the number of yellow and red cards and so on – then the opportunities are there. Footballers sometimes can't arrange this sort of thing themselves, and there are one or two agents only too willing to help and take the risk of sharing the dock with their clients.

But gambling isn't usually a laughing matter. One manager called to tip me off that my player was betting on matches. Now, the FA don't approve of that and you can understand why. The stupidity of this particular instance was that my client was consistently placing losing bets even with so-called inside information. By the time I'd had a word with him and found out the extent of the addiction it was too late. He'd remortgaged his house (well, houses actually as he'd bought whenever he moved clubs) and somehow or other had forged his wife's signature each time. He was left with literally nothing and when his wife left him too with the kids he actually had less than nothing. It affected his playing ability as well and he tumbled down the league ladder to a small club who paid him peanuts. He did stop gambling (probably because he had nothing left with which to gamble) but his life and his career were in ruins.

Drugs are rife in football – or at least in footballers' lives – and again there are several agents quite happy to provide them to their clients. We are talking about recreational drugs, usually, which is not to say there are no players who don't get involved in the harder stuff or that there are no agents with the capability of obtaining them and providing them to their clients.

It's all a question of timing. Players know there's a real chance of being asked to give samples before or after matches or occasionally at training. But if there's a match on a Saturday they may not train again until the Monday or sometimes even the Tuesday, and that means that whatever they've taken gets through their systems and is undetectable.

I know at least one agent who finds it hard to function unless he's high. He seems to work 24/7, is at a match every day when one is on (which is most days) and his only social life is going to clubs where he knows he'll be able to meet more players. And offer them drugs. And offer them girls.

Sometimes the line between player and agent becomes blurred. The agent so lives the life of his client that he fools himself into thinking that he's the client, forgetting that the client has a unique talent which he'll never have. Unless you count making money as a talent, which I suppose it is – although unlikely to draw crowds of over fifty thousand to watch.

I suppose somebody has to protect players from themselves and it might as well be us agents. Certainly their parents and their wives won't, as they're usually too busy feathering their own nests. Again, I'm not apologising for what we do or how players behave. I suspect musicians and movies stars are very much the same, only their agents charge them twenty per cent. So what we provide is a real bargain and you'd think they'd be grateful. You'd hope they'd be grateful. But not a bit of it. I've dealt with getting clients and looking after them and I'm about to look at how to keep them. Short of clamping them in chains (some of them might actually like that knowing their sexual predilections) and taking away their passports, it's a real challenge. Just as few players are one-club men, the number of one-agent players is also a minority. The grass is always greener and there's always a competitor waiting to pounce. Agents as brothers in arms? I don't think so.

EIGHT

LEARNING TO FLY

I'LL NEVER FORGET the first time R took me to a contractual negotiation.

'Look and learn, son, but keep your fucking mouth shut. You may have your own ideas, but believe me, I'm really not interested in them and nor is the bloke we're going to see.'

The club was a Championship club in the Midlands and we were meeting the CEO to effect the transfer of a player from a League Two club. It was unusual for R to bother with a player so far down the pecking order but he'd spotted something in this kid and, as usual, he'd been proved right.

There are agents who never venture above the lower Leagues when it comes to representation. It's almost as if they hit their own personal wall and just don't want to climb over it. I used to wonder how they made a living, but I suppose if, like some of them, you act for fifty players and earn two grand a deal it mounts up and can make it worthwhile. But that seemed like too much effort for too little reward to me, and certainly R was generally long past that stage.

R, to be fair to him, had shown me what he intended to ask for before we got there so none of it came as a surprise except the level of what he wanted. He saw me raise my eyebrows.

'Always ask for everything, son, 'cos then you might get something. Never start where you're prepared to end up and never accept it when the club says they've gone as far as they can go because they'll always go that bit further if you put it to them in the right way. And I've put stuff in there that I can give up to get what I want.'

The CEO clearly knew R and was on his guard.

'None of your fancy dan London tricks up here,' he said by way of greeting. 'We've not got fortunes to spend and I've given you my best shot.'

R totally ignored him and asked for a cup of tea.

'Didn't think you'd be staying that long but I'll get one for you. Does the lad want one too?'

'He's my assistant and he can speak for himself,' R replied and I really loved him at that moment for that, which made what I did to him later even worse.

Tea delivered, we got down to business and I realised just how professional R really was under all the mockney behaviour. There was no signing-on fee in the offer and R told the CEO he had to have one, but he'd accept less than he'd asked for if there was a loyalty payment tucked in at the end. Signing-on fees are capital payments made at the start of a contract to induce the player to sign, and if he leaves without asking for a transfer then the club has to pay them. Better still, they count as guaranteed income upon which agents can charge commission. A loyalty payment is kind of what it says on the tin: a payment after the player has been with the club for a while and isn't payable if the player leaves. That makes it non-guaranteed and so R was actually doing his best for the player to his own disadvantage. I could see that was why he kept his players, or at least those who were bright enough to understand what he was doing.

He didn't like the fact that the salary was the same right through the contract so he wanted uplifts to be guaranteed (again where he could charge) and uplifts to come after a certain number of appearances (where he wouldn't be charging). He wanted appearance money to which the CEO replied, 'Fucking hell, R, we're paying him a salary to play so why do we have to pay him more money to "appear"?'

R didn't miss a heartbeat. 'Because you're not paying him enough salary. If you want to pay him more then we can reduce the appearance money.'

And so it went on for most of the afternoon. The CEO got hotter and hotter as did the debate. R asked for goal bonuses, promotion bonuses, part of any future transfer fee for the player, relocation costs, a minimum of double salary on promotion, international cap bonuses, reviews of the contract after so many games, and if he'd thought that the player might have needed a new kitchen sink then doubtless he would've asked for that as well.

The CEO finally crumbled around seven in the evening. I figured it was either because he wanted to go home for his supper or because he just wanted R (and me, I suppose) out of his room and out of his life. He gave R a lot of what he wanted, far more than I'd ever have thought possible and then, just when he must have thought that he could get home for his egg and chips, R started in on his fees.

He had five per cent in his contract with the player and, to be fair to him, he hadn't tried to niggle away at what he'd got for the player. I know now that there are some agents who go into a room and say, 'My fee is a million quid, so let's see what's left in the deal for the player.'

That wasn't R's style at all.

'OK,' he said, 'I've delivered to you a top-class player and one that quite a few clubs were after. So five per cent is cheap.'

The CEO didn't agree. 'I'll agree we can do it on duality, but that's it.'

What he meant was that the club would pick up 2.5 per cent

and the player would only pay tax on the other half even though the club would pay the whole five per cent.

'Yes,' R concurred, 'duality is good. So let's call it five per cent from you and five per cent from the player.'

Ten per cent was a lot and I didn't understand then how R was going to square it with the player as it would cost him more tax. But he had a plan. R had a plan for everything.

At nine in the evening, when the CEO's dinner was probably already burned to a cinder and in the bin, R agreed on eight per cent. The two men shook hands and the player who had been patiently waiting outside was called in to sign off pending his medical in the morning.

R took the player aside and told him what the deal was. The player was delighted as R had achieved a package beyond his wildest dreams. R put his arm around him. 'I've agreed a bit more commission for me with the club. It might cost you a bit of tax. Most agents wouldn't tell you and just hope you wouldn't spot it when it gets taken out of your pay packet. But you know me. I always like to be up front and open with my players. Are you OK with that?'

Of course the player was OK with that. He was earning big bucks for the first time in his career. What did it matter if R took a little more? Later, when he had to pay the tax, he might think about it again but probably not. It was a masterclass in negotiation and client management – and one I never forgot.

It was also a good moment to get the player to sign a new representation contract even though the existing one still had a year to run. That meant the two year cycle started all over again. The player was on such a high that he didn't even bother to read it nor notice that he was not really signing in triplicate, but was in fact signing another blank contract into which R could insert a date when the new one was also about to expire. Dishonest?

Maybe, but nowhere near as bad as one agent who slid a sheet into the papers of his contract that was in fact a loan agreement saying that he had lent the player a substantial sum. If any player tried to leave him he'd simply call in the so called 'loan' unless the player re-signed. It said a lot for the naivety and vagueness of the players that none of them ever went off to get advice from a lawyer who would certainly have asked the agent to prove that he'd actually handed over the money which was claimed to have been loaned.

That was what made me go along with whatever R did. He was no angel, but there were others who were so much worse that they almost seemed to be agents of the devil.

NINE

CUTTING THE APRON STRINGS

I T TOOK ME nearly two years of working with R to believe that I'd learned all that he could teach me and it was time to move on. He wasn't happy when I told him I was leaving. In fact, he was incandescent and told me I was an ungrateful cunt and that he'd do his best to make sure that I never sign another client ever again. Nice. But I also knew R blew hot and cold, and I doubted he would ever actually do anything about it. He'd been very philosophical when players left so why should he be any more difficult with me?

However, he was even less impressed when he realised that I'd never signed a contract with him, mainly because in his caveman approach to business he'd never bothered to send me one. That would've meant paying his lawyer a fee to draw it up, and R was never one for spending money, only on raking it in. Anyway, the absence of a contract meant that I had no covenant not to compete and even more important than that, there was nothing to stop me taking 'my' players with me.

That doesn't seem fair, you may well say. Well, in football there's not a lot that's fair. It's every man for himself. Yet, in this instance, I was simply using the rules and regulations to help myself. The Football Association Agents' regulations might have been pretty restrictive, they might have been rubbish when you were working for a company and trying to comply with them (or at least keeping up a pretence at compliance, as the good old FA didn't realise that most agents were driving a coach and horses through them), but when you were moving on, then, wow, could they be helpful!

This is the way it works. Neither FIFA (the world governing body of football – and I use the word 'governing' in its loosest sense) nor any of the domestic regulatory bodies recognise the existence of companies. To be an agent you have to be a warm and breathing human being. Not that many of the agents I've come across can be described as warm. Or even human if it comes to it.

Before the coming of the intermediary the FA only issued licences to individuals, but still did its best to get its hooks into the companies through which many agents traded. It had a really odd rule which stated that when an agent left a company, even if he was a director or shareholder, then any players who had signed representation contracts with him were automatically released and became free men with choices. The FA, in its generosity, gave them multiple choices (a bit of an intellectual challenge to some players), namely that they could either stay with the company and sign with another agent, sign with the departing agent whether he went out on his own or joined a new company, or they could say a plague on both of them and simply do their own thing and represent themselves. What is it they say about lawyers? When they do their own work then they have a fool for a client? I'm thinking you could say exactly the same about footballers. Things changed once the new Working with Intermediaries Regulations came to town and a limited company could register itself as an intermediary. The advantages are obvious as it now makes no difference if an individual leaves a company or not because the player is contracted to the company which just goes on and on. I say it makes no difference but of course that isn't quite right because if one individual has acted for a player within a company then the player isn't going to be happy if he gets foisted off on somebody else, and the directors of the company are going to have to use a huge charm offensive to keep him – even though on paper they may have the absolute right to keep him to the letter of his contract. When the guy who has left is also moving heaven and earth to find a way out of that contract there's a whole war erupting, with the player as the battle field. It's never pretty and it's always going to be expensive for both parties as they throw all sorts of incentives at the player and his family to keep him, or prise him away as the case may be. That is the problem for the FA and FIFA (though FIFA in particular has other problems at the moment) – they just don't think things through. But that's largely because they've never worked at the coal face of the industry.

Against the background of both the old and the new regulations most prudent and sophisticated agencies (and, yes, there are quite a few of those around) try to tie up their employees every which way but loose. It's not as simple as it appears because covenants have to be reasonable and enforceable and, generally speaking, in this country at least, you can't make them so restrictive that a bloke can't earn a living. The situation is made even more complicated and fraught with danger (at least as far as the company operator and owner is concerned) by the fact that many agents working for companies aren't actually employed in the normal sense of the word. Agencies appoint them as self-employed consultants or, as is more likely when they're unlicensed, as scouts. The same rules don't quite apply to the self-employed, so it's a minefield, but in any event R did fuck all which gave me a licence to kill as well as a licence to be an agent.

It was as surprising to me as it was, eventually, to R that he took his eye off the ball in this instance because he was such a wheeler dealer and cunning operator in every other way. I think he was so upset because he was really angry with himself: a) for trusting me; b) for not putting anything into writing; and c) as it transpired not even knowing the bloody rules.

I confess I felt a bit bad about the whole thing. On the whole R had been good to me, if not exactly generous, and my conscience was salved when I thought about just how much money I'd actually made him. I'd come to like him a lot and I could never forget his leaping to my defence with the Midlands CEO or what he'd taught me. But nothing stays the same forever. I had to leave the nest now and learn to fly on my own.

As I've discovered since I left, so many of the bigger agents, the high rollers, not to mention the wildly successful footballers, are just not ones for detail when it comes to their own affairs. Which is, I guess, why so many deals end in tears and why so few player–agent relationships last for the whole career of the player. As I say, one-agent players are as rare a breed as one-club players, which is why you have to squeeze as much out of your representation of them as you can while the going is good.

So many of the big agencies have suffered in the same way as R. They've taken someone in, trained them up, allowed and even encouraged them to deal with the players directly (often because they can't be arsed themselves) and then suddenly one day, *whoosh*. The bomb drops, and the player and the agent are gone in a puff of smoke.

Without the right paperwork, and sometimes even with it, there's very little that can be done about it other than to lock the doors on an empty stable and vow not to make the same mistakes again.

It's hard to say if it all comes about because the older agents are mean or because the younger ones are just plain greedy. My thinking is that it's six of one and half a dozen of the other, because in this wonderful world of football there are very few innocents and those that exist soon get trampled underfoot.

I know of one young agent (and he's probably typical) who was supported and encouraged by his boss in everything he did. He was given a job, leads when he'd none of his own and even given a car to get him around. After a long wait, and a not inconsiderable investment on the part of his employer, he finally landed a Premiership player who was fast-tracked into the first team and then into the international squad. At that point the young agent went in to see his boss and told him that unless he got eighty per cent of all the deals for the player (instead of the ten per cent he was getting on top of his basic salary) then he was off. His boss, not known for a calm and measured approach to life, told him to fuck off – which he did and within days the player gave notice to leave the company complaining about the lack of service and the fact that he'd never even spoken to the head of the company let alone met him.

On that occasion you might have had a bit of sympathy for the boss (not me, I don't do sympathy except at funerals and even then not always as there are one or two people I know who are better off dead), but then you have to realise that the situation whereby the old guard don't want to give anything away always prevails. To invest to progress is not a motto that they work with. They keep their agents on low wages and low commissions and even delay in paying them when they've banked the fruits of their labours. And even when they begrudgingly shell out they try to deduct all the 'expenses' they've incurred off the top. Not just a percentage of them equal to what the agent gets, but all of them. Generous.

When they've finally written the cheque out with great reluctance they can hardly be surprised when they get a knife squarely between the shoulder blades. I get that because it's payback for the metaphorical (and in a few cases physical) kicking up the backsides they've delivered to their young protégés over the years.

Just like others before me, I'd planned my escape from R carefully. I spent a lot of time quietly whispering in the ears of all the players – both those I'd found and signed myself and those who'd been with R for a while but found my instant service more appealing than the distance R tended to keep from them – that I was thinking of moving on and setting up on my own. R had taught me that there was no loyalty in the game and I took that particular lesson to heart. There's gratitude for you, as they say. If I'd been honest with myself and had a good long hard look in the mirror I'd neither have recognised, nor liked, the person I'd become in just two short years.

What I'd also done was to get as many of the players as I could to sign with me personally to ensure that my departure triggered off their release and so they were able to sign with me all over again. I also let players' contracts run out and then got them to sign blank contracts so I could insert the name of my new business and date them when the time was right. Wonder where I learned that trick? I guess the moral of that story is be careful what you teach your children.

I was pleased, although not wildly surprised, when even some of the players who had been with R for years jumped ship. I knew he'd regarded them as friends as well as clients and that had made him smug and complacent. A big mistake in our industry. He'd been to their weddings and christenings, had held their hands during their divorces and tabloid exposures, but he'd also been a greedy bastard with a liking for cash who too often had gone for the short-term hit rather than playing the long game.

One of his favourite tricks was to be paid by the club through the FA, thus doubling the percentage that was in the contract on the duality principle (something I'll explain later) and then having the gall to go back to the player and plead that he should've got more and ask the player for a 'top-up' in cash. He'd explain that he could only be paid a commission on the basis of the basic salary and the signing-on fee (the guaranteed income) but he'd got the player all sorts of bonuses and loyalty payments that weren't guaranteed, and that the player should provide the brown-envelope money to compensate for that. He was utterly convincing when he explained to the players that he'd constructed the contract in a way that benefited them, and almost every player bought it. But only once. After that they'd talk to their teammates and get wise. That was a huge mistake by R, because he was giving the players and anybody they told power over him. He gave me power as well because I knew he stashed all the money away in a deposit box at one of those security places that look like Fort Knox. I took some pride in the fact that I never threatened to expose him to the Revenue for that one. Perhaps the fact that I took pride in doing the right thing when the wrong thing would have been basic blackmail shows just how far my moral compass had shifted and how far I had fallen in such a relatively short space of time. But did R even think about the chance he was taking with me and the players who gave him the cash or did the colour of the money make him blind to the risks? Who knew? But it did play into my hands as I'll explain in a moment.

I played on that with the clients. I assured them they'd just be charged what was in the contract. No more, no less, and I'd make sure the club paid it all. I never mentioned that the player would pay tax on half (assuming I convinced the club to do the deal on duality) as the payment by the club would be a benefit in kind to the player. If and when they called me (and some wouldn't even notice it) to question why they'd had a tax deduction that month because of what the club had paid me, I'd have a ready answer. But that was a bridge I didn't need to cross – and as far as I was concerned, tomorrow's problem wasn't a problem right now. My concern was to ensure that I had a business moving forward. My business. Even if it was one that I'd substantially nicked from R.

R's rage continued to grow. I received threatening texts and even more threatening phone calls which, under normal circumstances, one might have reported to the police.

'You ungrateful little wanker. You were nothing when you came to me.'

'I don't think so,' I replied. 'I was obviously something or else you wouldn't have taken me on.'

'You won't get away with this. I will fucking destroy you. And I know you well enough by now to be sure that if I don't do it you'll do it to yourself. You're a cocky cunt and you'll make mistakes. One day you'll come crawling back to me and I will shove my boot down your throat so far it exits your arsehole. And that's all you are. An arsehole. I thought you were something different. I thought you were better than the rest, but I was wrong. You're even worse than the rest because you actually know what you're doing is wrong. Watch your back and don't go out alone at night. I'm warning you – which is more than you did for me.'

I didn't go to the police, of course. I just faced down the charging bull elephant by puffing out my chest and telling him that he should consider himself lucky that I didn't go to HMRC and give them the address where he had deposited his security box containing all his cash.

You may think that I was behaving badly, that I was the ungrateful cunt that he thought me to be, but I prefer to think of my actions as some kind of free education to him. He would never make those same mistakes again. As for me, I didn't intend making them even once. I was out there on my own in the big wild world and that was exactly where I wanted to be and wanted to stay. If you operate without partners and staff then you reduce the risks of anybody cheating on you. From now on I was going to be a lone wolf. Looking after Number One; and I'd make sure that there wasn't going to be a Number Two. And I suspected R would be exactly the same. What I did not know then, but came to learn all too painfully, was that he was right, that I would come crawling back to him, with all the risk of that boot shattering my face. Only you can never tell with people, and that in itself, that element of surprise in the world of football, is ultimately what makes it all worth while.

TEN

THE VULTURES CIRCLE

WHAT I DISCOVERED, just three months after branching out on my own, was that there were a fair number of sole operators out there who were just as unscrupulous as I'd been with R. You always know you have a problem with a player when he stops replying to your texts and then blanks your calls. It didn't take me long to find out what was happening. I was young. I seemed inexperienced. Just as I'd seemed like a breath of fresh air to R's players, now the vultures were circling to try to get to mine.

One of the lads to whom I'd become closest called me up and relayed the dialogue in such a way that I told him he might well have a career on the stage when his footballing days were over.

'I am X's agent [X being an established England international]. Gather you've left R and joined up with his young gofer. Nice lad, but not a player, if you get my drift. Has he told you that United have been watching you? No? I didn't think so. Well, I can tell you that they are interested, very interested indeed. I've got the manager there in the palm of my hand and I can tell you that nobody signs there unless I'm involved. If you want it to happen then I can make it happen – and I'm afraid your young man simply can't . . .'

And so on and so on, the poison dripping into the player's ear until, despite them wanting to stay with me, they'd truly believe I couldn't get them where they wanted to go while X's agent could.

I'd written contracts with the players all lodged according to the rules with the FA, so you would've thought that I'd be OK, but it's unbelievable the strokes players try to pull to get themselves out of a contract they were so keen to sign just a few months before, when you were the flavour of the day.

I've known them to claim that their signatures have been forged.

I've known them to claim that they didn't even sign anything. We'll get to footballers' selective memories when we look at the advice they say they didn't get when they've made a financial investment.

But sometimes you get the total reverse of that. One player simply couldn't say no (certainly not to the inducements being offered to him) and signed with three different agents. One of the agents decided to be clever and didn't date his 'contract' so he could have the option to say he was acting for the club rather than the player he was really representing (I'll come back to the reason for that in due course). The only problem was that when he saw that wasn't going to happen and sent his contract into the FA for registration somebody else had got in before him and the FA had already received two 'signed' contracts, coincidentally signed on the same day, which was the day that news of the player's impending transfer had hit the papers.

Given that the two agents were at different ends of the country one had to wonder how the player could've been in two places at the same time. The truth, of course, was that he'd signed on different days and the other two agents had also held back (though not for as long as the third one) until the deal was imminent. That also extended the term of the contract (which could only be for two years under the rules – go figure the reason for that one), but the player, at least, remained consistent. He simply said he hadn't signed for any of them and on the actual day of the transfer ended up speaking to a fourth agent who then represented the buying club in the deal while the player completed the documentation by stating that he'd acted for himself. He almost dared the three agents who had lost out to sue but, of course, none of them did. They didn't want what they'd done to come out and they also didn't want the player bad-mouthing them in the dressing room and on the training pitches to all and sundry who would listen.

The new intermediaries regulations regarding contracts is even more confusing. As I say, I'm not an intermediary and given my track record am never likely to be one, but because I manipulate one or two I've made it my business to keep up to date with the mess that, with the help of FIFA, the FA have created. This is how it works now. There isn't even a standard form of representation contract. A couple of paragraphs will do. Date, length (still not more than two years), name of the agent and the player, and the commission rate. You can bung in more if you want, but sometimes less is more, particularly when players aren't slow in coming forward to tell you that the other agents they are talking to are happy with a single sheet of paper. Each intermediary has the equivalent of his own web page at the FA but it seems that they don't even check any more to see if a player has already signed with another agent. If he signs with you and you upload that contract onto your page then that's it. You've registered it. The death of paper (meaning less work for the FA) has meant the birth of chaos when a deal comes to be done for a player who has got three contracts uploaded with different intermediaries. Good luck with all of that when the shit really hits the fan.

As the FA were only interested in Agency Activities, doing deals for players or clubs in other words, and had only a passing interest in commercial contracts, I took to getting players to sign two contract with me. One for two years for the playing stuff and another for five (or ten if I could get away with it) where I earned twenty per cent of all commercial deals. That way even if a player didn't want to re-sign with me to do his playing stuff I still had something over him and his new agent, particularly if there was some serious shit happening with his commercial profile. If he did a tv advert for a hundred grand, even if I didn't do the deal, he owed me twenty thousand, and as you can imagine, even though it didn't happen too often, it led to some serious debate with the new agent fucker who'd knicked my client.

'You don't think you're going to get away with that,' one said.

'Try me,' I replied. I was seriously pissed off as I'd worked my bollocks off for this player to get him a move from the lower divisions to a Championship club and now he was moving without me to a big Premiership club where I knew his new agent had a thing going with the manager. He'd been called into the England squad, was a good looking boy and there was a lot at stake.

'We've taken legal advice and they tell us your contract won't hold water.'

'Fine. I'll see you in court then. My lawyer is very happy with it.' And if he's wrong, I thought, I'll sue the balls off him because he drafted it.

The pissing contest continued for another half an hour before we got down to the nitty gritty where I not only got Mr Clever Dick new agent to buy me out of the commercial contract but also to throw in ten per cent of what he was going to make from the playing contract. I got that when I threatened to sue him for an illegal approach to my player while he was still under contract with me, and the threat to expose his relationship with the manager of the Premiership Club to an investigative journalist.

None of that very nice but sometimes an agent just has to do what an agent has to do. Law of the jungle. Kill or be killed.

A slightly more sophisticated excuse, and one that seems to be becoming very popular where a lawyer is involved, whether as the wannabe agent or as a part of the company seeking to sign him, is that the player claims he wasn't told to take independent advice before he put pen to paper.

'This contract was just shoved in front of me and I was told there was nothing in it to worry about and if I didn't sign right away then the deal wouldn't happen.'

There was a clause at the end of the standard Agency contract under the old rules where the player acknowledged that he'd been told to take independent advice, but invariably said he'd chosen not to. And you know what, generally speaking, he really didn't need to back then because the FA would only register a contract if it was in the standard form with a few approved additions. As I've said, that's all changed now and even I can see it's not a change for the better.

Yet I've known shrewd operators looking to get players out of contracts use the argument that while the player was an ill-educated professional footballer knowledgeable only in the art of kicking a ball around, the agent was a wily, sophisticated businessman who simply took advantage by telling his potential client to trust him as to what he was signing. And now the trust is gone. Because it suits him to say he didn't understand and doesn't trust his agent any longer. Footballers are very adept at reinventing history and providing a revisionist view of what actually occurred.

That's true as well when they find they have to pay something to the Revenue for a great deal the agent did for him. This is the scenario. The player is delighted with the deal and can't wait to put his signature on the line.

'OK,' the agent says, 'the club are paying my fee but to save you VAT on half the bill I'm also putting down that the deal was done on a duality basis. Means I acted for the club and you.' He didn't but if everybody says so and HMRC agree, then who is the agent to argue?

'There's one thing though,' continues the agent. 'Because the club are paying half my fee that's a benefit in kind for you (as if they were providing you with a house or buying you a car) so there will be tax to pay on it. But as my fee is 100k, instead of you paying the whole of that you'll pay tax at, say forty per cent on half of that so this whole deal, which is making you two million a year, is going to cost you about 20k in tax and the club will deduct that from your salary at some stage and send it on to the Revenue.'

'Yeah, great,' the player will say and might even add, 'Thanks!'

Then a few weeks or months later the agent gets a call

'Can you call the club for me?'

He'll never talk to them himself, of course

'Sure,' says the agent, 'what about?'

'They've fucked up on my wages. I'm about twenty grand short this month.'

Now, there are a lot of players who wouldn't even notice. I mean what's twenty grand? An afternoon's shopping for the wife on the credit card? A new car for a mate? A deposit on a holiday villa to entertain twenty buddies? All through the great deal that his agent has got him. But this player (or more likely his wife or girlfriend) had noticed.

'Yes,' says the agent, 'I did tell you at the time we signed off the deal.'

'All I remember is you saying the deal wasn't going to cost me anything and here we are and it's costing me twenty fucking grand.'

'But you were on ten grand a week and now you are earning forty thousand every seven days.'

'But you didn't tell me . . .'

And so the seeds of discontent are sown and when another agent homes in that will be the first thing the player says to him while agent number two says, 'Well, if you'd used me you'd have certainly paid nothing because I would just have acted for the club, let you represent yourself and trusted you even without a contract.'

Job done and player gone and with him thousands of future revenue.

There are loads more examples of the my-hamster-ate-my-homework variety. 'I was told I'd only get a move to this club if I signed.' Or on a slight variation of the theme, 'I was promised a move to this club if I signed. And I didn't get it.' 'I was blackmailed into signing because my potential agent knew I'd been with a bird after a night on the town and threatened to tell my missus if I didn't.' 'I signed because the agent promised to give me back half of his commission.' Substitute 'my dad' for 'me' and that's another option. 'The agent said he'd buy my mum/dad a house/car/holiday of a lifetime.' Et cetera, et cetera. You get the picture.

The fact is that I've known all of these to be true in the case of some agents and some players, but whether or not they're true when a player is trying to wriggle out of his contract who on earth actually knows? That's one of the more exasperating aspects of being a football agent. The thin line between truth and fiction so often becomes blurred.

One agent developed a particular scam to perfection. I've mentioned the guy who slipped a totally fictional and fraudulent loan agreement into the papers. Another agent, in his impatience to get players signed up to him, he seemed prepared to offer them a substantial signing-on fee. Sometimes it went to the player himself and sometimes to a parent, and the agent always weighed up the amount against what he thought he could earn. But he wasn't one for taking chances so what he did to cover all bases, was to slip a 'loan agreement' into the papers, and the players just blithely signed everything stuck in front of them. If the player's moves didn't recoup the loan or if the player dared to leave him then the lad would find himself faced with a lawyer's letter demanding repayment of the 'loan' with interest. The player couldn't deny he'd received the money and the agent would protest that he'd done nothing illegal but simply say that he tried to help the player who was desperate for money at the time. It didn't do a lot for agent–client relationships but it all helped to make this agent's wheels go round. That is until he came off the road when one player with whom he tried it on sent some heavies round to sort him out and after a few weeks in hospital he decided that enough was enough. Still, I suppose the redeeming feature here was that the player had actually received the money, in contrast to the guy who was willing to chance his arm to get the best of both worlds.

It can be pure fiction when an agent either tries to sign (or steal) a player by telling him that he's done a better job than his current agent and actually found him a club. But he can't actually tell him which club it is unless he can be sure that he's going to be involved. Usually, the agent on the make is winging it. He's just plucked the name of a club out of thin air and even if he doesn't disclose it at first he has it up his sleeve to produce, like a magician, when the player gives him the nod that he's buying into what he's offering. Then he'll try and put the two ends together. Namely, the player he didn't have and the club that didn't exist, and it's surprising just how many deals do come about in exactly that way.

In any event, there I was with my newly acquired (if somewhat illicitly acquired) clients, in my newly acquired business, trying to repel all boarders and knowing that at this stage in my career I was only as good as my next deal. Given that everything I'd done until then had been for R, I didn't really have a last deal to use as a calling card – just my youth, enthusiasm and dubious charm.

Players are notoriously impatient, blaming anybody but themselves if they don't get the deal they want either by way of a transfer or at their current club. Top of the blame list is invariably the poor old agent. Unfortunately, we're not equipped with magic wands and we can't turn a donkey into a thoroughbred or a crap player into a world beater. But you'll never find a player, even at the lower levels, admitting he's crap or a donkey.

I realised I couldn't just rely upon the fact that the players had liked me enough to abandon R and sign for me. I needed to have a few aces up my sleeve; the one that trumps them all is to have a manager as the wild card in your pack. That acquisition never comes cheap. I knew what R was paying, and he had deals going with at least half a dozen managers that I knew of. I was prepared to settle for just one to start with and once he was in the bag I could start to build up my collection.

Like in every other business, although more so in football, success brings success. And failure brings failure. Both winning and losing are habits that are hard to break once they get a hold. I'd come this far and I wasn't prepared to fail. I couldn't afford to fail. I wasn't trained to do anything else. I wasn't going to fail and my meeting with manager M was going to ensure that. Whatever price I had to pay.

ELEVEN

THE BUNG

I WASN'T A stranger to managers. I'd met a few through R and just by listening to gossip at agents' meetings I was pretty much able to put together a list of managers who were, how shall I put it . . . approachable. And amenable once approached. Amenable, that is, to what in the bad old days would've been called a bung and now in these modern times is called – a bung. Or, if you're trying to police the business and want to be unkind, you might call it a bribe.

Nothing really changes in an industry such as ours. Except that my lawyer told me I had to be careful of something called the Bribery Act. (Yes, I'd also acquired a sharp West End legal eagle along the way to deal with some of the shit that was being chucked at me as well as advise on some contracts to ensure no further shit was launched, unnecessarily, my way.) The Bribery Act did pretty much what it said on the tin. It worried me to the point that I actually went to a lecture on the subject, but then I thought fuck it. Although what I had in mind seemed definitely to be a criminal offence I figured they'd have bigger fish in their sights than me; and if I ever got big enough to be a potential target for the authorities then I might review the situation.

Meanwhile, some four months into my sole enterprise, I decided to take my chances. Yes, it was reckless, but in this business if you don't take your chances then you lose your opportunities. I had to balance the risk and work on the basis that the managers I'd be approaching had been on the take from others for so long that they were clearly made of Teflon. Nothing was going to stick to them no matter what the authorities, both inside and outside football, might think. After the Harry Redknapp case collapsed in February 2012, you couldn't see the CPS rushing to bounce another manager into court, and they weren't going to knock off the agent without the manager. The dock would contain Punch but no Judy.

The thing about managers, well, the thing about most people in football, is that they can never get enough money. You kind of understand that philosophy when it comes to players. I mean, you wake up one day, you're thirty-five years old, your legs won't take you out of bed and into training, and you have to accept that it's over. Just like that. The money machine has stopped printing the fifty-pound notes that were so easy to come by. But managers in theory can go on forever and some of them seem to. If it's not one job then it'll be another.

I think the fact that the survival odds are a little bit longer than for those of a First World War infantryman or those of a bomber pilot in the Second World War may be a factor in a manager's desire to stockpile cash at every opportunity. They seem to grab at whatever is offered to them, particularly as they often feel that, compared to the players they manage, they're criminally underpaid. Which may explain in some part why they turn to crime and, in some cases, actively seek out agents to work with them.

One agent, whom I'll call 'the Bagman', acts for several managers, laundering their ill-gotten gains and making a very nice ancillary living out of it in addition to his own legitimate agency activities. The crazy thing is that everybody knows who this guy is and what he does, and yet nobody seems inclined to stop him. It may be because he runs with a rough crew and is a bit of a gangster himself, but you wouldn't think that would scare off the authorities; although rumour has it that he has one or two of the FA administrators on his payroll as well. Useful guy to know, but not a man to cross as he's not averse to threatening with a crowbar or a shotgun if the mood takes him. I've heard it whispered that he thinks everything belongs to him and therefore he's entitled to first dibs at it. So far, our paths haven't crossed, but I'm sure they will given time and an upsurge in my career and fortunes.

As I say, I wasn't new to this tame manager lark. When R had been starting out he told me about one high-profile manager whose fall from grace, although not unexpected, came from a most unusual direction. He would always ask for a 'sweetie'. This individual had huge balls, as he not only expected these backhander 'sweeties' from agents but from players as well. A player would be offered a new contract provided a proportion of the uplift found its way back into the pocket of the man who had graciously granted the right to the new deal.

The odds were also on the player in question never having found his way into the club without his agent having also shared his commission with the manager. That gave the manager some comfort because if the player ever discussed his demands with his agent then the agent would reassure him by saying that there was nothing wrong or unusual about what was being asked. The player got a better deal, the manager got a rake-off, and the agent got a fee. Everybody was happy, including the club who didn't have a clue what was going on but had secured a player that its manager had said was decent on a long secured contract. The gravy train only stops occasionally and then just to spread the gravy around.

Now, the days of the brown paper bags have been well documented. They made an example of poor George Graham years ago, and while they were doing so there were quite a few who said, 'There but for the grace of God [or whatever divinity watches over football] go I.' But there are far more sophisticated ways of going about things. R used to explain to me that he'd never dream of making a payment directly to a manager. It would've been all too obvious from his records if the Revenue or the FA or even the police came calling. The trick was to get an invoice from somebody overseas for scouting fees and then to pay the money into an offshore account. That way it could be used as an allowable expense, but it also achieved the successful task of money laundering.

There are various schemes out there but the Bagman seems to be at the heart of most of them. Even if he's not involved at the start of the deal, somehow or other he worms his way into the loop and then earns some extra on top for the delivery on behalf of the manager. It does not even necessarily end with the money in a numbered account earning minimal interest, as properties get purchased abroad in the names of nominee companies and they make the money work to provide a pension for the day when the manager runs out of clubs. That can also be for any number of reasons: he's fucked it up on the pitch, the club's been sold and the new owner wants his own man in place, or, as was the case with one Premiership club, he'd tried it on once too often and had been rumbled.

Mind you, if the manager is successful on the pitch and if the bent agent delivers a steady stream of talented players then the road to departure can be a very long and lucrative one with all the dodgy dealings overlooked in the pursuit of honours.

However unpleasant the agent may be, if he gets a reputation as a man who delivers, then the club will use him. And if he gets a reputation for spreading the rewards around amongst the manager and his immediate staff then, for sure, the manager will make him his agent of choice. The corrupting influence can move all the way up the club hierarchy. Directors, CEOs, club secretaries and chairman are not necessarily immune to the persuasive charms of a generous agent.

Whatever it takes to make the wheels go around, I suppose. All I knew was that I really needed to establish such a relationship – or relationships.

Sometimes dodgy managers come in the most unlikely of guises. They can appear smooth and sophisticated in the media, lovable, even well educated, often well groomed and softly spoken, but as old Bill Shakespeare said, a man may smile and smile and still be a villain. Or something along those lines. I just remember it because it was in my GCSE play.

Agents don't get time to go to the theatre or the cinema as a general rule. They stick to the drama of the football stadium. There's rarely such a thing as a social dinner and when it comes to entertainment the lines blur because a good night out is when you go to a match and land a new player, or spot a new talent that you make up your mind to land, or get or develop a new relationship with a manager.

That was how I came to invite manager M out to dinner. I'd been encouraged to choose him because once I'd gone to see him to discuss an unhappy player. He'd been a big move transfer, a young kid with great potential, but he hadn't kicked on in his career and now spent more time on the bench than on the pitch. M had said he wanted to be helpful, accepted the kid wasn't in his plans and seemed willing to take a loss on him (whether the Club Chairman was so willing didn't enter the conversation, but I assumed that M would be able to persuade him in the silver-tongued language managers use to cover their mistakes in the transfer market).

'OK. This is what we'll do,' M had said. I was encouraged that he used the word 'we'.

'You find the lad a club and I'll either let him go out on loan, as long as they're serious about buying him when they can, or just find a punter at . . .' he named a price that was half of the fee the club had paid to bring him in.

'I can do that,' I said, absent-mindedly scratching my head and revealing my very expensive limited edition sports watch which had been a present to myself after my first major deal. I mean, who else is going to buy an agent a present except himself? Especially one worth several grand.

'Nice watch,' M said, 'I've always wanted one of those.'

And you can afford it, I thought, thinking of the salary he earned and all the bonuses he'd had after a lengthy and successful career. But I said nothing. I didn't need to. We both knew what he meant. *If I help you get this lad out of the club then you buy me one of those watches.* And he did and I did and nothing was said between us, but after that we both kind of knew what sort of people we were.

As I watched him down a bottle of very expensive Merlot I also watched, and listened, for any tells that might suggest he'd be ripe for the plucking when it came to a more permanent 'arrangement' that involved cash rather than a watch which might have been regarded as just a very generous Christmas present doled out in the same way as a receptive bank manager used to be looked after in the good old days – when there *were* bank managers, receptive or not. R had told me all about the days when he used to go into the branch of his bank just before Christmas and you could hardly get to the counter for the crates of expensive wine, hampers, electrical goods and all sorts of thank you presents from grateful customers – who in due course doubtless rewarded the bank by going bust and not repaying the loans.

It was to take another bottle of wine before he relaxed enough to accept that I genuinely wanted to do business and wasn't a journalist with a recorder. I saw that he was wearing the watch I'd given him which was a good start. So then he told me how it would work.

'You're a young agent, but if you look after me then I'll look after you.'

His looking after me would take the shape of his recommendation to some of his better young players. I asked what would happen if they already had an agent, and he just shrugged as if any such contractual attachment was a matter of insignificance.

'I'll tell them they'll do better at the club if they use you. And if they try to stay loyal to their old agents then I'll let them see that the players who come to you do better than them. Sometimes it may take a while, but I know a good player when I see one, and trust me, it'll be worth it for both of us in the end. You'll pay me [he named a figure] for each one I get signed to you and you'll give me half the commission you earn from him at this club or any other. I'll persuade the chairman to give our players the best deal possible and I'll also try and get you involved in any other club deals I can. Same terms.'

I knew it was highly unlikely that I was the only agent with whom he'd cut a deal, and I was pretty sure that some of the more experienced guys had secured better terms for themselves. But I've always known an opportunity when I see one and this was a chance for me to take a short cut into the grown-ups' tent. I'd been on my own for a while now and had come to realise that this could be a very lonely business. These sorts of arrangements of convenience were what so many seemed to be entering into, and so, after a brief wrestle with my conscience, which I won, I was committed.

That was going to help my chances of getting established players but most managers have little or nothing to do with the kids coming through the Academy system. That's left to the Academy Director. He's usually unheard and unseen, surfacing only when a club in desperation after the dismissal of a manager puts him in temporary charge. Yet, with players being courted at earlier and earlier ages he can be a vital piece of equipment in the agent's armoury. He's close to the players and their parents as the future of any young player rests in his hands and his alone. Youngsters will sign with a club on schoolboy terms and work their way up to the Academy but the big moment is when a club decides whether or not to offer them a scholarship. If it doesn't then they are out on their ear at the tender age of fifteen or sixteen. If it does, they've got a bit of grace until they get offered a professional contract (or not) at the age of seventeen onwards.

The big thing for the club is that by offering them a scholarship they secure compensation if another club comes in for them. The big thing for the player is to see whether or not there is anyone else out there wanting to offer them a scholarship and the huge thing for the agent is to get them signed up almost before anyone else has a chance. So after I got M on board my next target was to get an Academy Director – but that proved to be harder than I initially thought. Not because they were incorruptible, but because so many of them already had a beneficial relationship with my competitors.

And then I had a huge stroke of luck. I went to watch a Premiership Academy game and happened to get chatting with a dad who actually knew my parents. He told me that his son was on the brink of being offered a scholarship and thinking that I had more experience at this level than was actually the case, asked me if I could advise in the background.

'We've had a few of the big boys sniffing around, wanting young (let's call him Ritchie) to come for a trial, but they've all approached me through agents and that makes me really uncomfortable.'

So, he'd been approached by agents. Which made me realise that clubs were using agents to deal on their behalf for kids who must at times be well below the age of consent – and that meant another avenue I needed to explore at club level. Anything anybody else could do, legal or not, I felt confident I could do better. The arrogance of youth? Maybe, but it hadn't worked too badly for me so far, although something inside was telling me that I just might be getting a little reckless.

Anyway, that was how I ended up at a meeting at the club training ground with its Academy Director and his inevitable entourage of coaches and ex-players who were all making themselves out to be more important that they really were. The fact that the Director insisted on seeing the boy and his parents on their own at first did not auger well for my chances.

So I was a little surprised when I got invited to the inner-sanctum and found that the boy and his dad had been wafted away through another door and it was just me and the Director. He'd been an assistant manager at lower clubs in years past and was vastly experienced and knew exactly what he was doing when it came to choosing a potential star.

'I don't usually talk to agents about kids as young as Ritchie, but his dad tells me that you're a family friend so I'm making an exception today. Look, I'll be honest with you (that makes a change in football, I thought, not believing him for a minute; he'd been assistant to a right villain of a manager who'd taken him with him from club to club, which told me a fair bit about him – in our game you're generally judged by the company you keep) we really want Ritchie to sign for us and anything you can do to make that happen and get this nonsense about other clubs out of his head would be much appreciated.'

I decided to take the humble approach.

'Look, you've got a great reputation for bringing young players through and giving them a chance in the first team and I know the dad hasn't been impressed that these so-called bigger clubs are dealing with agents, so why don't you set out the terms of his first professional contract now, even though he can't sign it for a year or so. I'll tell them I've got you to agree to that and then you can tell them that you like me and have been impressed and that you wouldn't object to the boy signing a rep contract with me.'

I knew for a fact that at the very start of the season all the kids at this club had been gathered today in front of a representative of the PFA and been told in unison by him and the club that they would not look kindly on the boys having agents at this early age. The fact was that many of them had been committed to one agent since they were thirteen, but obviously Ritchie had been an exception.

J nodded, stood up to reveal a huge roll of fat at the top of his track suit bottoms and shook my hand.

'You're a bright lad, you'll go a long way,' he said.

Although my hand was hurting from his grip I smiled and asked for his phone number, which he willingly gave me. I called him the following week and suggested dinner; he accepted with alacrity and I knew I had my man and a regular pipe line of young players at that club.

I was beginning to realise I wasn't the same person I'd been when I'd started out so bright-eyed and bushy-tailed with R. I was becoming more and more like the 'others'. But was that such a bad thing when the others were successful, when the others made big money? Did it really matter that I was smashing my way through the rules and probably the laws of the land as well? Not really, I decided, and that would prove to be a decision that would change my life forever.

TWELVE

FOREIGN DEALINGS

A S IF DEALING with English or other home-grown UK players wasn't tough enough, representing a foreign player, particularly one from one of the African countries, is a total nightmare. And no, I'm not in the slightest bit racist, just a realist. For one thing, you're never sure that you're acting for the player, and then he may not actually be the player you thought he was.

Agents live or die by their reputations, and one of the great certainties in life is that if you persuade a manager to have a look at somebody who you claim to be the best thing since sliced bread and he turns out to be a cross between a plank and a Muppet then you can be fairly sure he won't take your word for anything again – even if he's sort of on your payroll.

I made that mistake very early on in my career with R when I was chasing each and every deal that came my way. I was contacted via Facebook by a player with some of the most impressive YouTube clips I'd ever seen. He looked like Pelé, Messi and Best all rolled into one package and seemed to have the looks of Beckham to go with it. With hindsight I should've asked myself why he was reduced to contacting the likes of me if he was such a brilliant player, and also why Real Madrid, Paris Saint-Germain, Barcelona and Bayern Munich hadn't fallen over themselves in the race to get his signature. Had I bothered to ask the questions and listened to the answers, it was very simple.

The answer would've been the same to both questions. He was fucking crap.

I put him into a Championship side in the Midlands where R was close to the manager, and even persuaded them to fork out for his flight and accommodation – unheard of for an unknown triallist. If I tell you that the club booked him in for a whole week for a trial and then cancelled the booking after one night you get the picture. I knew something was wrong when R called me in as he'd had a call from the manager and said I needed to get to the Midlands by lunchtime and that I'd be picking up the cost of any speeding tickets I might gather en route.

When I arrived at the club's training ground I soon discovered the reason for the manager's call and R's response. The player who had looked so good in his videos did, at least, have one thing in common with David Beckham. He had tattoos. In fact he was so covered by them that he looked like the cover of a science fiction book I once saw my dad reading, Ray Bradbury's *The Illustrated Man*. He was also carrying a paunch that reminded me of the player in a betting company TV ad where the background music is 'Hey, fatty boom boom'. With his man breasts he looked nothing like the bloke in the clips and as he confessed to me . . . he wasn't the bloke in the clips.

When I pinned him up against the wall of the changing room and virtually choked the truth out of him I soon became aware that he had some serious mental problems of a delusional nature. The thing was, he really believed he had the talent of the bloke on YouTube but that if he sent footage of himself as others saw him (rather than as he saw himself) then he wouldn't be given a chance.

In fact R made it all right with the manager (not too tricky when the manager wasn't going to kill the goose regularly laying golden eggs for him). The manager saw the funny side and even when I'd left, R always asked me if I had any more tattooed, overweight players I wanted to send him. It was a good lesson for me and I was always more cautious after that, checking out any players with more than one source before I recommended them.

However, all agents are chasing the same dollars and the same dreams, so there is still the faint temptation when you get the chance to represent a player who looks good on paper and on film to take a chance. Yet, as I say, I still remind myself that football is played in the flesh, on grass and not on film or on paper – and that has stood me in good stead.

So, back to Africa. I was once in the States watching a Major League Soccer game and said, 'That black boy looks good,' and I was told that if I had said that to a non-white I was quite likely to have my lights punched out for my trouble. But this is the point I want to make. Players from different countries have a radically different approach to the game and to representation.

There are some great players around from Nigeria, Ghana, the Ivory Coast and Cameroon all playing at the highest level of the game, represented by some decent local agents who are usually working with influential agents in the UK. However, there's also a cottage industry of one-man bands out there trying to persuade you to work with them and sending you the names of players they can bring to the table, who, again, often look quite attractive on paper. Plus, they all claim to have access to so-called 'academies' dotted along the length and breadth of the African continent and from which they claim to have the pick of the crop of the emerging young talent.

I'm sure that some of these kids are talented, but the approach of some of the agents who do actually make a living out of them does smack a bit of a cross between human trafficking and the slave trade. Anyway, like a lot of other agents I get regular invitations to come out and visit and see for myself – and maybe I should just brave the vaccinations and do just that.

But there are all sorts of problems attached to representing these foreign players whether they're kids or adults anyway. The UK exercises tight work-permit controls outwith EU players, and even experienced players have to be regular internationals for their national side and sometimes, if the nation is only a small footballing country, even that isn't enough.

Apart from the fact that you're not supposed to move kids that young across borders and certainly shouldn't be earning from them, there was, for years, a scam of placing the kid in a convenient EU country and then applying in due course for a passport. R had great contacts in the likes of Spain and Italy in the shape of dubious immigration lawyers and other officials who seemed able to conjure up EU passports at the drop of a hat (or at least at the drop of five grand or so) for the least likely of candidates.

The other route was to place them temporarily – or 'park them' as the saying goes – in a Scandinavian or Benelux country who for a long time made that possible. Again, once the player had played there for a while, often gathering a local wife along the way, he could sneak into the UK under the radar having acquired a suitable passport.

However, when it came to South American players, what I soon discovered was that I was coming up against what the FA and FIFA call third-party ownership. It's commonplace in South America and some other jurisdictions, but the FA simply don't like it and have declared war on anything that even suggests it might be happening.

So, what does it mean and how does it work? Like a lot of UK agents I've got myself a partner in South America and I'm not just dipping my finger into the honeypot . . . I'm plunging my whole hand in right up to the elbow.

Just examining the likes of Brazil and Argentina for the moment, where there's a heady mixture of young talented footballers, they almost invariably come from unbearably poor backgrounds, if not the *favellas* themselves, and are there for the taking by rich predatory agents. In fact, they're there for the taking by anybody – and by anybody I mean unlicensed individuals who seem to take a delight in putting two fingers up to the global football authorities as they continue their uninterrupted march towards multi-millionaire status. Forget *Twelve Years a Slave*. These kids can become slaves for their entire careers.

This is how it works. There's a talented youngster from a poor background. He can sometimes be as young as eight or nine. The agent comes to his family and offers to give him money or, more likely, give the family money. From that moment on, the player effectively belongs to the agent to do with as he wants – football wise, that is. I've come across a few gay agents in my time, but no paedophiles. We can be accused of everything else but not child molestation. We leave that to the TV stars, media celebs and politicians.

Anyway, some good does come out of the 'ownership'. The lads do get some education and generally keep out of the clutches of the gangs and the police, but from a very early age the focus is on turning them into money-spinning, football-playing machines. There's a Dickensian feel to the whole system. It's not toiling in the workhouse or being shoved up a chimney, and it's not the poor house either – whatever a footballer may earn he's unlikely to go to debtors' prison – but in many ways there's still something of the Oliver Twist about it with the agent cast as the wicked and manipulative Fagin.

As the kids grow up, the local agent will probably place them with a domestic club. He won't earn a fortune, but whatever the club pays for the youngster will end up in the agent's pocket. The agent may argue that he deserves that for his investment and ability to spot the talent, and it's hard to dispute that really.

When the kid starts earning there's a bit more payback as well, but the real jackpot is yet to come if and when the lad is good enough to move to a European club. As I've said, by then he may well be travelling on a passport of convenience, and the local agent will almost certainly have a European agent (or an agent from some exotic tax haven) with whom he'll be dividing the spoils, having made sure to recoup the investment he's made over the years.

If you have followed everything I've been telling you – sorry if that sounds condescending, but I've got so used to dealing with footballers – you may wonder how the agent can earn anything given that third-party ownership is frowned upon in so many jurisdictions and carries a penal sentence in the UK. Well, here's the plan. If there's any kind of fee paid by the European club to the player's home club then because the agent, rather than the club, owns the player, the agent takes the lion's share. If for any reason there's no fee then the payment for the player is concealed in the agency fees in acting for the buying club and the successful delivery of the player. What is a given is that until the player becomes a super star, the agent (or agents) will earn considerably more than him from his career. And even when he is a superstar they may earn just as much if a massive transfer and commercial opportunities come along.

Never mind that it's all against the rules. If a club wants a player, really wants a player, then the rule book goes out of the window along with the club's high moral stance. One thing I learned pretty early on was that clubs have totally different rules in different situations: when the agent has a player they really want, to the situation where they already have the player and it's simply a matter of renegotiation, or where they're prepared to be persuaded to sign a player but aren't all that bothered if they don't.

As my work in this business has gone on, I've realised that when it comes to hypocrisy, clubs take all the prizes. At the same time as its chairman/CEO/manager is going public slagging off some agent or other for easing a player out by unsettling him, then that same club is paying a barrow-load of money to another agent (or quite probably somebody unlicensed) for easing a player in and dishing out exactly the same amount of dirt to another club.

I've strayed off the subject of foreign players and ownership a bit, I know, but ownership can come in all shapes and sizes. One very high-profile player was totally controlled by his agent throughout his career. The agent managed to get media headlines by saying the player wanted away. The club went ballistic, not least its excitable and seemingly totally unforgiving manager. They said publicly they'd never deal with this agent again and all their other players were specifically warned not to deal with him, but however hard the club tried, it could not drive a wedge between the player and his agent. Within less than a year the club had been forced to grit its teeth, buy a very long spoon and sit down with the same agent who had been barred from coming anywhere near the stadium or the training ground to negotiate a brand new extended and much improved contract. Talk about expediency.

However, I think every agent in the country, many of whom intensely disliked the agent in question, was actually quite pleased when he made the club pay in spades for their actions by building in a penalty fee to compensate him for all the crap they'd thrown in his direction.

Now, when an agent controls a player like that, when he makes a fortune out of his commercial deals, isn't that really a kind of ownership? And is it any worse than taking a slice of a transfer fee in one way or another? Yet one is perfectly legitimate and the other totally illegal. Go figure.

It's a lovely business, isn't it? Such nice loyal people in it from top to bottom. But it's what I do and you know what? I love every minute of it.

THIRTEEN

SMOKE AND MIRRORS

I T MAY COME across as a bit xenophobic, but believe me, dealing with home-grown players and their agents is a doddle compared to dealing with foreign agents.

I've already explained how the overseas agent who controls the player interacts with his UK-based associate or partner. It's difficult enough dealing with somebody you know and trust; when you get involved in a transaction with somebody for the first time you have to watch your back. And your front. Not to mention your middle and any other vulnerable piece of your anatomy.

Somehow or other you have to sum up the other agents involved in a transaction and try to establish whether or not they're who they claim to be and if they really do act for the player they say they represent. None of which is helped when the player arrives with an entourage that may or may not include the actual agent with whom the English guy has been dealing. And may also not include anybody who speaks English. An interesting challenge.

When I'd been with R, I'd watched from the sidelines open-mouthed as he managed to get himself involved in a deal involving a South American agent who claimed to have a player wanted by a Premier League club. The player duly arrived, having demanded four first-class tickets, but there was no sign of the agent with whom R had arranged the transportation. The other three tickets had in fact been used by a trio, one of whom claimed in very limited English to be the player's mentor and/or guardian and/or representative depending upon the time of day R spoke to him and also depending on how much of what he said R actually understood.

The other two companions were even more sinister and incomprehensible, consisting of two burly South Americans who appeared to be related either to the player or his wife. R never did find out. The three of them created a major problem for R because they made it quite clear that all communications with the player had to be through them and there could be no direct conversations between the player and R. That might have been tricky anyway, as the player spoke only Spanish and R's grasp of that language was limited to two words: 'sangria' and 'paella'.

With everything being done via the 'representative', R had no idea what he was telling the player or even if the details of the deal were being correctly relayed to him. He had no idea what the player was really looking for, although it was certainly more than the club had to offer, as everything had to be 'net'.

R had explained to me early doors the concept of 'net' or 'netto'. If you told an English lad he'd be earning three grand a week he immediately understood he wouldn't be getting that amount into his bank account and that the Revenue would take their slice. But tell that to any player outside the UK and he assumes that the club (or some other beneficent being) will be paying the tax on his behalf and that what the gross salary is in his contract is exactly what he'll receive. Talk about cultural differences.

On the day of the transfer we all squeezed into the office of the club chairman who said he wanted to see the correct documentation to know he was dealing with somebody who actually had authority to represent the player. And, by the way, who are you all?

R phoned the player's original agent – who quite clearly hadn't been invited to the party – who expressed astonishment that the player was even in England let alone about to conclude a deal. So the chairman's question became highly relevant. Who the fuck were all these people? R never actually found out, but the player still insisted he wouldn't sign anything unless his 'representative' not only agreed to it all but was also paid a million pounds. Which was unlikely to leave very much for R.

The guys who were there with the player gave varying assurances: from saying the old agent had released him to claiming that the agreement had expired, had never been signed or had been induced to be signed pursuant to fraudulent representations and/or promises of payments which had never materialised. Take your pick basically. Who knew?

Eventually, R, by consummate negotiating, managed to get the club to agree that he could act for them and receive a comparatively modest fee. The club, having flatly refused to make any kind of illegal payment of one million quid to a bloke they'd never met before, then doubled the signing-on fee they were going to pay the player so that he could pay the representative directly. And for a while it appeared to have ended reasonably happily, although with a few bruised egos and damaged pockets.

But football is not the land of fairytales and is rarely filled with happy endings. The original agent simmered like a volcano for a while and then erupted. He sued the player for the commission he claimed to have lost because he'd been excluded from the transaction. He would've sued R as well, except that R actually gave him half of what he'd received, so he was off the hook.

The player audaciously counter-claimed against the agent, saying all the things that the 'representative' had said in the meeting with the chairman were false and then adding, for good measure, that the deal he'd secured was no good because he'd understood that the monies he would be paid would be 'netto' and not gross. How on earth the poor agent could've checked that, when he'd been excluded from the negotiations, heaven only knew.

Whether or not the 'representative' ever got paid, whether he'd even told the player accurately what the deal really was, R never discovered. R was never one to give up and did have a tilt at getting the player to sign with him as he'd been the only one who'd known what he was doing during the whole deal, but he was tainted by his relationship with the real agent and by then the player had already moved on to yet another agent, who had rampaged his way into the club to try to renegotiate the deal up to the level the player allegedly thought it should've been.

Anyway, the whole fiasco was a real eye-opener for me in the world of international transfers. I promised myself I'd never get involved even in lifting a phone unless I was satisfied the paperwork was airtight. That was easier said than done. At the risk of sounding like a potential UKIP parliamentary candidate – again – the worst confusion often arises in relation to players coming from African or South American countries. However, as a general rule in the world of football, and agents in particular, nothing is ever what it appears to be.

One international player, for example, appeared to be controlled totally by the owner of the club for which he played. The owner would decide if and when he'd play for his country, and despite any international regulations would simply send in a medical certificate to say the player was injured if his absence did not suit him. He was also determined to control the identity of any agent who might come to represent him. The player, somehow or other, came to sign for an English agent. The chairman did not approve and consequently decided to instruct his own tame agent to sell the player at the price he wanted – an inflated one at that (the price that is, not the tame agent – it has to be said that he was a bit overweight). The English agent, foolhardily, totally ignored the chairman and got the player a trial at an English club, omitting to tell them that: a) the chairman had appointed another agent; and b) that the price was one that no sane club would ever pay. Not that in my experience I've ever come across what you might call a sane club by normal standards.

The player did well on his trial. The club was interested and tried to make an offer to buy him, which fell so short of what the chairman had wanted as to be insulting, but probably reflected what he was really worth. The chairman ignored the club and demanded that the player return. Instead of increasing the offer, the English club cut its losses (having paid for the player to come over) and, deciding that this was never going to be a straightforward transaction, simply pulled out. The poor player, whose English wasn't great, did not know if he was coming or going, and was left in limbo. Which really is neither coming nor going.

The agent appointed by the chairman started phoning other clubs to get some interest, only to find that the player's English agent had got there before him, suggesting a price that was half of what he'd been delegated to obtain by the chairman. Not unsurprisingly, none of the clubs were interested.

The chairman became impatient, as chairmen tend to do. Imagine the Fat Controller in *Thomas the Tank Engine* and you get an idea of the temperament of the average club chairman anywhere in the world. His agent finally succeeded in finding another English club sufficiently interested to offer the player a trial. The chairman agreed but then told the English club that if they wanted to see his player in action – yes, he really did regard him as 'his' – then they had to pay his fare over. The club, not being entirely convinced and having only agreed to see the player because of the persuasive powers of the chairman's agent, declined to pay. The chairman's agent, being unwilling and scared to piss off the chairman, not to mention having spent an inordinate amount of time in trying to place the player, agreed to buy the ticket himself. In for a penny, in for several hundred pounds.

The player duly arrived, and the club promptly phoned the agent to ask him why he'd sent them a player carrying an injury. The agent called the chairman, only to be told that he'd had to make an unexpected business trip for an indefinite period of time but would call as and when.

The call did not come. The English club assessed the injury and was told recovery time would be at least a month, so back the player went. You wonder who got the air miles. Once he was back, calls to ascertain his fitness were stonewalled by the club and the chairman remained steadfastly uncontactable. Meanwhile, the player's own English agent refused to give up and reactivated his own efforts to place the player. Clubs, having been contacted by two different agents quoting conflicting prices became increasingly wary about the whole thing.

I've said it before and I'll say it again: football is a village. Everybody knows everybody else's business, and every club knew the player hadn't only been on trial twice but had collected an injury the second time around, and had two people punting him about. They also knew that even if he was given a trial and proved his fitness that the transfer fee was likely to be a great unknown.

At this stage, the chairman's agent and the player's agent hadn't even spoken to each other or considered pooling their resources. They each felt they were operating within their own individual bubbles and racing against time. In fact, there was a race but, as it proved, neither of them had even got to the starting blocks because, to their mutual astonishment, they awoke one fine morning to discover that the chairman had miraculously surfaced and bypassed them both. He'd personally flogged the player off to a club in a totally different country for a fee which bore no resemblance whatsoever to that which he'd demanded, nor even to that the English agent had optimistically quoted to get the attention of clubs.

Faced with the choice of either bringing an action against the chairman and his club in his own third-world territory or trying their chances with a complaint to FIFA (about which more later), they both decided to cut their losses and retire to lick their wounds, with interesting stories to relate to their grandchildren in the future.

As I say, nothing in the world of football is ever what it seems to be and although a contract may say 'contract' on its outside cover, it doesn't necessarily mean that when you open it up. I worked out fairly quickly that a deal is only done when the money you have earned finds its way into your bank account. Until then it's all potential, and potential doesn't pay the bills or impress bank managers.

FOURTEEN

PROMISES, PROMISES

I'D BEEN OUT on my own for over a year and had convinced myself I was doing pretty well. I hadn't made a lot of friends among the other agents mainly because I was picking up their players with alarming regularity. You're not supposed to approach a player who's contracted to another agent, but if you don't, how on earth are you ever supposed to find out if he's ripe for the picking?

Sometimes you need to substitute 'belonging to' for 'contracted to'. I once flew to meet an African player who was scoring goals for fun for a European club. He was a nice young man but his English was not the best and he had an older guy with him who he introduced as 'mon ami'. This 'friend' seemed to be a lot more than that.

'Are you an agent?' I asked. We'd decided to use French as a common language as I spoke a bit, it was the player's second language and the friend's first.

'No, but I've looked after the boy here for all of his career,' and with that I realised that to win the confidence of the player I needed to do a deal with the friend.

Now, I don't know to this day whether it was the language barrier or a genuine misunderstanding, but I came away from that meeting with a signed representation contract (I'd explained that I couldn't, and wouldn't, act for a player unless I had a contract lodged with the FA. Not true but it worked a treat when

I used it as a ploy to get a player to sign with me) and without any firm agreement with the friend. So, back in England, I got busy and soon got a club interested in the player where I had a friendly manager who was happy to offer a trial where, if it led to a signing, there was a back-hander for him. I set everything up and then got a call from the friend.

It was hard to understand much of what he said because he was so angry, but the gist of it was that I hadn't asked his permission and hadn't told him anything and that if I didn't call the whole thing off then, and this bit I did understand, he was going to have me killed.

I weighed my options and thought, fuck it, if he wants me dead he can just join the queue. But in fact instead of killing me the friend killed the deal by finding the player a club in France. It didn't do a lot for my relationship with the manager who'd offered the trial and when it came to suing the player for a breach of my exclusive world wide representation contract then discretion as the better part of valour did kick in and I let it pass.

The most valuable asset for a football agent is his phone book. Mobile numbers of players are pure gold. They tend to change them more often than they change their underwear or their women, but just to get the number of a player you have targeted puts you in with a chance. A text is a good way to start, either mentioning another player known to the target or a high-profile player you already represent, preferably an international. Some agents don't even bother with the nicety of representing the player they mention, and just hope the target doesn't check, and that they'll be able to blag their way through things right up to the point where the target signs a rep contract. Even if the text doesn't get a response, at least you have an excuse to call the player to see if he received it.

The conversation usually goes something like this (assuming

he actually answers, although with some players you never really figure out if they're on the line or awake or not): 'Hi, hope you don't mind my calling but I've got something that may interest you.'

You either get a grunt in response or, if you're having a lucky day, 'How did you get my fucking number? I'm busy.'

To be honest, either of them could mean anything, and so you plough on into the unknown just hoping the player isn't shagging some bird while he's taking your call. And yes, I've known that to have happened more than once. Footballers always show such respect towards their women. I'm amazed they don't make them walk at least one pace behind them – when they let them out, that is.

'I hear you might be a bit unhappy,' you continue. He might well be if you've interrupted his sex life, but there you go. You're in hot pursuit and are you really going to let the odd orgasm get in your way? Anyway, your comment as to his happiness could refer to his situation with his agent or his club, and it's amazing how often he'll tell you. He tells you because, generally speaking, players are miserable bastards and greedy to boot, and they wouldn't want to miss any opportunity to put some money into their already well-lined pockets.

Now you've awoken their curiosity, you've got their attention and you're one step away from getting a meeting. Just as it is with double-glazing and insurance salesmen, once you have them eyeball-to-eyeball then you're in with a real chance. They'll have made a real effort and, trust me, for a footballer to get off his arse and come to a meeting is an effort, particularly when he could've been playing golf. And if you get the meeting then you need to make sure that you deliver.

So you need to find somewhere to meet where you won't be seen. Unauthorised meetings in public may be good for your ego and your profile, but if you're spotted, as one agent found out to his cost a few years back, it can prove to be a very expensive mistake. He met a player in a hotel with a view to tapping him up for a club who wanted a transfer, and although the agent in question may have stood to make a small fortune from the ultimate deal, he committed the ultimate transgression of being spotted – and hence found out – and received a not insubstantial fine and lengthy suspension from the FA. Not, I suspect, that either penalty cramped his style or really interfered with his business methods or acted as a genuine deterrent.

So, assuming you have found somewhere totally out of the way to meet, this is how the conversation goes. You offer them a drink. Sometimes they accept and, to be fair, it's usually just a juice rather than anything alcoholic. That comes when you're meeting the father of a young player. Be prepared for an endless evening of beers, shorts and boredom then. If the player you have come to meet doesn't accept a drink then he'll most likely just sit there, avoiding eye contact while checking for messages on whatever latest electronic gadget he's brought with him. The pressure is on you to make the running, to keep (what may well prove to be a one-sided) conversation going.

I've discovered that footballers never open conversations (well, at least not unless they want something), never make small talk and never show the slightest interest in who or how you are or what your personal family situation may be. All they care about is what you might be able to do for them, so it's best not to forget that. Although you need to sell yourself, you also need to have something that the player actually needs otherwise you might as well not bother to open your shop doors.

They don't even really care what you've done for other players, although if you have no track record you're probably wasting your time, unless you have a sister they might like to shag.

However, a few calling cards of previous deals does at least set the scene even if it only leads to them asking you what sort of deals you got for the players in question. You can try and take the high moral ground and say it's confidential, but if you think they'll be impressed by that, heartened that you won't be exposing their financial secrets to others, then you're fooling yourself. They want to know because they want to make sure they're not earning anything less.

You have to put into the equation of your courtship that players have the attention span of a newt and the egos of a dictator of a medium-sized, troublesome Central American country. This means that the time of the audience you have been granted with them is limited, and so you have to speak quickly and make them realise as early on as possible in the conversation that the very universe revolves around their individual careers and that you'll devote your own life to ensuring that planetary state will continue.

First of all, you find out who their current agent is. Once they tell you, then you come right out with it and ask if they're happy with him (or her, and yes, there are more and more women coming into the industry). If they say they are, then you tell them you understand; you understand, that of course you don't want to drive a wedge between them and their current representatives, but that, he, the player, has a duty to look after himself. Loyalty is a great virtue, but the deal that you alone can offer has to be given some thought. You tell them that you also like their current agent. That he's a good bloke and that you're sure you can work something out with him, that you'll look after him, and as you'll get everybody more than he would then he, the agent, won't lose out. You say anything to keep the conversation going. Promises in football come cheaper than anywhere else. They're not just two a penny, they're a hundred a penny and they're nearly always broken.

If the player tells you he's not happy then you've hit the jackpot. You run the other agent down and then you run him over again and again until it looks like he's been hit by a steamroller. And by now you can be fairly sure that the player has given up texting, emailing, surfing the web, tweeting or posting on Facebook (or whatever by then is the current fad). He's no longer playing video games because he's now the central character in your game and you're the only one pushing the buttons.

He's the game. He's the prey and you're the hunter. He's in your sights but he's far too valuable a commodity to kill. You'll only use the stun gun, and when he comes round he simply won't know what has hit him.

You tell him that you're 'in' at a Premier League club. That you, and you alone, can get him a move there. The sort of thing other agents say to your players. Tit for tat; dog eats dog. You tell him all the other things that you can do for him that his current agent can't. And then, when he's almost in your grasp, there's just one small problem left to address. The fact that he's already contracted to somebody else.

As I've made clear, footballers are hardly queuing up to participate in *Mastermind*. They might even struggle to join the dots to make a picture in a kids' comic. So once you have their ear, they tend to believe whatever it is you have to tell them. That is, until somebody else gets their ear.

So, particularly when what you're telling them is something they really want to hear, they aren't going to be too bothered about something as mundane as a previous contract if you have already told them it's the only impediment to their getting the move of their dreams. You have them on the hook and you just have to reel them in until they're lying at your feet, fresh from the water and gasping for breath.

'Don't worry about a thing,' you say. 'Just leave it to me and it won't cost you a penny, because I'll act for the club and you'll represent yourself. Because you can, you know, and the beauty of it is that you don't even need to tell your agent until after the deal is done because that's what it says in the contract with him.'

You don't add: 'You remember the contract? That's the one I've just torn into shreds and put in the incinerator.'

'What if my agent has a go at me?' the player might ask, if he's not totally devoid of intelligence.

'Leave that to me as well,' you reply in honeyed, reassuring tones. By now you're his saviour, he wants to trust you and you are there for him. Almost over the line.

The fact of the matter is that his agent may well sue him for breach of contract somewhere along the line, but by then you'll have banked the hefty fee you've earned from delivering him and that then gives you several options. One is to get him a specialist sports lawyer who can pick all sorts of holes in the representation contract. Although the FA check through all the contracts before they register them, to ensure they comply with their regulations, what they don't do is dig any deeper into the circumstances which led to them being signed. Nor once it's signed and registered do they monitor the agent's due performance of it and whether or not he's fulfilling his obligations.

Another approach is to bankroll the player to a certain degree (obviously not to a huge one as you don't want to give away too much of what you have earned, otherwise what was the point of the whole exercise), so that he can offer it to his old agent as a consolation. He's not really the old agent anyway as the poor bastard still has a contract which he thought was watertight, but he might just take it as an easy alternative to bringing a claim against his player and having the player turn things around in the dressing room to make the agent look like the bad one and ruin his chances with anybody else at the club. And if he does take it, then you're even more of a hero to the player than you were for finding him the club and ensuring he got a great deal. So, your contribution is a very small price to pay.

The third course of action is, in fact, one of total inaction. You do nothing, take the short-term view that it was a good deal for you and just leave the player to his fate. If it gets really nasty, he has no proof of what he claims you said and all you've done is act for the club and you just move on, somewhat the richer.

I know quite a few agents for whom that third option would be the preferred choice, but to me it seems just plain silly – not to mention plain greedy and short-sighted. However attractive it might be not to give away any money, the fact of the matter is that players talk. They say good things when you've delivered (even though their memories of the good things may be cut short when a predatory agent comes along to offer the earth, as illustrated above) and they'll certainly say bad things when they've been shafted. In fact, my experience is that they'll say bad things even when they just perceive they've been shafted because they've had to lay out a bit of money by way of a fee or tax, but there you go. I acted for one player where the club had a thing about paying agents. So, what I did was to get them to add a few grand to the player's signing-on fee so he could pay me directly. I even worked out the tax on what he'd have to pay on the extra I got him and I invoiced him for a net sum after taking off that amount of tax. He did pay with a cheque in a grubby envelope and the wrong amount of postage so I had to pay extra when I went to collect it from the Post Office, but still. In the envelope there was just a cheque, not even a thank-you note, and then, as soon as he could he dumped me. And when I asked him why, he said it was because I'd charged him. I tried to explain that if the club had paid my fees on his behalf I'd still have, in effect, been charging him, but he wasn't having any of it.

The truth is, you can't carry on in this business for too long if bad things follow you around from deal to deal, leaving a nasty smell. There are one or two agents who specialise in foul-smelling deals, and because they deliver they're still allowed into the room, and I suppose you get to a point where you're so successful that nobody has the balls to talk about your BO.

Me, I give a bit away of what I get every time. The old agent might be left feeling a bit down, but something is better than nothing, and you know what, I'm starting to get agents I've taken a player off talking to me again and even wanting to work with me and tap into my connections. People tend to be pragmatic in this industry. You don't have to like the folks you work with. You just have to make money with them or out of them.

Going back to the sort of deal I was talking about where you nick a player by sweet talk, the odds are that many agents who do just that don't have a club ready and waiting, and certainly not the attractive club they mentioned. The player giving them the nod is the signal for them to put the two ends together to make fire. If they can, then great. If they can only do it with another club then they'll probably be able to substitute that club for the one that hooked the player. And if they can't find any club at all, well, all it's cost them is the juice they bought the player and a bit of time, and his old agent can have him back and is welcome to him because there's nothing to be made from him.

I'm not going to embark on what the word 'agent' means in legal terms because in football it seems to mean something quite different. My dad was a sales agent and quite happily signed contracts for the company for which he worked and it was bound by them. But a football agent can't bind a player, as I found out.

I had a player whose contract was running down at a club. A manager at another club liked him and made him an offer which was attractive. I went up to see the new club, met the manager and the chairman and we knocked out and agreed on terms for my player which far exceeded what was on offer at his current club. A formal offer was made and typed up. The club signed it and so did I. We rejected the offer on the table from the old club and then disaster struck. The manager who had liked him got the sack and the chairman of the club brought in somebody else who clearly did not fancy my player and wanted to find a way to get out of the deal. The FA Regulations gave him the perfect escape as they clearly state that only the club and the player can be parties to a playing contract, which has to be signed by both of them. My magic piece of paper was worth Jack shit and the club just put up two fingers, leaving me to explain the situation and scurry around to try and find another club at what was, by then, an advanced stage of the transfer window. I managed to pull it off, albeit for less money, and then was told I didn't have a snowball's chance in hell of getting any compensation from the club with which I had signed on behalf of the player. The player did stay with me because he knew I had meant well and, indeed, he was one of the first to come forward me and offer me help when the roof began to fall in on me.

Anyway, despite that minor blip, I guess I must have been doing something right because I was being noticed. Not just by players, but agents as well, and not just the agents who couldn't help but notice me because I now had their players. And that was how I came to be having lunch with Agent B who had gone beyond the foul smells of reputation because he could afford to have his own deodorant and after-shave designed for him. So I took with me the longest spoon I could find, rolled up at the Mayfair restaurant he'd chosen, and crossed my fingers that he was picking up the bill. Which, indeed he did. In cash of course.

AGENT B

EVERYBODY IN THE business knew or knew of Agent B. His nickname was 'The Lizard', because every time he got the merest sniff of a deal he crawled out from beneath the nearest rock. B was not the most pleasant of individuals. In fact, let me put it another way, he was the sleaziest, greasiest man I'd ever met. Somebody described him as 'unctuous', and after I looked it up in a dictionary I had to agree. Charles Dickens would've smothered him in adjectives.

Yet, the one positive thing you could say about him was that he knew how to make a deal happen, and although he rarely directly recruited players of his own to represent, he was often sought out by a club to act for them when they wanted to source a particular player and needed to untangle the log jam.

As one fairly decent chairman told me when I asked him why he'd anything at all to do with B he said, very succinctly, 'He delivers. He may cost, but he delivers.'

He didn't add that B also had scant regard for any rules and regulations – which he truly believed had not been put in place with him in mind. He wasn't licensed out of England so unless he did something wrong here when he'd had to register for a particular transaction as an overseas agent, the English FA had a hard job pinning anything on him. He ducked in and he ducked out, bobbing and weaving like an overweight heavyweight boxer, but deliver he did, albeit at a price. And the price was often paid by an innocent agent who had thought he had a player or transaction in hand only to see B swoop down and take it out of his grasp.

It did not matter one jot to B that he was taking the bread out of the mouth of an agent who actually represented the player and who had worked very hard (sometimes for years) for that privilege. B was just focused. Show him an opportunity to make money and he was like a dog with a bone. Sometimes he would even move on to the next deal before the ink was dry on the paper of the last. He was a man obsessed.

There were many stories told about him, some of which seemed like pure fiction until people who were there or were involved confirmed their truth.

On one occasion, he actually kidnapped a player and quite literally wafted him off on false pretences to his remote, albeit palatial, home. The player in question had been with his agent for years, but the opportunity came along for him to move to a top club abroad. B had it all planned out. He convinced the player that his own agent just couldn't do a deal of this magnitude. He got himself a retainer from the buying club where he was well known, so that was all fine and dandy. He then approached the selling club and asked them what they wanted for the player. They named a price, and he said he'd try and get it for them, but anything above that would belong to him. So, having got control of both ends of the transaction all he now needed to do was to get the player as the last piece of this very remunerative transaction. But there was a problem. The player's agent was honest and reputable, and to see this deal through B had to control the player as well. Hence the drastic step of taking the player away from his loved ones and, in particular, from his agent.

This was in the days before representation contracts had to be registered, and the player had enjoyed a long relationship with his old agent which was so based upon trust that neither of them had felt the need for a written contract. Consequently, he was there for the taking, and take him B did, both metaphorically and physically.

It didn't take B too long to persuade the player that he, B, was the only one who could actually make the deal happen, and, I suppose, with him acting for all the parties, that was actually true. You may wonder why the player was so amenable, but B was very convincing and assured the player that everything was being done with the knowledge of his agent and that when the time was right he would be called in to the deal – but to bring him in now would prejudice everything. It was a great chess move.

At first everything went swimmingly. For B. He added a million pounds to the asking price of the selling club. He then gave an even higher figure to the buying club and asked for an extra commission from them if he reduced it to what the selling club wanted (plus his million of course). Naturally he knew he could reduce it because the selling club were not expecting it.

He then asked the player what he wanted and applied the same technique, telling him he'd be charging a 'super commission' (payable in cash of course) on the excess he might obtain for him. It was all so terribly simple, as long as he could keep the parties from talking to each other (and keep the old honest agent far from the scene of the crime, because crime it was) – and why should they when good old honest B was there to enable them to communicate? Just like Hannibal in *The A-Team*, he was able to say he loved it when a plan came together.

I suppose, if you were taking a pragmatic view of the whole situation, you could say that nobody really lost out. One club sold a player and got the price it wanted. Another club acquired a player it really wanted (and who in fact helped them both to a domestic title and a tilt in Europe), and the player doubled his salary in the move – and with the tax-free advantages, he had no worries about life after his career ended. But the biggest winner of all was B, and here he was in the flesh (rather a lot of it after a life of expensive dinners and even more expensive booze) and he'd asked me out to lunch.

R had told me, quoting the old Hollywood adage, that there was no such thing as a free lunch, so I never really relaxed, told him I didn't drink when he offered me wine and never for a moment let my eyes move from his face. He wasn't one for eye contact, so that rather put him off as his eyes slid all over the place and ended up staring intently at the crisp white tablecloth.

He told me he liked my style, that I reminded him of his younger self, and after a few questions about my business and the level of my turnover he asked me if I'd like to work with him. And I have to say I was tempted. Despite everything I'd heard about him he came across as sincere, and much more pleasant than the reputation which preceded him. But my brain finally engaged over my heart and I said no. I'd heard too many stories, so many that some of them just had to be true.

Like when he dashed off to a transaction he'd set up very much like the one I described in detail before, only to find that the player had got there before him. In this case the player was very much his own man and told the buying club (which had been assured by B that he controlled the player) that he'd never actually met him. B arrived, breathless from his last killing, only to find the player sitting down with the club officials and his father, the terms already agreed. The only words that passed between B and the player were as follows:

PLAYER: 'Who the fuck are you?'

B: 'I'm B, your agent.'

PLAYER: 'No, you're not. Just fuck off.'

Some you win, some you lose, I guess, and B did not have a reputation for sensitivity or a thinness of skin.

On this occasion I trusted my instinct, told B I'd let him know (given that I didn't want to decline there and then in case I got lumbered with the lunch tab), and when I did let him know it was by text and read, thanks, but no thanks.

I knew I'd made an enemy, because he wasn't a man who was used to people saying no to him. Don't get me wrong. I'm not saying B was totally dishonest or dishonourable. In fact, if he agreed a deal with another agent he always kept to it. It was just that he tried very hard to avoid having to agree a deal. I'd heard that on one occasion he'd arrived in the middle of a transaction and grabbed it by the scruff of its neck even though he didn't act for any of the parties at its start. One startled agent suddenly realised that all the money in the deal was going to B, even though he was entitled to half a million pounds.

'Look,' he said, 'I don't really know you. In fact I've never met you before today.'

'Are you not trusting me, son?' B had said, pulling himself up to his full height and looming over the by now trembling agent.

The agent assured him that he'd trust him with his bank account, his child and the keys to his house while his wife was alone and naked in bed upstairs.

B rose and went over to his briefcase, which the agent noticed was full of cash. He pulled out a sheet of headed paper and signed it, and then handed it over to the agent.

'There you go, son. You just fill in the amount you think you're owed.'

And sure enough the money was paid over as soon as B received it, although if it hadn't been paid the agent would probably never have dared to sue B on the basis of the sheet of paper. Or, indeed, on any other basis, given his reputation.

I really wasn't prepared to give B the chance to show me what a good partner he could be even though, as it transpired in the future, it would cost me a deal. Quite frankly I had the feeling that if I'd gone in with him it might have cost me much more, including potentially my liberty. That particular asset of mine I managed, in due course, to fuck up all on my own, or at least just with a little help from someone I thought to be a friend. But meanwhile, let me tell you what the Lizard actually did to me.

I'd started to build up my own little network of contacts abroad, and one of them had introduced me to a player in one of the European leagues. He wasn't top class, but he scored goals consistently at his level and he was certainly good enough to play in the Championship.

I began to make some enquiries, although his current club was a bit reticent about the level of the fee it wanted; I eventually got a figure out of them which was fairly realistic. A few clubs showed a bit of interest, but none of them were sufficiently keen to make an offer, or even to pay up front to get the player across to have a look at him. But I soldiered on because that's what you do. You live in hope and you never give up: those are the two mottos that every football agent should have on his family crest.

Then, one day, I was sitting at home minding my own business when a friend called me and told me to switch on Sky Sports.

To my astonishment, there on the screen was B at Heathrow walking though with my European player, taking him to a club to which I'd already spoken, a club whose manager had told me he didn't fancy the player. As you can imagine, I got to the phone in a heartbeat and called the CEO of the club who expressed total ignorance of the transaction and thought it must be the manager winging it on his own.

This news did not surprise me, because there were already hot rumours in the industry that B and this particular manager were in cahoots. However, the CEO said he'd investigate and get back to me, and to be fair to him he actually did. He told me that the club were not proceeding because the price was too high. I asked him the price he'd been quoted, and he told me it was fifty per cent higher than my figure and that the player was heading home.

I let the dust settle and then got back to the player's European club who told me that B had contacted them and told them the price they'd quoted me was too high and had got them to agree to a lower figure, only then to ask the English club for even more than the original price to boost his own potential profit on the deal. Yes, B had been up to his old tricks again and had agreed with the club that whatever he got above the figure would belong to him. Only this time he'd been too greedy, and instead of making money the little jaunt had cost him the expense of bringing the player over (although I did hear that such was his nerve that he invoiced the English club for the costs of the flights).

Having got the selling club to see sense, I tried to resurrect the deal, but the buying club was now suspicious of the whole arrangement, and despite the player having done well in his trial, decided to pass. However, seeds of doubt had been sown about the manager and his relationship with B, and it wasn't too long before he got the sack. On the face of it, the dismissal may have seemed to be performance-based, but I knew the truth. You might have thought the club would look closely at all the players B had brought to the club in the past while this manager was there, but, not for the first time, the club didn't want to wash its dirty linen in public, didn't want to look foolish, and just closed its books on the whole sorry episode. It appointed a new manager in due course, but I knew that this guy was hand-in-glove with yet another agent, so I wondered how long that relationship might last – unless they were going to cut the CEO into their nefarious dealings, which was always a possibility at some clubs.

B was relentless and actually had the gall to phone me.

'Son, I'm really disappointed in you.'

I have to say I was lost for words for a moment.

'*You*, disappointed in *me*?' was all I managed to splutter out.

'If you'd have called me we could have worked out a deal between us and my pal (he mentioned the manager by name) would still be in a job. He's not happy with you and I reckon you owe the pair of us an apology. So the next deal you get, I expect a call and for you bring me into it on one side or another. Understood?'

'Go fuck yourself,' I replied.

'Not nice. We may have to teach you some manners. Maybe a phone call or a letter to the authorities about one or two of the deals you boasted about might help.'

I felt physically sick. Nobody had ever tried to blackmail me before, but I came to learn that for certain agents it was a standard tool of the trade even if they never carried out the threat.

'And what about your deals?' I replied

'Are you threatening me, son? *Nobody* threatens me,' and then the line went dead.

I have to confess that for a while I avoided dark alleyways and put a security system into the Shoreditch flat I had bought for myself, but apart from coming down to find my tyres flat one morning (simply could well have just been par for the course for the area) and some late night number-withheld calls, I managed to keep all my body parts together and nobody came knocking at my door from any of the authorities. At least not then.

I'd like to say that justice caught up with B, that clubs kept their distance, that the Revenue was hot on his heels, that he was yesterday's man, but the fact was that he lived (and continues to live) happily and prosperously ever after, and even today he's still in demand as the man who delivers where others fail.

But he wasn't for me. I might have been losing my moral compass but I didn't feel ready to descend to his murky depths, however much money it might make me. At least, not just yet.

SIXTEEN

THE FRONT

I HAD PLAYERS signed to me, decent ones at that; I had a couple of managers I was 'looking after'; and I had gained the grudging respect of some of the more experienced agents who could see by now that I was a young man on the up. But there was something missing from my armoury. The ex-footballer who could act as my scout, talk the talk and walk the walk with the young players because he had the experience, had done it all before.

It had become apparent that anybody who was anybody was utilising one or more of these ex-players to a certain degree. Sometimes they were on the payroll, sometimes on commission and sometimes it was hard to tell which of the operators at a company was actually the licensed agent. Indeed, as far as some companies were concerned, forget the 'ex', it was actually current players who were involved. Or, in a couple of cases, were the true owners hiding behind a fronting agent.

One international player was absolutely blatant – calling player after player and asking them to join 'his' agency. I didn't give a toss until he called one of mine and I hit back with a threat to report him both to his club and the FA, and after that it subsided for a bit. At least as far as I was concerned. I mean, the guy was on about eighty grand a week and here he was trying to take deals away from me worth about twenty grand at most. Greedy or what? Well, definitely not 'or what'. He was also making sure that any of the youngsters coming through the club were 'his' almost as soon as they could talk, and in that respect I heard he had visited the parents of an eight year old prodigy to 'book' the future representation. I guess he had enough money to ensure they were looked after for another eight years until the kid was old enough to sign, but as a long game that was almost without a horizon.

Some of these players even went so far as to tap up players on the pitch or in the bar after a match. They'd butter up the player by telling him how well he'd played, how good they thought he was and then innocently ask how much they were earning and who was acting for them. They'd express surprise at what they called a low figure and then say that they weren't surprised at all given the identity of the agent who had negotiated the deal. Shortly thereafter electronic devices would be out to exchange information with a view to setting up a meeting, with the agency with which the player had a deal, or of which he owned a slice (or even sometimes a majority share).

I may have given you the wrong impression on occasion about the relationship between agents and the FA. They're definitely not our friends. They may offer small crumbs of kindness, in much the same way a prison warden might bring a prisoner a message from home, but generally speaking we're simply not on the same side. We're trying to make money. They're trying to stop us. Those at Wembley who have been, and are, responsible for the Agents' Regulations have to sit and watch some of us earn fortunes from our deals while they put in their nine-to-five shifts, overlooking a huge car park in which they've parked their modest family saloons, for a comparative pittance. Sometimes I kind of get why they might feel a bit peeved and why at times they seem to be creating and enforcing regulations just for the hell of it, but mostly I don't. It didn't come as any great surprise when they recently had a major reshuffle that saw at least one of their fairly senior number put himself about to find a job with an agency. Gamekeeper turned poacher doesn't come close to describing it. Now, I am not in any way suggesting that this guy, who I rather liked, did anything wrong, because who could blame somebody for trying to better themselves financially? But the fact of the matter is that he must have had access to vital information about every agent's clients, including the length of the representation contracts. I know exactly what I would do if I had that: I'd make a list of targets with a count-down to when they became available. But as I've always said, it's one law for the FA and another for the rest of us.

I've seen too many of my fellow agents suffer at their hands. You'd think I might be pleased, but in fact all I generally do think is, who's next in line? And I guess it could be me with some of the business practices I've started to adopt. Not that I'm doing anything that anybody else doesn't. And I don't reckon I'm as blatant as most, but one of the things the FA seems to like least (and believe me there's quite a lot they don't like – usually things that earn us our living) 'fronting' is what they called it.

With the advent of the looser Intermediary Regulations and no entrance exam being necessary for the industry it's nowhere near as relevant now. Why bother to front or have someone front for you when you only need five hundred quid to be an intermediary? But then there are some individuals, like myself now, I suppose, who can't even get over the ridiculously low bar that the FA have set to get registered. I know of people in the game who have criminal records, who've been or are bankrupt or, for one reason or another, have found their faces don't fit in the FA screening process.

Now, I never called it fronting when an unlicensed guy who worked for me found a player, got him to sign with me, found him a club where he knew the manager, and virtually did the deal leaving me to come in and sign it off. I called it then – and call it now – deploying staff to maximise income; a mutual co-operation. And where was the harm in that?

Indeed, the thinking behind the whole intermediaries nonsense seems to suggest that FIFA didn't really have a problem with it either because all those guys who couldn't be agents for one reason or another have now flooded into the 'agency' business under the guise of being intermediaries. It's kind of a reward for having failed the exam a few times. Prizes for everybody. Not the first time that the world of football reminds me of Wonderland, with the FA threatening to cut of people's heads whilst at the same time showing all the awareness of the Dormouse, the sanity of the Mad Hatter and the consciences of the Walrus and the Carpenter.

The FA said back then, and say now, that only a licensed agent (or a Registered Intermediary) can carry out what they in their wisdom, have designated as 'Agency Activities'. Someone at HQ must have a real sense of humour (or sadistic nature) because they've made the definition so wide that if an unlicensed agent (i.e. your ex-pro) even meets a manager of a club (maybe somebody with whom he played and who is his mate) and mentions a player while winking, then the FA could argue that it was an agency activity and consequently a breach of the rules.

So, the agent has to contend with that and the financial demands of the ex-players who work for him as a scout. They know their price and their value, and as they quite often control the players, their demands can be fairly outrageous. They think nothing of taking up to ninety per cent from a deal, leaving the licensed agent who has fronted them with a mere ten per cent for his trouble and his risk. The argument is that he's done fuck all except put his name to the paper and the ten per cent is generous because he wouldn't have got anything at all were it not for his scout's ability to spot a young emerging talent and cosy up to the parents.

After I got myself some ex-pros in my team I thought I had a great relationship with them and that they might appreciate that I gave them their first break. I paid generous commissions, or so I thought, of forty per cent and I bore all their expenses. But not a bit of it; after the first phone call from one of these guys I knew what to expect.

'I think I should be getting more than what I get.'

You could tell this individual had been bottling it all up because there were no niceties. It just all came flooding out as if he'd been turned over and wanted to put right a moral wrong.

'Ok,' I said, 'what do you think is fair?'

'I reckon the other way around, 60–40 to me.'

I thought for a nanosecond, weighed the consequences of saying no and then agreed.

And that was that for a month or so before the same individual cut me down to thirty per cent and then twenty-five and then finally put the icing on the cake by telling me he'd been approached by another agent (the Lizard as it turned out, so he did get back at me in a way) and that he was prepared to pay him a retainer as well as eighty per cent of what he brought in.

'Good luck with that,' I said, although it might well have cost me a fortune. 'You deserve each other.'

The fact was that once the player could register as an intermediary he shafted the Lizard as well and set up on his own. I managed some damage limitation by bribing a couple of clients who the player thought were his and ensuring they stayed with me (I had them under contract anyway so the player couldn't have signed them at the time, but I'm not sure that would have meant an awful lot as I've illustrated before).

The cosying up to players and their families can go quite a long way, as I know of one scout who got to a player by shagging his mother. The only problem there was that although the player did make the big time, the scout was married and had to decide if his marriage was more important than his investment in a player. I'm told he did hesitate, but eventually his wife made the decision for him by way of an ultimatum and he stayed with her while the player moved on to another agent – who didn't have his mum in his sights and could actually focus on his career. The player later found out what his mother had been up to and having given her a black eye (which was carefully kept out of the media's eye) he then swung a punch at the scout in a club car park and eventually had to be dragged off him by his teammates before he inflicted permanent damage.

Clubs get on their high moral horses about how much agents earn and allegedly take out of the game, but they were more than happy, when they wanted a player, to deal with an unlicensed individual and put the agent down on the paperwork even though they knew he was just the middle man in the deal.

Sometimes, even now it's even more obvious than that, and clubs deal directly with any old unlicensed bloke who controls the player but hasn't bothered to get a contract signed or even apply to have himself registered and find a way to pay him by making him their scout and giving him a payment for helping to introduce some commercial deal. Football is all about consensual pragmatism. If a club wants a player they'll use any means to get him and won't be bothering to take up references on the person who can deliver him. If somebody, whether an Intermediary or not, gets a sniff that a club wants a player they'll move heaven and earth to deliver him by fair means or foul.

These 'unlicensed agents' (many of whom are now open and above board intermediaries operating within the system and having managed to sneak their way in under the FA's radar) came at the time, in all shapes, sizes and colours. Many of them were, as I say, former professional footballers who didn't feel able to pass the agents' exam or simply couldn't be bothered to take it. Then there were those who had taken the exam and failed but didn't see that as a real impediment to carrying on a 'shadow' business of a football agency and could because they controlled a few players. And they certainly can now with the unbelievable encouragement of FIFA and the FA. As I say, there are times when you simply couldn't make it up.

As I say, one or two of these unlicensed guys were really high-profile and even talked publicly about 'their' players. The problem faced by the FA was that those individuals weren't under their control or jurisdiction, because they'd not signed up to the rules, so all the FA could do was to punish clubs or players if the FA could prove they've actually worked through an unlicensed person. And proving any such thing was much easier said than done. If a player said he represented himself and the club confirmed that they'd only ever spoken to the player himself, or his dad, or a licensed agent, then there was fuck all the FA could do about it. And not a lot's changed in the Brave New World of the intermediary. The FA see what the clubs and those involved in a transfer want them to see and the only way I can see that changing is if the FA can persuade some poacher to turn gamekeeper as at the moment nobody who works there has a clue as to what it's like to work at the coal face.

Innocents could get suckered in and were actively sought out by unscrupulous unlicensed individuals. I've done exactly the same since my fall from grace, about which more later, and I can tell you that it really isn't that difficult as long as you have a carrot with a stick in the cart in case things get a bit tricky.

One agent had recently got his licence, but as yet had no

players at all and was holding down a regular job to earn enough to keep his family. He was approached by individuals who told him they were agents but needed to keep their names out of the transaction. They offered him a small share of a deal bringing in a player from abroad, and the newly qualified agent gratefully accepted. The 'agents' did everything: negotiated the whole deal and even picked up the player from the airport when he flew in from abroad. All the 'innocent' agent did was to sign off on everything. He got the shock of his life when the FA opened an inquiry and charged him with fronting because the so-called agents had no licences and, indeed, had even failed the exams. The FA threw the book at him, and the club claimed, quite properly, that they should not have taken the unlicensed guys at face value. Probably for the first time in living memory the real agent lost his licence before he'd even got himself a client, while the club was fined a six-figure sum. The two individuals to blame got off scot-free because they were outside the jurisdiction of the FA, and it beggars belief that it's people like that who the FA have now allowed to become intermediaries.

Don't get me wrong. I'm with the FA on this one. You may not think so from what you've read so far, but I did at least try and pay some lip service to the regulations (well certainly in the early days) and operate in a fairly (well, comparatively fairly) open manner. We've also always been a bit buggered because we could only be paid through the FA after the club has paid them to pass the money on to us and once they've checked that everything is hunky dory and above board. Those unlicensed guys were flying below the radar and sometimes their bombing raids caused us real damage.

Whilst I wanted to put an end to it back then and felt that the lunatics were running the asylum; as you can imagine, I don't feel that way now. Now, it's an opportunity, a spider's web of loose regulations through which one can creep and crawl safely if you know how the industry works and how much the authorities or the Revenue ever want to dig into a transaction.

Back then, it didn't take me too long to stumble upon 'Mr Fixit', who was not only unlicensed but seemed to control an inordinately high proportion of deals involving players coming into the country, largely because he seemed to own a slice of the said players. The FA were helpless to deal with him even though he was breaking all their third party ownership (TPO) rules, but clubs fell over themselves to find ways to pay him because of the quality of the players he could bring them. Since I became an outsider myself I have to admit that he's become a bit of an inspiration to me. Not the sort of role model or hero you'd want for your kids but pretty effective for all that.

There was one deal due to complete on a transfer deadline day, and Mr Fixit knew of it and clearly had something on the player involved, even if he didn't totally own him. Everybody was sitting around in the buying club's offices when the phone rang. It was Mr Fixit.

His message was loud and clear and he was that brazen that he didn't care who heard it.

'Unless I'm paid a fucking half a million pounds the transfer isn't going to go through.'

The buying club said they'd committed as much as they could with what they were paying the selling club and the player himself. Efforts to persuade the player to sign anyway fell on deaf ears.

'I'm not doing a thing without Mr F,' he said, so whatever it was that Fixit had on him was good enough to make him put a very lucrative deal on the line.

After much bartering, all parties agreed to put something into Mr Fixit's pot. He got his half-million, and the deal went through without any of the relevant authorities knowing about the payment to Mr F. Talk about protection monies; talk about the mafia. Mr F could give lessons to all concerned. And, I thought at the time, he'd managed to stay above the law: both the law of whatever land in which he chose to do his business and the law of football. How naïve was I.

Football is a honeypot and attracts all sorts of strange creatures around it trying to get a jarful of the amber nectar. (Or is that whisky? I rarely drink so I don't know.) It just all looks so easy to make money. Financial advisers, lawyers and accountants who have worked with agents look at the deals and, having seen just how much the agent has made, wonder why they should settle for paltry commission or fees based on time when they think they could do a more professional job of negotiating and concluding the deals themselves. It may mean biting off the hand that has fed them, will certainly mean the end of the relationship with the agent or agents in question but, hey, you know what? It's a small price to pay when they can walk off with the players once they've gained their trust – either by making their money work for them, saving them tax, or winning a legal action. We'll return to making money by investments (or losing it as the case may be) further on in my sorry tale.

Then there are the player's 'mates'. They've grown up with him, played in the street with him, been in the same class at school, been teammates at various levels of football clubs before he moved on to bigger and better things, and just hung around to become part of his entourage. That entourage, those mates, have to be brought on board by the agent, whatever the cost. But, even if the agent mixes with them, gets pissed with them, pulls birds with them, even has threesomes or foursomes with them (as one agent regularly does), the fact remains that the player will usually trust them more than any Johnny-come-lately agent. I've been out on the town with some of my players, and trust me it isn't a pleasant experience. I'll come back to that even though I've tried to erase a few incidents from my memory.

Such players often refuse to sign with an agent, telling him that when he brings them a deal they might consider it but that he should work on the basis that when it comes to the paperwork he'll say that he's acted for the club. Apart from the fact that the player then pays no tax on any fees, it also means that he can expel the agent from his inner circle at any time. So the agent is constantly on trial, walking on eggshells, and forced to work with the entourage or its leader. And even if the player does finally sign a representation contract it might just as well be with his mate or mates given the influence they'll exert. The agent therefore has to work through two layers of approval – player and entourage – and any deal he negotiates is subject to scrutiny at both levels.

The players listen to their friends. Generally speaking, they can't be bothered with the trivial details of the deal, the small print. They just want the bottom line. I've been told by a player, 'If so and so [i.e. his mate] says it's OK then go ahead.' And the inference is that his mate has to be looked after financially, even though that's also a breach of the rules because it isn't something you're going to want to disclose.

That's how an agent finds himself cosying up to some tattooed thug who in a parallel universe would be serving time for armed robbery, drug dealing or worse. That hasn't happened, because he's found a better way of life, stroking the player's ego and generally doing whatever he tells him.

Players can be cruel, and even their agents aren't guaranteed to avoid that. They know the agent can't tell them to fuck off (well, they can, but it would be a brave one who would), so I've heard of tales where they get a mate to piss in the agent's expensive car (for a laugh, of course) or, in one case, put the poor agent in the boot of his own car and drive him around for a whole afternoon.

The player may dispense some beneficence. He'll buy his mates rounds of drinks or pay for their hotels (although if the agent is with him then he'll be expected to pick up the tab), give them freebies like boots, trainers and tracksuits from the kit deal his agent has negotiated, let them smash up his sponsored car (which his agent acquired for him), hand over the young women he's done with (which sometimes the agent is expected to acquire), but who has to sort out all that mess? Yes, you've guessed it: the agent who made it all possible and who on many occasions has created this monster into which the player has turned.

You might think that the player would look after his mates from the remunerative deals he has both on and off the pitch. Like fuck he will. He usually expects his agent to spread the cash around out of his fee, and although that can be substantial it quite often only equates to a week's salary of the player's own deal. The cost of a night on the town, the rounds of drinks at a club (often including total strangers) and the hotel rooms afterwards can make big inroads into the profit. Girls and drugs – no surprises there – can swallow them up altogether.

Now, don't get me wrong. Not every friend of every player is a total idiot. Some of them are really bright. They may even have gone to university or a college at least, and in a way they're the most dangerous to have around. In the same way that the professional advisers can see what the agent makes, so do the more intelligent members of his entourage. I've known these guys to take over the player's management and squeeze the agent out into oblivion, no matter the good work he may have done or how close he thinks he's come to them.

I got one of my players an amazing deal with a club and as soon as he'd seen a six figure loyalty bonus hit his account at the end of his current contract he dumped me for his best mate.

'He needs the money more than you,' he said. 'I just wanted to give him a leg up; and anyway, to be honest (I hate it when anybody in football says that to me because they never are), I reckon I've learned enough from you over the years to be able to know what I want from a deal.'

I don't think he even realised what he was saying and I doubt he had ever heard of the phrase 'damning with faint praise', but you can well imagine how that made me feel.

I have to say I felt sorry for the mate of another player who gave up a really good job to work within an agency with him as his biggest player. He was in a bar one night when someone started taunting him about his mate, suggesting he was gay (and yes there are some gay players but don't expect me to out them here, that's for them to do – and I've not reached the depths yet of selling them out to the press). Anyway, the guy threw a punch and it all kicked off and spilled out on to the pavement. More punches were thrown, more insults exchanged and the player's mate got a bit carried away, landed and huge right-hook and the recipient fell to the floor and hit his head. Unfortunately it killed him and the mate ended up doing a deal, pleading guilty to manslaughter rather than murder, and got a ten year sentence. I gather he'll be out in a year or so and the player has pledged to trust his affairs to him when he does. I don't see him being able to register with the FA any time soon but I guess, despite the catastrophic outcome, you have to have a grudging respect for the player sticking by him in those circumstances.

Meanwhile, these mates become the power brokers, sometimes legitimising themselves by bothering to get a licence, although more often not. Not because they're incapable, but at the end of the day a licence to do what they do is irrelevant. They may not have the bit of paper and the registration number that's issued by the FA, but they've got something much better than those. They have the player. And, in the words of Meatloaf, 'in the land of the pigs, the butcher is king'.

SEVENTEEN

THE TOOLS OF THE TRADE

AFTER ALMOST TWO years of trying to build my
business I was well into the psyche of players (at least
those of them who actually had one). They have strong
likes and even stronger dislikes. They like money, of course; that
goes without saying. And generally they're young and fit-looking
heterosexuals who like young and fit-looking (and amenable)
women. They like Nando's, and Red Bull, and tattoos. They like
expensive fast cars and the latest gadgets. They like loud music
playing from the best stereo system. They like smart clothes,
expensive footwear, jewellery and baseball caps. They read the
tabloids but hate the journalists who write for them. If you put
all that together then you get the picture, but with one notable
piece missing. They love, absolutely fucking *love*, freebies. Even
if it's something they have no use for whatsoever. Provided it's
free, they want it.

Freebies can vary in accessibility and cost, but any agent who
can't provide them might just as well give up the day job and
go to the nearest Jobcentre, because football agency is most
certainly not for him.

Starting with basics, the first question almost every potential
client has asked me is, 'Can you get me boots?' If you're meeting
a parent then they're programmed to ask the same question. I
understand that in a way, because they're normally working-class,
if working at all, and they've scrimped and saved to get little

Johnny his boots since he was first old enough to stand upright and kick a ball. Now you've come along with your flash car and your smooth talk and your nice suit and the track record you've reeled off in front of them, so why shouldn't they expect you to assume this particular burden? I suppose it's also not unreasonable for the player himself to expect you to provide them because, after all, they're the tools of his trade and it's become something of a trade practice for the bloke most likely to make a barrow-load of money out of the player's career to provide them for him.

R used to reminisce fondly about the good old days of his agency work when the big boot companies like Nike, Umbro, Puma, Adidas and so on used to give a pair of boots to any Tom, Dick or Harry (must have been the good old days with names like that) who could kick a ball – and indeed to some who couldn't but whom the agent told them could. They worked on the basis that if you gave boots to a hundred youngsters then the odds were that two or three of them would reach the top echelons of the game which made the whole investment worthwhile. By the time I hooked up with R, and certainly by the time I branched out on my own, those days were sadly, at least for my pocket, long past.

So, many agents, me included, had to buy footwear for their clients. Now, boots don't come cheap, and even the youngest of players won't be fobbed off by the cheaper brands, even though they may do the job just as well. It's all about peer pressure, pride and ego, even when the kids are just in an academy – or even before. They all want top-of-the-range branded boots in the brightest of colours as worn by whoever may be their latest international idol, and they certainly won't settle for some foreign brand willing to spread samples around in an attempt to break into a saturated market.

When I first started out on my own, I did, just like everybody else, promise players anything (the Earth included) just to get them to sign up with me. You want boots? Sure, no problem. Any brand and as many as you want. Add that to holidays, cars, insurance, designer clothes, looking after their mums and dads, and you get the extent of what I had to do. If you miss a heartbeat in telling a player what he wants to hear, in selling yourself through your pitch, he'll spot it in a nanosecond. As you'll have gathered, I don't have the highest regard for footballers as academics, but they do have a built-in antenna for any lack of confidence or anything that might sound like bullshit. Even if it is. It's all a bit like taking a lie-detector test and beating the equipment. However, once you have their signature on the dotted line then reality kicks in.

I once had a young player who seemed to have real potential. I managed to sign him in the face of fierce competition by persuading him (and of course his parents, not to mention their new partners as they were separated) that I could give him a much more personal service than any of the big agencies with their hundreds of clients all vying for attention. I was absolutely delighted to have signed him, even though I knew at this early stage in his career I wouldn't be making a fortune out of him. I just hoped to be able to impress him enough in the initial two years I had with him to re-sign with me just when his career was likely to become more lucrative for both of us.

The first problem I encountered with him was . . . boots. He asked for a pair of top-range Nike, and having tried and failed to get him an early sponsorship deal with the company, I bought him the boots with the discount on the price that most of the big companies offer to agents. He didn't even bother to say thank you – par for the course – but to add insult to injury he told me that he needed a second pair, this time moulded ones as he liked to carry both studs and moulded styles depending on the conditions.

Fair enough, I thought, sensible young man. Tools of the trade. The better he does on the pitch then the more likely I am to cash in when I do his next contract. And if it takes two pairs of the most expensive boots to make him a better player then who am I to argue or rock the ship for a halfpenny worth of tar. Whatever a halfpenny ever was. Long before my time. Bit like loyal one-club, one-agent footballers. I may have been set back over three hundred quid by buying these boots, but I'd convinced myself that I needed to look upon that expenditure as an investment.

But there are investments and investments, and less than a month later he was texting me again – cheaper than phoning me and also not giving me the chance to ask him for an explanation. 'All my mates are getting their men ('man' is what most players call their agents. 'My man is better than your man,' etc) to get them boots in whatever colour they want. So I want orange. And I've got a match tomorrow, so get them delivered to the ground will you.'

What he was really saying was that if I didn't cough up, then there were agents out there, representing his teammates, who, given the opportunity, would perform hand-stands with bells on for him.

Anyway, four pairs of boots later (two studs, two moulded, one of each in bright orange), I was asked for another four pairs of boots and began to wonder if he was either into eating leather or was running a sideline on a local market stall. I'd always kept in touch with the lad's mother – a good ploy to always remember birthdays and so on – and in passing, having found an excuse to call her, I say, 'Your boy seems to be getting through a fair old number of boots.'

'Oh, yes,' she replies, 'he's always been heavy on shoes. Is there a problem?'

'Oh, no,' I say, gritting my teeth. 'Always willing to help. Your son is one of my favourites.'

They all were, as long as they made me money, but I wasn't going to be sharing that thought with her.

Fast-forward another month and a request for four more pairs. And he would like – for 'like' read 'demand' – some leisurewear thrown in. Because that was what all his mates were getting through their super agents. If Carling did agents then they'd be like mine.

Now, this lad had done very little in his career to date. He'd got some schoolboy caps in the Victory Shield, been picked for an Under-17 tour but had never played, and the nearest he'd got to a first-team debut (and thus the renegotiated contract I'd built into his current deal and which would hopefully provide some payback for me) was a place on the bench for a League Cup tie when the manager chose to field eight reserves in his starting squad.

So, I'm starting to think he might or might not actually make it, and at this rate, in terms of footwear acquisition, I was likely to be about a grand out of pocket before the day he got released and ended up playing in what was then the Football Conference and is now The National League. (I'll talk about talent spotting there a bit later). So, I seized the bull by the horns, or more accurately the player by the balls, and asked him if he really, really needed so many boots. And, you know what? He comes right out and tells me that some of them have been for his kid brother who takes the same size, although there the similarity in football skill comes to an abrupt halt. But he wasn't ashamed, wasn't apologetic. I'd never asked so he had never lied to me and he kind of assumed that's what agents do. After all, wasn't every other agent doing it as well?

I guess you're thinking, a whole chapter devoted to agents and players and their mutual relationship with footwear? Sounds like an extract from a book on foot fetishes. Well, as I always say to my players, you have to keep your feet on the ground and I suppose if you do then your shoes (or boots) are likely to wear out.

So I had to find a way of minimising my expense but without letting my rivals maximise the competition. Seek and ye shall find may be a religious tractate but it is also as good a motto as any for making a success of a football agency.

Before I tell you what I did, let's make it quite clear that I'm not slagging off the whole of the sports-goods manufacturing industry or suggesting everybody involved is corrupt. The last thing I want is to be banned from their Christmas parties or to invite a class action for defamation. When I've typed the last word of this book they'll have to join the queue of lawyers around the block waiting to serve writs on behalf of their outraged clients. And what I was planning could hardly be regarded as corruption anyway, at least not by the standards of my own industry.

Most of the people at the sporting companies are decent honest folk with a genuine enthusiasm for not only their own company's wares, but also the developments and designs of their competitors. Everybody wants to develop the perfect, innovative boot, and just when you think there's nothing new under the sun a boot appears that tells you you're wrong.

But when a large company gives an executive the power to make gifts then it surely must be apparent that somebody is going to give them gifts in return to be sure they'll be the recipient. It's then that the temptation to break the corporate rules arises – and break the rules is precisely what the odd few do.

I could never understand why a whole clutch of young players at one club would go with one agent. Knowing some of the agents to whom these players migrated, I was sure that it wasn't because they were better at their job than me (or anyone else for that matter). There just had to be another reason. Was it the academy director, the youth team manager, the manager himself on the take? Maybe, but I worked out there was also another common denominator. Same club and same brand of boots.

This hadn't been an angle R had worked, so I had to figure it all out for myself – and this is how it works and how I made it work for me. The companies tended to put a couple of their guys in charge at each big club with one having a specific remit to look after the young players. The kids coming through are in their pockets because these are the men who supply them with boots and kit and so on from an early age, often well before they're even eight years old. Now, I know I've talked about kids as young as ten or eleven with agents sniffing around them, dare I say, grooming them. Yes, I dare, because grooming it is. Not for sexual favours of course but for another kind of control. Player representation.

That's not always the case for a kid with real potential, because somebody may well have got to him before the agent. That somebody may just be the guy from the sports manufacturing company who has got his trust and also that of his parents by spreading the gear around. He's given him boots, maybe a tracksuit, a sweatband, a T-shirt, sunglasses if the company makes them, perhaps even a watch. These companies have such a wide range of products nowadays that they can totally equip a young lad for the big wide world. I'm half expecting them to develop their own brand of condoms any day now. Maybe they do already and I just don't know. As with every free gift there's always a catch, and the catch here is that all the time the kit guy is whispering in the lad's ear, 'I know you're looking for an agent. You don't necessarily want to leave that sort of decision to your mum and dad. They're not football people like you and me, and they're not at the heart of the business like I am. I know who's good, who's bad, who's in and who's out, and more importantly who's right for you.'

That's the moment when they hit them with the name of the agent and the trick is to ensure that the agent is you. Or me, in this case. Yet, as you have probably gathered by now, nothing is for nothing in this dog-eat-dog world of ours. As I've said, there are many decent guys working their arses off for the big companies. But fortunately for us there are also a few who, as was put in a court case a while ago, 'like a bung'.

The bung (I really hate that word, but I suppose it's less sinister and sounds less criminal than a bribe) can take several forms. Either the agent simply pays the introducer from the boot company a lump sum for every player who signs with him (the sum varying according to the status of the player) or he puts him on his payroll permanently and gives him a retainer and/or a percentage of everything he makes from the player in question.

Yes, I know. Don't bother to tell me. It's a bribe and it's illegal, but so is driving at eighty miles an hour on the motorway and everybody does that. And so much of our business is illegal that you kind of get immune to thinking of it like that. This is a victimless crime all round, anyway, so there's little need for a sleepless night about it. The general rule in football agency is that if you stick to the rules you won't make any money. So, to get on in the business you have to bend or break them, simply roll the dice and take your chances.

Unlike in many other sports (the so-called gentleman's game of cricket for example, or the drug fuelled world of cycling and athletics), I've never heard of any agents being prosecuted for bribery and corruption, while I have heard of a fair few making enough for an early retirement, so I'm thinking the risk of breaking the rules has to be worth it.

Lately a fair number of the experienced guys from the sports manufacturing industry have come across to the so-called 'dark side' and become licensed (or unlicensed in some cases) agents themselves. They've generally spent their whole working lives playing it by the book, earning a living wage but no more, and watched the agents for the players they service raking it in. So you can hardly blame them for waking up one morning, smelling the roses and realising that their contacts within the game are pure gold dust and can be sprinkled around to make pure gold for themselves.

I don't have a problem with that. There's nothing wrong with competition – as long as it's fair. I don't think it's fair when the PFA come down to see a whole group of Academy players, at the invitation of the club, and give them goodie bags containing all sorts of sports stuff together with an invitation to be represented by the agency arm of the same organisation. Again one rule for the establishment and another for us.

So, to level the odds, I've got myself a real live boot guy. He didn't come cheap. These boys know their value and he's screwed me for half of everything I get from the players he introduces to me. But, as I've said before, half of something is better than a whole of nothing, so we'll see where it goes. I don't see it being a long-term relationship because tomorrow he'll want sixty per cent, the day after seventy and so on. And when he gets to ninety he'll think, let's push it to a hundred and strike out and I'll start my own business, just like the ex-pros I mentioned before. Greed is an epidemic in this industry and it spreads faster than the Great Plague of London. I'm prepared for the day the greed gets the better of him because I know it's coming. I've become very cynical in my few years at this game. It's the only way to survive. Optimists become complacent.

Pessimists don't get off their arses because they think they're going to fail. It's a world for cynical realists. Which led me to the conclusion that if my guy left me it wouldn't be the end of the world because there would be another one waiting in line. There always is.

EIGHTEEN

VICARIOUS LIVING

YOU MAY BE wondering if there's something missing from my life and you'd be right. I have no real friends, no down time, no social life whatsoever. I mix only with footballers and their families, managers, coaches and just about anybody else who can make me any money, or who I've put (or want to put) on my payroll. It's all about the deal and the pursuit of the next one.

I live in my car, and in fact I've just checked and seen that in the last twelve months (I may have lost my agent's licence but I've still got my driving licence) I've driven over 50,000 miles. Even now, I work 24/7 and if 25/8 were on offer then I'd take that too. I don't see my parents, and they have to phone just to check I'm still alive. Of course they were upset about what happened to me, particularly my mother. Her main problem with it all was that she didn't like the photo they used when the story of my problems hit all the newspapers. That's when I found out who my true friends were amongst the journos. It's a pretty sorry state of affairs when I call reporters my friends and can't name any others outside the industry. Anyway, parents know to try my mobile first because who uses a landline nowadays? My mobile bill last month was over £600 and that was without me even leaving the country. There are all sorts of deals for people like me on offer but who has time to sit down and consider them? My life is a series of questions I ask myself but don't even have a minute to answer.

I even began to question my own sexuality. Was I so obsessed with footballers that I actually wanted to sleep with one? Another question. This time I answered with a resounding no. (I've only known a couple of openly gay agents during my time in the business.) To be honest, I've slept with the sister of one player and had an offer to sleep with the wife of another, but that would be pissing into the tent and I'm not that stupid. I even had the mother of one of my players come on to me when I arrived at their house for a meeting a bit early. And her one-year-old was asleep upstairs in his cot. I confess I was a bit worried about how to deal with that one. Having declined her offer, I was petrified she'd tell her husband that I'd tried to come on to her as some kind of revenge for the rebuff, but as it transpired she was all sunshine and light when hubbie got home, and I still act for the player. I just make sure I'm never left alone with her.

As I briefly mentioned earlier, nights on the town with players are a nightmare. You have to protect them from too many groups. Fans want to buy them a drink, ask them personal questions, become their new best friend. Opposition fans want to lure them into a fight. Girls want to make them the next notch on their footballers' bedpost. The paparazzi are always at the ready and gossip columnists cling to every word. But most of all you have to protect them from themselves.

To be honest, it would be easier herding cats and mice than trying to control a bunch of footballers out for a good time. They're like kids on the day school breaks up. Even though, in their case, they have to return to school the next day or the day after if they're, at least, going out the night before a day off. I went out with one of my players who'd had a stinker the previous Saturday and who'd also had the mother-and-father of all rows with his missus just before he closed the door of his house behind him. He wasn't in the best of moods, that was for sure, and his first words as we got into the car (and I realised instantly that I wasn't just the minder for the evening but also the dedicated driver) were, 'Right, let's get some down us.'

I'd already arranged access to the footballers' venue of choice (there's one in every town and the photographers camp outside), so off we went with three of his mates, one of whom was a convicted drug dealer. Cocktails mixed with beers followed by some drinking games soon had my player ready to take on the world. I'd arranged a roped-off area, but he still had to get to the loo, and when he did, somebody told him he was crap and he thumped them. He thumped them again for good measure to the point that I wondered if he might have killed the guy. This led to my contact at the nightclub looking for me and dragging me over. They didn't want bad publicity any more than I wanted my client in jail, so we took the victim to the manager's office and cleaned him up, and while he was still a bit woozy I did a deal with him and got him to sign off on something I cobbled together there and then. It cost a few bob and a few free tickets (the player said afterwards that I'd been too generous), but it worked.

The player then carried on as if nothing had happened and managed to pull three different girls before the club closed. He shagged one in the same loo in which he'd just had a fight, one in the manager's office which he now seemed to regard as his own, and another on the back seat of my car while I stared straight ahead, blocked out the noise and just hoped they wouldn't do too much damage to my leatherwork.

He then wanted me to take him on to another place where he knew they did lock-ins, the drug-dealing mate offered me a line of coke, and I knew that somehow or other I had to get him home, which eventually I did only to be greeted by his still raging wife who had been calling him all night.

'It's all your fault,' she screamed at me. 'You just want to be seen out with him so he can help you get some more clients. When he sobers up I'm going to tell him he needs to dump you.'

And, guess what? She did exactly that. The player saw it as a way to appease his wife, and I was made the villain of the piece on both sides. If you had the time to ponder it all you might also contemplate slashing your wrists or buying a one way ticket to Switzerland and checking in at Dignitas. But you make sure you don't have the time. You keep running, sometimes just to stay on the same spot, and as long as you're not going backwards, as long as you're not looking at the arses of your rivals as they're disappearing into the distance then you're kind of winning. And in my case, back then when I was on the up, winning was everything. Players sense losers and don't want to hitch their coat tails to their wagons, that's for sure. Which is why you don't just have to behave like a winner all the time, but you have to look like one. Expensive cars that you can't always afford, particularly when you've had to pay a huge fine imposed by the courts and the FA, and when you've no idea where the next penny is coming from. But you duck and you dive, you bob and you weave and somehow or other you make it happen.

As you can imagine, agents spend a fair amount of time dealing with the women in their clients' lives. Footballers tend to get married early and have children even earlier. Almost every wedding I've ever attended has had the couple's kid (and sometimes a kid who only belongs to one of them) as a pageboy or bridesmaid. The girlfriend of a footballer can see his potential as a meal ticket as soon as she realises he has a bit of talent, and even if he's never going to be the perfect father or husband, the credit cards, the nice house and the expensive car are more than compensation for nine months of pregnancy.

What they don't realise (and believe me, everything you hear about footballers' wives is true with bells on) is that while it may have been easy to pick up a player who has been on the lash in a nightclub it's a damn sight harder to keep him interested. Players like arm candy, and a pregnant wife or girlfriend rarely looks her best during or after the nine months of gestation. She may think she's been really clever trapping him into the commitment and even cleverer when she gets a second bun in the oven when he's grown a bit bored and started to waver, but that tactic, ultimately, only makes him feel more trapped. More to the point, it means that she's stuck at home more than ever, giving him the time to play away – in all senses of the word.

Players travelling to an away match and staying over in a hotel have the perfect alibi if they have a co-operative roommate who knows when to vacate his bed and let some groupie in, and then knows to say nothing after. To be honest, his teammates are unlikely to gossip as the odds are that the girl would've serviced them both and put another couple of notches on her footballer shag list.

Yet, when it comes to alibis and after illicit sex fallout, the poor old agent is first in line to be telling the fibs and shielding his player from the wrath of his wife. The alibis first because they'll, hopefully, defuse the situation. The first time I did this I had a twinge of guilt because the wife was so sweet. I'd met her at the same time as I'd first met the player because he'd brought her along to 'approve' me. They looked like the perfect couple. He was a decent prospect at a League One club and she was a trainee beautician. They'd been going out since school, and once I got him a move to a Premier League club they actually got married. For once, this couple did things the old-fashioned way, and he got her pregnant on their honeymoon.

Money, fame and opportunity do an awful lot to most footballers – most people, if it comes to that. Right after a pre-season tour he phoned me in an absolute panic. They'd been playing in the States, and he'd met a girl at a hotel bar, and what followed was a story as old as hotel bars and men on their own. It wouldn't have been so much of a problem had the girl been American and just fancied a quickie with a good-looking young guy with a nice physique. But she was from Leeds and she knew all about football. She also knew all about the media and she'd heard that a certain publicist did a nice line in placing kiss-and-tell stories about professional sportsmen. So there I was with Publicist T, lying through my teeth and telling him that on the night in question I'd been in the States and at the team hotel, the only drink my player had consumed was Diet Coke and that I'd been with him all night. I got the story backed up by another of my players on the team, and without any evidence of the liaison no paper would touch the story. The girl was dismissed as a fantasist, but I couldn't really feel any sympathy for her because she genuinely was trying to make a quick buck out of a meaningless shag.

That was an easy lie and not one likely to get me into trouble, but I've told worse than that. I had one player whose lovely wife was safely ensconced in the north while he plied his trade in the south. He went out to celebrate a win, and after over-celebrating somewhat, he woke up in a strange woman's flat where neither he nor she had a surfeit of clothing. Again, whatever the morals of the situation, nobody would've been hurt – had the girl not waited until my client had dressed and left, and then called the police to accuse him of rape, which led to his immediate arrest.

Now, as it happened, he hadn't raped her. He hadn't even had sex with her as a police swab eventually proved. And one of his teammates had been in the same room, albeit on the couch. I had to piece all this together while fielding frantic calls from the player's wife and trying to make sure she didn't become his ex-wife.

I had to think quickly. I couldn't say he was in hospital because she was the sort of loyal companion who'd be down in a shot. The best I could come up with was that he'd lost his voice. I went to the police station and managed to persuade them to give me his mobile phone after they'd checked all the messages and calls (none to or from the girl but quite a lot from the distraught wife). I began a text conversation with the wife pretending to be her husband. I must have been quite convincing because when the police released my client without charge the next day – and he'd miraculously recovered his voice – he told me that his wife had said she wished he lost his voice more often because he was so much more romantic when he was texting.

It didn't always end so happily. Another player was sexting a girl he'd only met the night before and sent her an explicit picture of his impressive private parts. She claimed to be so shocked that when she arose from her swoon her mobile automatically dialled a tabloid newspaper, who then called him, who then referred them to me. I decided it was time to use my brief acquaintance with the celebrity publicist to good use, and for the modest fee of ten grand he managed to tone the story down to one where the paper just reported he'd been sending drunken messages.

There is truly no justice in the world, because his wife blamed me for leading him astray and encouraging him to communicate with strange women. It seemed the player had told her that he and I had made a bet on the subject. As it turned out I was the only loser, having laid out the ten grand and then receiving a termination letter from the player which had clearly been drafted by his wife. Some you win and some you lose. You just have to ensure the wins outnumber the losses, a bit like a football manager.

I've been a bit unfair to the WAGS as some of them do have a fairly astute grasp of business. Certainly more than their husbands. One of them called me and started the conversation by saying, 'Don't tell my husband that I've called you, but I'm really worried about him. We had some guys over last night. He particularly didn't want you to know . . .'

Interesting that. Players are easily embarrassed and really cowardly when it comes to upsetting people. Even the ones who are the frightening leaders on the pitch. He may be pictured as a wounded warrior with a blood stained bandage around his head, but the same player didn't have the guts to dump a girlfriend and got me to do it. Another hid in the toilet when he called me over and asked me to sack the nanny because his wife didn't like her and thought she was too pretty.

Anyway, this player's wife was worried that he was being pressurised into buying a pig in a poke by way of an investment and she wasn't wrong . He was too scared to say no and too scared to tell me so he'd ended up signing up to buy a piece of real estate in some remote island in the Pacific that he was unlikely to ever visit even if he got it built. He been told it could be rented with ease even if he didn't want to use it himself.

He'd actually written out a cheque for a deposit and I asked the woman to get me a copy of the paperwork. Fortunately, it had a seven day cancellation clause in it and I decided to take a gamble, tell the sellers that the player had changed his mind and with some threats got them to find an excuse to tell the player that they'd made a mistake and the development wasn't right for him. As you'll see when I talk about other investments sold to gullible players others were nowhere near so lucky.

So, as you'll gather, most of the women in my life are either with somebody else, are blackmailing my clients or are my mother, and none of those scenarios form the perfect basis for a meaningful, lifelong relationship. I know, I need to get a life. And I will. But not just yet.

NINETEEN

MATA HARIS

I'M HALF WAY through my story and I realise that when it comes to women I sound a cross between a male chauvinist pig and a misogynist. I am actually neither, though many footballers are certainly MCPs. But the fact remains that I've painted a dark pictures of the wives and girlfriends, the wannabe wives and girlfriends and those girls who just have dollar signs light up in the eyes when they see a footballer. That and another notch on the bedstead. I once went to the wedding of a player who was marrying a girl that everybody but him could see was just in it for the money and when he said 'I do,' the girl's mother could clearly be heard saying, 'Yes!' and I'm sure she wanted to add, 'Got 'im!'

Although the only woman who comes out of this book with any great credit so far is my mother (after all if it were not for her there would be no book), there are an increasing number of women coming into the game. Everybody knows Karen Brady who has been a trail blazer in proving that there is a place for women at the top end of the football industry. Yet she is still the exception rather than the rule, and I am sure I am not the only one who cringes at some of the bimbos chosen by television stations to act as football presenters. Again, there are exceptions as a few of them do clearly know their game but so far they are not proving the rule.

José Mourinho made headlines over his treatment of Eva

Carneiro, a female member of his medical staff, and obviously he was unimpressed by her knowledge of football tactics or at least *his* football tactics, but I guess if you really believe you are the Chosen One then anybody who disagrees with you is going to be wrong. Yet, more and more women are entering into the world of football agency and some of them are doing very well. Although, in some cases, you have to ask exactly what that may be.

I've called this chapter Mata Haris. Now, as you know, Mata Hari was a spy (and I suppose that is just another name for a secret agent) and she did not hesitate to use her feminine charms to further her career. Now, there are some women agents who actually take the opposite route to that. They want to be one of the boys, to out-drink them, out-swear them and generally work as hard as they can to make others in the industry, whether they be players, managers, chief executives, owners or fellow agents forget that they are even women. And to a point they succeed; but only to a point.

Yet, some of the more successful female agents do work on the basis that if you've got it then you should flaunt it. Players think their charms are undeniable, that any woman is there for the taking and if an agent can make them believe that up to the point that the player signs with them then I suppose you can't blame them for that. But some do cross the line.

One young female wannabe-agent found a player who she thought was going to be her entry card into the business. At the time he was the first player she'd signed and on an evening out one thing led to another, drinks flowed, hands touched and she took him back to hers and let him shag the living daylights out of her. His wife had never liked the idea that he'd taken on a fairly attractive woman to represent him, and when he didn't come home she tracked him down to the agent's flat and told him that he could stay there.

Unfortunately, that did not seem such a great idea to the agent, who was truly regretting her one night stand, but she realised that if she also asked him to leave then she would lose her only client. The player was looking for a club move and so she decided that the best way to get him out of her flat was to find him a club as far away as possible. The only problem was that she'd launched into business without many connections. She'd been a fan, and sort of become a groupie – and we all know what happens to groupies. Anyway, she couldn't find him a club, he showed no great appetite to find himself alternative accommodation and although she persuaded him that ongoing sex wasn't going to happen and moved him to the spare bedroom, that didn't solve the problem either. He began to regard her flat as his and when she returned home one day to find him in her bed with some other bird the camel's back was well and truly broken.

She threw his clothes into a case, ripped the representation contract in half and tossed it on top and then called a locksmith to change the locks. He told every player he met she was a slag and even gave one or two her number, but she never tried to seek to represent them. Lesson learned.

As in most professions, women agents feel they have something to prove and can be pretty aggressive, not just in their mode of client representation but in their ruthlessness in trying to poach clients. One woman phoned one of my clients so often that his wife took to answering the phone when she rang and told her to fuck off and leave her husband alone.

Yet, sometimes persistence pays off and I know of one agent who was left shaking his head in astonishment, not to mention disappointment, when one of his players was wined and dined by a fairly experienced female agent. She had taken him to one of the most expensive restaurants in town, dressed to kill and been treated with such deference at the private members' club that they adjourned to afterwards that he had decided to sign for . The upmarket, exclusive private members' clubs in London have an unwritten 'no footballer' member rule, and her promise to bypass that thanks to connections with the membership selection committee had been the winning card. As it happened she did a really good job for him, and I know for a fact that even the most difficult chief executives dreaded having to negotiate with her.

It makes no difference to me if a fellow agent is a man or a woman, straight or gay, black or white, Jewish, Christian or Muslim; to me they are all competitors and I watch them like hawks. But if any of nicks any of my clients then they need to watch out. Beware an agent wronged.

TWENTY

PLAYER AGENTS

A S IF THE business wasn't tough enough already, FIFA and the smug fat bastards (of whom many have been shown to be totally corrupt fuckers) who run it made it a whole lot tougher by making the Licensed Agent an extinct species and turning my first effort at writing my story into a history book. Do I hear you say, good, you deserve it? Well, maybe so, but it's the only way I know how to make a living nowadays and a hell of a lot of the other agents plying their trade and trying to turn an honest buck are a lot nicer than me. Not hard, do I hear you say? Well, I promised myself that I'd be honest in this book so I surely get a few Brownie points for integrity in that respect.

I've talked about the raggle-taggle bunch of gypsies who operate unlicensed and unqualified. Well, in the perfect illustration of 'if you can't beat them join them', as I've mentioned before, FIFA has invited them into the football family and wants to legitimise them and called them 'intermediaries'. This lot will include all the various villains I've described in this book and a few more besides, not to mention the hundreds of wannabe agents who have never been able to pass the exam. As I've said before (and you kind of realise I feel strongly about this) it's a reward for working under the radar for so long, a reward for failure. That, in itself, wouldn't be so bad except that at the same time they want to delegitimise all the other agents and call them, er, 'intermediaries'. No idea what they call me because I simply operate under the radar in No Man's Land.

But everything the guys have worked for now counts for nothing, and all those guys who have been putting two fingers up to the FA for years not only have an amnesty but an actual reward – the chance to go out there and compete against the established agents on what is an allegedly level playing field. Only it won't be. Whatever the shortcomings of agents, they do generally know what they're doing, not just for themselves but for their clients as well. These chancers think they can make quick and easy money at the expense of the players and the clubs. Oh, and at the expense of those of us who've been at it for years.

I don't have a crystal ball, but this is how I see it panning out. A current footballer, who's been tapping up your players during his own playing career with a view to persuading them to leave you and join another agency, can now retire from the game and seamlessly set up his own business alongside all those established businesses. I say 'his own business', but the truth is, as you'll have gathered by now, that there are quite a few footballers out there who have happily run their own agencies for years, even while playing.

You can imagine the conversations at the club and in the dressing rooms. The experienced pro (quite often a high-profile international) tells a young emerging talent that he'd like to look after him both on and off the pitch. You know, 'Stick with me, kid, and I'll see you all right.'

Managers tend to listen to their more experienced players who often, as their club captains, are their mouthpieces on the pitch. If the captain suggests to a manager that he's got a nugget in the reserves or even in the youth team and academy, then that kid will have a better chance of getting noticed. Of course he has still got to be a decent player to get on but he definitely has a better chance than another decent player with the same ability who doesn't have a senior pro batting for him.

Players know they're generally done in football at thirty-five unless they're a keeper. In fact, from thirty onwards it's generally a slippery slope, and in the descent they can see their salaries slip from twenty, thirty, forty, fifty grand a week right the way to a grand or even less. Once a player goes beneath the Championship then he's playing either because he's so hooked that he can't stop or (and this is far worse than any addiction) because he needs to carry on. He's had the money and for one reason or other he's blown it – a bad business decision, a dodgy tax-shelter investment (sometimes actually suggested by his agent in return for a not insubstantial commission), an expensive divorce or worst of all a serious gambling, drug or alcohol problem.

So, if you're on the outside looking in, you may not blame a player for seeking to feather his nest while he has the chance to get his hands on the material with which to line it. All he's doing is making plans for his life after football and if that afterlife is representing players and doing it totally for his own benefit, ridding himself of the agent he's used to front for him during his playing days, then who can blame him? Well, all the real agents, all four hundred of them (that's roughly how many there were of them before the system got bombed into oblivion).

Nobody had a problem with the players who'd retired, passed the exam and done everything right, gaining their experience within a reputable agency on the job. It's these snakes who've slithered around nicking clients to which everybody objected.

Footballers who wanted to muscle into the agency game were for years the biggest threat. A really high-profile player, a household name and a so-called 'respected international' specialised in trying to persuade players (whoever represented them) to leave their agents. He did this by bad-mouthing all agents, saying they were leeches taking money out of the game and in particular out of the pockets of the poor players. For a time he even said he'd never used an agent during his playing days because he didn't trust any of them. This didn't stop him then getting them to sign up to another agent he nominated just as soon as the player was free to sign (and sometimes even before that to get him to sign an undated contract to be dated as soon as his old one expired). Suddenly it appeared he had someone who could be trusted. Yeah, right. Makes perfect sense but players were buying into it.

While he's waiting for the old contract to run down player/agent/intermediary guides the player through the troubled seas of the current agent's wrath.

I know the conversation goes something like this because one of my players told me of an approach, and in fact he was so bright he actually recorded it on his phone. 'Listen to me, mate, and you'll be fine. If your man calls you don't return any calls or respond to any emails or texts. In fact, change your number – I'll arrange that for you – and don't give the new one to your agent. If a new deal comes along I'll advise you because I know what everybody at the club is earning. You can just say you acted for yourself and if you want to give me anything in cash out of the extra money I get you then that would be nice, but not obligatory. And if your agent threatens to sue you then I'll get someone to have a quiet word with him to tell him we'll make sure he loses all his other clients as well if he so much as calls a lawyer.'

I contemplated doing something about it but decided that my own hands weren't quite clean enough to take anything like that to the FA. So instead I rang the player, told him I had absolute proof of what he was up to and if he tried it again with any of my players he'd be sorry. I thought about telling him he'd get a visit from a couple of very large individuals with baseball bats who'd make sure he'd never play again, but although I knew of one or two agents who might have taken that approach (one of whom took it with me and made a point of telling me he had a shotgun in the boot of his car) it just wasn't my style then or now. I'm not the tallest or the toughest individual in the world and wasn't looking to get a criminal record – well, not before it was thrust on me, anyway.

The thing is that everybody knows this goes on. The tabloids are always sniffing around the story of a player secretly running (or at the very least, owning) his own agency. But as with so many wrongdoings, knowing is one thing and proving is another, and after the phone-hacking fiasco and the resultant pay-outs, the newspapers and their legal advisers are becoming increasingly cautious as to what they actually print. Even when they're certain it's true.

These wannabe agent-players are generally the brighter ones and know how to play their cards just right. There is the lead card of: 'All agents are thieves, and why pay one when you can get more money for yourself by working with the likes of me. I've been there. I've been ripped off. I can prevent it from happening to you.'

They're also not averse to playing the race card.

'Hey, I'm black, you're black. So come on, bro, why would you want to make your white agent even richer than the motherfucker already is? Let's keep it in the family. Right?' Right.

It's not just the players who are trying to be surrogate agents but the managers themselves. They can play one end against the middle as well. Tell the chairman that the player is worth more than he really is, put in an agent friend to do the deal, and Bob's your uncle. It works even better when a manager/agent wants to bring in a player from abroad. I've already explained to you how an agent can manipulate a transfer fee but how much better placed is a manager to do just that?

They bring the player in, recommend the financial package, get a friendly agent (either their English mate or his foreign partner) to do the deal and then take a walloping great slice of the commission from a totally inflated contract. Works every time.

I know of one case where a manager simply waltzed into a club with a player as his 'friend'. He sat quietly while the buying club made its offer and then told the player that he knew for a fact that there were players there on far more. He ended up getting the player double what had first been on offer and also ended up getting a very generous thank-you present from the player. I doubt the buying club or its manager were that grateful, but they still did fuck all about it.

That's one of the problems with being an agent who has never played the game. It's a them-and-us situation, and you're never going to be regarded as part of the football family which seems to be able to close ranks at the slightest hint of a threat from an outsider. They may seem to be deadly rivals when on opposite sides, but when it's one of their own against an agent they're suddenly all brothers in arms. That's the by-word of the PFA. We look after our own so don't trust anybody outside this private members' club. It's a bit like the medical profession. I'm told on good authority that one of the hardest things to find is a doctor prepared to say that another doctor was negligent and give evidence to that effect. I found that out when, before my fall from grace, I was asked to give evidence as to the level of earnings a player could achieve after the poor bastard had seen his career end with a horrendous challenge and then been the victim of what appeared to be some pretty badly botched surgery. I'd been asked to help by the player's lawyers and, having sat in a meeting with his old agent, the solicitor and the barrister, I got the impression they were finding it really hard to find another medic who would definitively say that it was the surgery more than the tackle which had finished the career.

The competition with agents can go even further up the ladder. There are directors, chief executives and even a chairman (or so I'm informed) at it as well. One of my players was arousing a fair amount of interest amongst other clubs. His manager told him that he was going nowhere, and although I did my best to persuade him to let him go he just wasn't having any of it. My player wasn't happy either with the club, or me for that matter. But then, suddenly, the chairman of his current club called him in and told him that he'd only allow the move to happen if he let him, the chairman, handle everything. Which he did, totally to his own advantage, and although the player got more money at the new club, there was no doubt that a fair amount which should've gone into his contract ended up in the chairman's pocket.

I did think about suing or going to the media, or even the FA, but I knew I'd get no sympathy, merely adverse publicity. It would cost me a fortune and I'd just be chasing my losses. And so, I had to be pragmatic and move on. Yet you never forget in this business. Jack Charlton used to talk about his 'little black book'. Well, I don't have the opportunity on the pitch to kick seven bells of shit out of those who have crossed me, but I sure as hell have made a mental note. What is it the Chinese say? If you sit by the banks of the river long enough then you'll see the bodies of your enemies float by. I was quite prepared to sit there – metaphorically speaking at least because I fucking hate fishing – until Doomsday.

What that chairman did to me was only one step away from the manager or the chairman putting in a close relation to set up an agency of which he owns a chunk. Or even if the relative has carved out a career for himself as a football agent, pushing players in his direction.

I read about one very famous manager who knew a club was interested in buying one of his players. The player's agent called the buying club and the manager expressed surprise that he was acting. He then, obviously phoned the manager of his current club and they seemed to cook up something between them because the current manager called the player into his office.

It seems the conversation went something like this.

'I hear you want a move, son.'

'I didn't ask for one, Gaffer. I'm happy here, but my agent told me somebody was interested, so I've got to look at things haven't I? To be fair, I'm not your first choice every week.'

'That's true son, and I'm not one to stand in the way of anybody, but I have to tell you, I really don't trust your agent and I only want the best for you.'

'I've been with him a long time, Gaffer, and he's always done well for me.'

'Too fucking well when it came to your contract here,' the manager said, meaning he was miffed that he'd not earned anything out of the deal. 'So, you're telling me you're going to ignore my advice?'

The player shrugged a gesture that this bully boy of a manager didn't like.

'OK. It's your decision – and your funeral. But I'm going to call the club who want you and tell them that you're not for sale. If you're not prepared to listen to reason and drop your man then I'm telling you here and now that I'm going to destroy your career and you'll be lucky if you spend the rest of it picking splinters out of your arse while you sit on the bench at reserve matches after training all week with the kids and doing double sessions – because, son, I reckon your fitness level is even shitter than your choice of a fucking agent.'

The manager, always ruddy faced because he liked his drink (don't they all) was getting redder and redder in the face until the player thought he was going to explode. The player cheekily asked him who he'd recommend if he didn't like his current representative and the manager mentioned an agent, who I later found out to be totally corrupt, as somebody of whom he'd approve.

The player stood firm. His current agent threatened to sue the bollocks of the manager and the club as well as claiming that his client had been effectively dismissed. The hierarchy of the club panicked, settled everything and it was all swept under the carpet. The player moved at a reduced fee, his current agent did the deal and so it goes on. Everybody wants a slice of the action. Everybody wants a piece of a player, a deal, and whatever else they've got – usually quite a lot in the case of a manager or a player – it's never quite enough. Money somehow or other breeds the pursuit of more money. It becomes another kind of addiction, another obsession. But then who am I to preach from the top of my high moral mountain? After all, was I really any better than those I looked down on?

Forgive me for saying that I truly thought I was. And it was that thought that drove me on, that kept me going straight down the road that led to disaster. I thought that being less dishonest was enough. As things panned out, it wasn't.

TWENTY-ONE

CORNERED

THERE ARE LOTS of terms for illegal cash in our business: readies, sweeties, chocolate. Whatever you want to call it, there's an awful lot of it about and an awful lot of it stashed away; just how much or where it came from or how it was used took me some time to discover. Whether it's kept in a security safe in a bank, a cardboard box under the stairs or one of the depositories that specialises in storing ill-gotten gains, it's still there and it's still illegal.

As I said, for a long while I couldn't figure out how it was generated but as I've mentioned before there are willing bag men amongst the agents (not to mention willing Swiss bankers) who are ready to facilitate its availability if not its creation.

I stumbled into a meeting once where a huge sum was about to be generated and I have to say, even though by that stage I thought I was unshockable, I was shocked.

I was acting – or thought I was acting – for a player moving between two medium-sized Premiership clubs. I'd spoken to the buying manager.

'I like the lad, but we need to sort out a few things first so why not meet me for a chat.'

He named a hotel that was owned by a manager (not directly, of course, but through and off shore-company controlled by his wife's trust). I thought it a bit odd at the time that rather than meet in the bar, the lounge or a conference room, he'd chosen a hotel suite as a location, but what was even odder was that when I got there he was sitting down for a drink with the manager of the club that was selling the player and my old friend Mr Fixit.

They were all clearly old friends, reminiscing about this player and that, and I truly felt as if I'd arrived at a private party without an invitation and inappropriately dressed. They had a few drinks, tried, unsuccessfully, to ply me with a few as well, and although none of them were drunk they were loosening up while I remained stone cold sober and felt very uptight. And yes, I have to say it, a bit judgemental. I just felt better than them, superior, because whatever I might have done or been prepared to do, I'd never flaunted it, never broadcast it. Whatever I'd done, in or out of Vegas, had stayed in Vegas, and I liked it that way. Liked the fact that nobody had anything on me to give them the power to make me do anything I did not want to do.

Somewhere along the line they exchanged looks and left it to Mr Fixit to do the talking.

'Listen, there's a deal to be done here. It might not be the deal you thought you were going to do, but if you don't do it our way then I'm afraid there won't be a deal at all.'

Nothing like coming straight to the point, I thought, realising they'd summed me up and arrived at the conclusion that foreplay was a waste of time and they might as well just rip my knickers off and go for a full gang bang.

He took my silence for acquiescence and then continued. 'Right, so this is the deal. I've seen what you want for your boy. [I was always efficient and had sent a deal proposal ahead of the meeting. Sometimes that had the right effect and made me look professional, and sometimes I'd seen a manager or a chairman rip it up in front of my eyes, or thank me for supplying them with toilet paper.] You can fucking forget that. K here [he pointed to the buying manager] is going to give him [he named a figure a good twenty-five per cent below what I wanted]. You said you wanted five per cent from each side [I always tried it on, hoping to get five per cent between the two sides.] Well, you can fucking forget that too. In fact you can forget putting your name on the deal. We've spoken to your boy, and he's agreed to act for himself. We're going to give you [he named a figure which was about two per cent of the deal]. It'll be in cash, so you won't be that out of pocket. After that you say nothing. You don't comment on the transfer fee paid, you don't say you did the deal. You just say you and the player fell out, and you didn't want to stand in the way of his career. You cancel your rep contract and we all move on.'

'And that's it?' I said.

'That's it. Take it or leave it. Don't even think about trying to negotiate with us. You're playing with the big boys, and all you've brought to the party are your soft toys.'

'And my player, as well,' I couldn't help but add.

'Yeah, but somebody snogged him and then fucked him while you had your back turned, so you won't be leaving with him. Just the cash we're offering. Or nothing if you prefer and want to be stupid.'

I hesitated for a moment, tempted to make the grand gesture and walk out, and then thought maybe I should speak to my player (or what was more likely, it seemed, my ex-player) first. I reached for my phone and saw just a flicker of emotion on Mr Fixit's face as, for a moment, he must have wondered if I'd recorded the conversation. No such luck. I'd not been expecting anything like this so I'd come unprepared.

'Go on,' he said, now anticipating my move. 'Call your lad.'

I did. It went to voicemail, so I tried again. All I got back was a text from the player asking me to leave him alone. I got the message.

Of course, I should've told them to get stuffed. But they

were offering me a choice between fifty grand in readies and a long legal battle to get my money from the player for breach of contract. I made my choice. A bad one in hindsight because now I'd stooped to their level and I was one of them, whether I wanted to be or not.

It was only afterwards that I worked out just how they were going to generate the money for my payout, not to mention making far more money themselves. The buying club was going to be delighted, because the manager would show them what I'd wanted and what he'd managed to get the player to take while forcing me (and my hundred grand fee) out of the transaction. He was on some kind of bonus deal when he saved the club money. On the other hand, the agent for the selling club's manager would've carved out a commission deal for himself with him advising the club what was a fair figure and the buying club's manager endorsing that. All very cosy. And very remunerative for all concerned – except me, who'd had to take a cut in fees, and the poor player, who had got a crap deal and foolishly been persuaded to believe it was as good as he was going to get, and was the only way the transfer was going to happen.

It wasn't to be the last time I'd have problems with managers, but after this incident anything seemed possible. I'd tested my own boundaries and found I didn't really have any.

When I tried to move a player to another club, I received a call from another agent telling me this was 'his club' and he had to be involved in any transfers there so what was I offering. To be fair to him he did, at least, come up with a solution – namely that I carry on acting for the player, but that he would act for the club and we'd pool whatever we got, with him taking sixty per cent and me forty. That was generous after my Mr Fixit deal, which saw what I would've earned reduced by half.

It beggars belief that shrewd businessmen who buy clubs and

bring in hand-picked managers then let them rape and pillage the club alongside their chosen agent. I guess it works, so long as the manager succeeds on the pitch and delivers trophies, but he can be very exposed once the results start going pear-shaped.

I've never been too sure how far up the tree this sort of corruption goes. I know there are one or two dodgy CEOs and I know at least one director who is right at the heart of the sort of scam I've described above. But who knows? If you buy a club, it's very hard to make a profit or take money out, so I suppose you could regard this as an inventive way of awarding oneself a bonus. Does it make it right? Is anything in football *right*?

But all of that was absolutely pocket money compared to what I discovered, years, later was Mr Fixit's most profitable hour,

He had a partner in a country which wanted a World Cup. Now staging a World Cup isn't necessarily the route to great riches for the actual country involved. Ask the poor South Africans who are stuck with empty and decaying stadiums. But people make fortunes in building those stadiums and doling out the sponsorship and merchandising and media rights for the event. So, one way or another there are big bucks at stake.

Mr Fixit had got somebody whispering in his ear just how much it was worth to deliver a World Cup so the next step was to work out who he could look after at FIFA to actually deliver it.

Years on there can't be a person alive (apart from my grandmother in an old folks' home in North London) who doesn't know just how rotten to the core FIFA became as an organisation. By the time the FBI and the Swiss police had moved in there was hardly anybody left at FIFA HQ in Zurich to answer the phone, let alone to make a decent cup of coffee.

Yet what nobody seemed to realise then, or now for that matter, was that the people concerned, whether that was at FIFA itself or the relevant country's governing body (or even government, because in one case it certainly went all the way to the top of the tree), they were not the sort of people to get down and dirty when it came to the nitty-gritty.

So, that was where Mr Fixit came in, this time fixing it on the international stage. He was the one who orchestrated everything, moved the money around, opened bank accounts, laundered huge sums by buying properties and businesses around the globe (even football clubs, where it was felt they could be profitable, and cashed out after a few years when the source of the money that bought them was long buried and forgotten).

I was never privy to the detail or the small print but this was serious stuff. Vote rigging of the highest calibre. No money-making stage of the World Cup process was ignored. Everybody who wanted to make money, who wanted to bid and feel sure that their bid or tender would be successful had to go through to Mr Fixit. He even set up his own corporation to make it seem reputable and at one stage was employing about fifty people – of whom only a handful knew what was actually going on.

There was a constant stream of masters of the universe traipsing through the marble halls of the corporation building. Some, who were simply too big to get embroiled in the house of cards, received a genuine contract for a genuine fee. That was to show anybody who poked around that there was nothing to hide. It was all above board and Mr Fixit was just using his years of experience as an agent of renown (if not repute) to turn and honest buck.

However, beneath that was the real money-making machine, as contracts for hotels were awarded, exclusive travel and clothing partners were appointed and all the time Mr Fixit took his percentage for, well, I suppose, fixing it.

What is most amazing is that even as the whole edifice crumbled, even as arrest after arrest was made and those accused were falling over themselves to point fingers and plea bargain to get their own sentences reduced, nobody mentioned a single football agent, let alone Mr Fixit.

I was going to say it shows how dumb the police, the football authorities (those of them who aren't corrupt) and the investigative journalists can be. I just wish they could have been so stupid when it came to my issues – but maybe I just didn't have the wherewithal of Mr Fixit to make it all go away.

I have no idea how much Mr Fixit made from the project or how many others benefiitted from the whole rotten process. All I do know is that the scandal will rumble on for a long time to come and that there are quite a few agents who won't sleep easily in their beds until the last column inch it written, the last arrest and prosecution has taken place and the heavy footsteps of Mr Plod which threatened to arrive at the doors in the early morning along with the milkman have finally receded into the distance.

TWENTY-TWO

THE MEDIA GAME

LIFE USED TO be so simple when it came to the media. The players would attend a press conference a few days before a match and then play, give a few interviews afterwards and that was it for the week. Not exactly stressful for the player or the agent, and if the agent was skilful he might even be able to manipulate a few bob out of a paper for an exclusive and charge his commission – twenty per cent of course.

How times have changed – and certainly not for the better. You have to satisfy not just the papers but also Sky and BT Sport and all the rolling news stations and of course the radio programmes and their phone-ins. There is a huge appetite for gossip and news about clubs, players and managers, and somehow or other the agent has to find a way to satisfy that. Every fucking day, if you represent a high-profile player or manager.

The problem is the unpredictability of your client and the all-seeing all-hearing eyes and ears of the press. I dread the danger hours at the end of the day when one of my players has either drunk too much and been thrown out of a nightclub or has been arrested for drink-driving or molesting a girl at said club. There are a hundred other scenarios that might happen and I keep a couple of lawyers' numbers handy. You'd be amazed at the number of times I need them.

There are some criminal lawyers who specialise in sorting out the problems of high-profile individuals, and footballers in particular. That doesn't make them bad people, but it does make them expensive people, and an agent is always torn between getting the money from his client or covering the cost himself. The player is almost always in a better financial position to pay, and it's usually his own fault that he's found himself up the creek without a paddle, but somehow or other he doesn't see it like that.

Forgetting the criminal or civil repercussions, it never hurts to have a couple of journos as mates. I was going to say 'in your pocket' but surprisingly, given the awful press the press gets from its own, they're a pretty incorruptible mob. I've never heard of an agent being able to silence a story with a bribe, although I have known of the sort of barter that the PR gurus indulge in.

'I've got a big transfer coming up and I'll give you the nod on that one if you take your foot off the accelerator on this one.'

The problem with that is if you think football is a village then Fleet Street and, indeed, the whole of the Fourth Estate is much worse. I know all about the phone-hacking stuff as I've had clients hacked. But somehow or other it's very hard to keep any secret from the media when it comes to football, and I've read about deals in which I've been involved in the paper before there was even a deal. The fact is that it isn't just agents and players to whom journalists speak: it's everybody from the kit man up at the club, and believe me, the kit man hears and knows everything.

Speaking of kit men I once negotiated a deal for a player which I thought was pretty good. The player then called me up to say it wasn't enough and he'd spoken to a few people about it who all thought I was suggesting a shit package. I asked him who he'd spoken to, and while he was at first reluctant to tell me, he finally admitted it had been the kit man. Oh well, when these new intermediary regulations come in, all the kit men can give up their day job and become intermediaries – as I'm sure they think they can do a better job than us lousy agents.

Back to the media. They also love sound bites from agents. The trouble is that the agents they pick to give them aren't always the ones the rest of us want to be judged by. They used to use the bloke with the long cigars a lot. Interesting guy, but one of a kind, and I've never met anybody else like him in the business. But he was entertaining, and the media loved him so that was the picture the public got of us. Recently they stuck a cowboy hat on another agent they interviewed and had him walking down a street market. What the fuck? Draw your own conclusions from how he fell into that one.

The thing is that when somebody sticks a mike under your nose you have to think in a nanosecond, and it isn't always possible to come out with what you really wanted to say. And you have to say something. The media rarely have direct access to a player unless it's at a club press conference, or they collar him going in or out of the training ground. Consequently, the second best route is through his agent. As I say, agents do have favoured journalists, and although that doesn't stop the bloodiest-minded and most vindictive of them writing what they want anyway, it does make them think twice before they burn their bridges irreparably with any given agent.

I've always been wary of the press but I do have a private rule that I'll give all and any of them one chance to show they're trustworthy by telling them something 'off the record' to see if it shows up in their columns. Of course, I've been let down. Every agent has. Journalists, particularly the younger ones, can't afford to play the long game so they'd rather go for the big story than the long-term relationship. That's their problem. Though on one occasion, it became mine.

I was trying to keep a story about my client's gambling and

womanising out of the paper and said, 'off the record', that I'd look after the journo on any future transfer deals and give him a heads up. The bastard printed his story in full including my proposed deal. Neither the player (nor the player's mum, in particular) nor the player's current club were best pleased, and it eventually cost me the player, who wouldn't sign a new rep contract with me because he claimed I couldn't be trusted to keep my mouth shut with the press.

Some agents I know get hooked on fame and being a Z-list celebrity themselves. They love giving interviews and sound bites, love seeing their names in the papers just as much as their clients'. It's not a new phenomenon. The agents of George Best, Gazza and more recently Wayne Rooney became household names but, just as with the players themselves, the British press loves nothing more than to put a person up on a pedestal just to knock them down.

That's why I try to keep myself to myself. I don't want to be waking up in the morning and finding myself splashed all over the papers for something that some sleazebag of a journo has dug up about my personal life. Mind you, as you'll have gathered, they might have a hard job given that I have no personal life.

I've seen it happen to other agents though. Tax scandals, criminal proceedings, gaffes in public speaking, racist allegations, affairs . . . you name it, my compatriots have either done it or been accused of doing it.

So far, the worst I've experienced is when somebody wrote that I'd taken half a million quid out of a deal where, at its start, I didn't act for the player or either club. I did know the player, and he'd asked me for some informal advice, and we'd met for a drink from time to time, but on this occasion, although the clubs between them were alleged in a tabloid to have paid a million quid of agents' fees, none of that had found its way into my pocket. The player was amused, the FA less so and I had to satisfy them that the report was wrong. However, I decided to do nothing about it because I thought it might help my profile. Big mistake. When my accountant filed my tax return for the relevant year HMRC got interested and asked why I hadn't declared the half mill that the paper had said I'd received. It finally got sorted out, but not before I'd had to pay a hefty fee to my accountant and endure the lovely guys at the FA watching me like a hawk for a while to see what I got up to next below the radar.

They might have been better off watching a real villain (I'm running out of letters so it might be easier to call him V). V was a real piece of work and how he managed to keep out of jail I will never know. I've written about players being duped regarding cars and jewellery but V went way beyond that. He had a brother-in-law who ran a holiday company out of Cyprus. As part of getting players in, one of the incentives that he offered was that he could arrange luxury holidays at knock down prices. You know what I said about there being no free lunches? Well, in the world of football there are almost certainly no bargains. Whether a club is buying a player or hiring a manager or whether an agent is 'selling' something to his players. The fact of the matter is that you will always get what you paid for, and usually get something worth a fair bit less.

In this case V had a player who truly was not the sharpest tool in the box. V suggested he should take a holiday to impress his newly found girlfriend and came up with an exotic location for a mere ten grand for the pair of them for a week (although for that snip he threw in the flights).

The player got a bit concerned when he'd received no documents by the day before his holiday, but V told him not to worry. It was all sorted and provided he and his girlfriend took their passports with them to the airport they could collect everything, including the hotel vouchers at check-in. As you can imagine to believe that one you had to be a very inexperienced traveller and the player, as it transpired, had never been beyond Magaluf, except when he travelled with his club side.

He duly turned up in good time, swimming costume and condoms all packed and ready, and was told to his disappointment that there was no booking in his name and that the airline did not really do hotel arrangements from its check-in desk. He tried to ring V and when he finally got through V feigned outrage and blamed the incompetence of the airline, the travel agent and anybody else he could think of on the spur of the moment.

V asked if they had their credit cards with them and when they said they did he took the numbers and the travel was duly arranged, miraculously, on the plane they'd thought they would be taking and at the hotel where they thought they'd be staying. So, effectively, they paid for the same holiday twice but in talking to others at the resort they discovered they were really on a package tour the price of which was about half of what they'd originally handed over. V and his brother-in-law had made a killing having been paid twice for a holiday that cost in reality a quarter of what the player believed the price to have been.

Upon their return the player complained to V, who promised to sort it out and then proceeded to delay and delay until he finally broke the bad news that the travel agency had gone bust in Cyprus; and on top of that he had the gall to claim credit for at least having rescued the holiday.

It wasn't something V could do with players who were more aware of prices and value, but as a scam it was nice work if he could get it and it wasn't the only thing he got up to earn his deserved being given the name V for villain.

It's all very well saying that anything you read in the paper is tomorrow's fish-and-chips wrapper, but you never know who reads the garbage. An agent acquaintance (I was going to say a friend but we can't afford that sort of luxury in this business) always used his media contacts to generate interest for any unhappy player. Unfortunately, for him and one of his clients, the player's current club used the articles to support their claim that the player had actually asked for a transfer, which meant that they were entitled to say he'd forfeited the balance of his signing-on fee (a small matter of two hundred grand). What had started as a favour to the player had become a serious liability. The player denied that he'd authorised or known about the articles, but nobody believed that. After some serious horse-trading the agent managed to get the club to agree to pay half, and also got the player a deal at a new club, which was so good that it meant he lost nothing. On that occasion the story had a happy ending but it's pretty unusual.

Another agent loved to play the system and act for the buying club when he was really always acting for the player. That sort of thing always sets off warning signals with the FA as well as the Revenue, neither of which are totally stupid and who realise that it's being done to avoid the player paying any tax on the agent's fees and also avoid paying any VAT. It doesn't sound the best when I put it that way, and I can see why the Revenue would be sore, although as with most 'avoidances' I really can't see why it should be any of the FA's business other than to stop an agent earning more than the bloke who is trying to stop him earning it!

This agent was taken by the smell of the greasepaint and the roar of the crowd and decided to play Billy Big Time by describing to all and sundry who'd listen that the player was 'his'. Now, there's a little man (it may be men, it may be women, it may even be a few of each) who sits in the department that HMRC have set up (I think in Birmingham), cuts out interesting little snippets from the papers about footballers (and other sportsmen and women and entertainers) probably between doing the crossword and seeing what time Strictly Comes Dancing is on the box, and then follows the trail to see if they lead to any kind of tax evasion. Somebody saw the agent's comments, and when it came to the deal saw the agent had acted for the club. Bingo! For the Revenue that was it. They hit the player with a tax demand saying that the payment by the club to the agent who said he'd acted for it (the same agent who'd said in the media he acted for the player) was really a payment on behalf of the player and therefore a benefit in kind and therefore taxable. I'd love to have been a fly on the wall when the player got the demand and called the agent.

That's the problem with most of the guys running around in this business. They only think of today, not tomorrow. If a deal looks too good to miss then why miss it? If you can play the system and try and fool the taxman (and sometimes your own client) while inflating your own ego, then why not? The answer is very simple. Because tomorrow always comes a-knocking and very often has company in the shape of the taxman or the football authorities or even the police. Whenever I read something like that I always vowed to be more careful. I vowed, but then temptation gets put in my way, and hey, I'm only human. And I'm a football agent, and while some people may feel those two identities don't really fit too snugly together I beg to differ. You remember that old driving advert, 'Carelessness costs lives'. Well, I became careless and while I'm still here to tell the tale, I certainly lost my old life and it's taking me a while to get it back. A long while and I'm still not there.

TWENTY-THREE

SWIMMING WITH SHARKS

I'VE NEVER BEEN one for gambling myself. I've always thought life to be a big enough risk on its own without stacking the odds even further against you. But, go tell that to footballers. Whereas an agent's time is precious, with every minute counting, footballers have all the time in the world to fill.

They will roll into training around nine in the morning, admire each other's expensive cars for a while, discuss their new tattoos and sexual exploits from the night before, have some free breakfast provided by the club (about which they will complain), run around for a bit, kick a few balls, have a free lunch (about which they will also complain) and then bugger off. Some of the more progressive coaches are now organising double sessions so they actually have to stay for a while after lunch, but, generally speaking, unless there's a match in the evening then the rest of the day is theirs to waste as they will.

The options for their free time, their 'me' time, are standard. Sleep, golf, more sleep, shopping some quality time with their agent or lifestyle coach (rarely happens), a new tattoo, snooker (a bit passé now), a DVD, thinking up new ways to make more money even though the top echelons struggle to spend what they're already making or . . . a bet. Or two, or three, or as many bets as they can make before the money runs out. I may be doing many of them a great wrong as I know there are players who are happy to push a buggy, take the older kids to the park to play football (of course), or even go to Tesco with the missus. It's just that I've never met any of them or was lucky enough to represent them.

I'm not the sort of agent who tries to interfere in my clients' lifestyle choices, so what they do in their spare time is entirely up to them. If they want to have an orgy or indulge in dogging, wife-swapping or a bit of S&M (and there are certainly some who do), well, good luck with that as long as they keep it to themselves and nobody takes photos. I've had to deal with blackmail attempts and investigative journalists, and neither situation is great fun. Only when their habits interfere with my lifestyle or my income do I start to get concerned. And a player who gets himself up shit creek with his gambling habits can be a real drain on his agent's wallet. And this is why.

As long as a player is making a fortune from a deal secured by his agent, then everything in the garden is rosy. When he loses that same fortune in one way or another, then the smell of rotting compost can totally overpower the sweet scent of the roses. The player may well have his back against the wall, will almost certainly not have told his free-spending wife that she needs to cut back on the pedicures and designer clothes, and will be looking to dig himself out of his situation. Generally this is done by the player seeking to get more money, one way or another, so that he can chase his losses because, like every compulsive, addicted gambler, he's convinced himself that his luck is just about to change. It isn't. But he won't believe that until he's run out of prospects from whom he can borrow.

There are plenty of loan sharks out there, many of whom have a connection to the sort of bookies who are happy to arrange preferential accounts for players with credit lines even beyond their astronomic means. Taking money from them is not a good idea. It is, in fact, a very bad one because they tend to get rather upset when the loans don't get repaid.

Another agent told me about a visit he received at his suburban home at two in the morning from a shark who suggested that if he wanted to have a live player to represent then he should consider paying the player's debt, as there wasn't a great demand in the industry for a footballer with broken legs and fractured kneecaps. The agent, wanting the visitors to leave, asked how much and was told it was sixty grand – but that the following week it would be sixty-five. The agent declined to pay, knowing his player was on fifty grand a week and, he thought, could well afford to pay the debt himself.

However, when he sat down with his client the next day to go through his finances, he discovered a very different picture.

'This guy isn't the only one I owe,' the player confessed.

'How many?' the agents asked and was shocked when the player replied.

'About half a dozen. Maybe more because some of my debts have been sold off so I don't even know some of these blokes who come calling. I've taken to coming into the club by the back door, working out escape routes, and when one of them came into the café at the club last week [which is open to the public] I had to hare off across the pitch. I can't go on like this.'

'Can't you sell your house and move to something smaller?' the agent asked helpfully.

'Mortgaged up to the hilt. Kept taking loans and even forged the wife's signature on a few of them.'

'Get rid of your car,' the agent advised, looking out of the window at the fifty grand monster parked just outside.

'Which car? I can't even remember how many I've got or who's using them at the moment. In any event they're all on HP and none of them are worth enough even to pay off what I borrowed in the first place.'

The player's form was being affected, his contract was up at the end of the season and the agent knew he wouldn't be able to match his current salary next time around so he took him off to an insolvency expert who patiently sat down with them both, carefully considered the situation and offered to help him make some kind of arrangement with his creditors.

You'd have thought the player would have appreciated it but instead he told his wife that it was the agent who'd got him into the mess by giving him bad advice and, using another agent, got himself a very rich tax free deal in the Middle East – and put his finger up to all the people to whom he owed money, his agent included.

Whereas with that player the agent hadn't had anything to do with his choice of house, agents do often get involved in property as well, as most footballers like to buy off-plan new-builds. There is always a developer around to look to for commission along with lawyers prepared to throw in an introductory fee to get the conveyancing. That's the situation at homes they will actually live in and I'll get to properties for investment and holiday homes a bit later.

As far as cars are concerned, footballers tend to stockpile cars in very much the same way as my nan used to hoard tins of baked beans. After she died we found over fifty of them in her pantry going back over a quarter of a century. I can't ever recall seeing her eat them, although on more than one occasion I did have baked beans on toast after school at her flat without ever knowing the vintage. Players will either get bored with the car they have or lust after bigger, better and more recent models than those their teammates are flashing about in the training-ground car park. They may acquire one for a girlfriend who then becomes an ex-girlfriend and departs in the seat of the very same car that has just been bought for her (that departure probably having been triggered by the player again lusting after a bigger and better and more recent model or the girl finding a teammate prepared to provide a more expensive car and throw a rock of a diamond in for good measure.

Another scenario is that the player has given a car to a mate or lent it to a teammate or even, in one famous instance, forgotten where he'd parked it. It's quite incomprehensible to the likes of me, who has driven the same car for three years or more, that expensive vehicles can simply vanish in transit, particularly when they belong to the finance company rather than the player himself. It follows that the hire purchase companies of the loan sharks, like the bookmakers, are going to get a bit antsy when the asset they've bought disappears and the person they've lent the money to in order to buy it stops the repayments.

One of my players was trying unsuccessfully to service three major debts to cover his bookies, six finance agreements and a bank overdraft, plus pay off his maxed-out credit cards, keep a mortgage that was a hundred grand more than the house it was secured on, and in between all this – it was hard to believe he'd actually found the time – had fathered a child for which he was paying maintenance. All in all he was in total financial meltdown, and when I sat down with him to try to help him sort things out, the player came up with a remarkably simple solution.

'I tell you what, mate,' he told me 'You've earned a fucking fortune out of me so why don't you sort it out.' Footballers aren't generally the brightest of individuals, but, as I've said before, when it comes to money they do seem to have the ability to cut through all the crap and get straight to the heart of the problem.

I was now faced with a major conundrum. I had, indeed, earned a fair old wedge from the deals I'd done for the player, but paying off his debts was going to mean giving most of it back with no guarantee there'd be more to come in the future. Eventually

I agreed to sort things out on condition that the player signed a new representation contract with me and that proved to be a shrewd move at the time when I did in fact manage to recover most of my investment when the player moved clubs. But then the cycle started all over again. Gambling, losses, loans and this time around I decided to quit while I was ahead, particularly because the player's loss of form (doubtless caused by his head being at the race track while his legs were at the match) meant any new deal was unlikely to be as remunerative as the previous ones.

As it happened there was no shortage of mugs willing to try their hands at representing him and inevitably, he played them all a good deal better than he was playing for his club. He borrowed money, got them to invest in schemes his mates came up with, shares in race horses and so on, each and every one of which was going to make the agent all his money back in spades – and none of them did. Last time I heard, the player was earning two hundred quid a week at a part time club in the National League and the agents who'd acted for him after me (I think there were four of them altogether), were left nursing their wounds and counting the cost.

Whilst gambling amongst agents is almost non-existent (even the ex-players who've gone into player representation seem to steer away from it), gambling amongst footballers is pandemic. It often starts with card games on the match-day coach when players can lose amongst themselves what would be ridiculous sums of money to you and me. They chase losses even there, trying to impress teammates (they all lie about what they're earning anyway as nobody wants to be seen to be earning less than the next man, any more than he wants to have a cheaper car) and it spirals from there.

Although the current regulations among football authorities in the UK to ban gambling by participants (players, agents/

intermediaries and managers) on football altogether, until recently the restrictions only extended to games where the player had potentially some influence, or some inside information. Given that all players and agents know somebody at almost every club, that should have been a very sweeping restriction, but it didn't work that way in practice. Footballers were and still are, are quite happy to shove their agents in the firing line when it comes to taking a bullet for putting themselves in the position where they stand to win money from a result they can influence in some way or other, or where they have inside information that can affect the result. An agent (or, as is the case now, one of his friends or relatives) placing a bet is likely to attract less interest than a footballer, and most of them don't want to upset their clients by refusing a simple request like that.

Unusual betting patterns will get picked up by the larger betting companies such as Corals, Ladbrokes, Paddy Power and so on, but many of the gambling players have their own tame bookie who can be licensed, maybe just a guy who stands on the rails at the smaller race meetings, or unlicensed, the old-fashioned street bookie with his own unique methods of collection, as illustrated before. It's hard for players or their agents to fix matches because so many participants are required. It's much easier in cricket, and agents there haven't been slow in coming forward to assist. Yet it's not so hard to fix an element of a match, given that bets can be placed on almost anything: free kicks, yellow and red cards, goal times even the first throw in and so on. A dishonest player working in conjunction with an agent to whom he's feeding information can make a nice little fortune on the side. And often does.

I've had my own experiences here, and although I'm not easily scared I have to say they gave me a few sleepless nights. It all started off innocently enough. A couple of African guys contacted me and asked me if I wanted to help them in setting up some friendly matches. They seemed genuine, dropped the right names, and I reckoned it was at least worth a meeting with them. They came across and told me that they controlled the national teams of three different African countries and could get me exclusivity for their friendlies. They also said I could have free rein in the dressing rooms. As I quickly worked out, that meant access to half a dozen Premiership players so it had to be worth exploring further. Then came the catch. I had to go to one of the countries and meet the president of its national association, as he always wanted to know with whom he was dealing.

I started to feel a bit nervous. 'Does he want anything out of this?' I asked.

The two men looked offended. 'Of course not. He just wants to be sure that he's dealing with the right sort of people.'

So I went ahead, had all the injections, and booked a ticket and I did indeed meet the president who was charm itself as we sat by the pool at the five-star hotel he'd arranged as the venue.

'I do need something in writing,' I said.

Everybody nodded. *Of course, of course . . .*

I got back to England and had some paperwork drafted. And then things took a turn. My two new chums said they had an agreement for one of the countries to come over to London and play a friendly international here in an area where many of their countrymen lived. But they needed a company with a track record to sign off on the deal and they were fairly new at the game, so would I do it, please?

I took a look at the contract and fortunately got my lawyer to look at it too. He soon spotted something very odd. There was a clause where the promoter (me) had the right to appoint the officials for the match. As he wasn't slow in telling me, that was really not normal.

I went back to my buddies and asked the reason for the clause, and by then they obviously felt I was sufficiently involved to tell me that if we had our own officials we could control the score in the game, and if we could control that then certain friends of theirs in the Far East would be so happy that everybody – me, them and the president – would be royally rewarded.

I pointed out that this was in essence match fixing and that was a tad illegal. They looked at me blankly (well I guessed it was blankly as they rarely smiled or removed their designer sunglasses) and tried to persuade me that it couldn't really be match fixing because these were friendlies and nobody really cared about the result.

'Except these guys who plan to bet millions on it,' I pointed out. 'Listen, guys, thanks for thinking of me, but no thanks.'

And I was out of there. It was then that the threats started. To my body, my business, and when they got to my parents I decided it was time to go to the police.

The police listened and then asked me if I'd be prepared to go back into the ring but wired up, so they could nail them. It was now like something out of a TV thriller and I really was out of my comfort zone, so I refused. The police said they couldn't make me do it, but I sensed I wasn't making friends on the Force and there was to come a time when I knew that for sure.

Such scams aren't always successful. One agent was told by one of his players that his team was decimated by a virus but the manager had managed to keep the news under his hat. Knowing that his team was going to be under-strength for a weekend game, the player got his agent and his mates to place bets throughout the week on the opposition. Although the bets were spread out over any number of high-street betting shops, it got picked up when they laid them off with the big boys. Betting was suspended, and the weakened team duly lost by a hatful. The match wasn't fixed as such, so the bookies were in a quandary as to whether or not they paid out. The regulatory bodies weren't subject to such hesitation and began an investigation into the source of the leaked information and who had been placing the bets, ensuring ultimately that the big winners became big losers.

One player I knew was always in debt. He'd inherited the habit from his father, a small-time shopkeeper who, when in arrears to an impatient taxman, tried to charge wannabe agents for the privilege of representing his son. Some poor mug paid in good faith – always a mistake when it comes to footballers' fathers – only to find that there was an auction going on, and not only was he one of several bidders but the father regarded his deposit as non-refundable.

The player joined the agent who was 'chosen' by his father, but then as he himself ran up all sorts of debts arising from a disastrous gambling streak, he drifted from agent to agent, always spinning them a convincing yarn as to why he was changing. The only consistent factor was the chaos he caused along the way.

One of the lucky agents was convinced that whatever he lent the player he would recoup from the next deal (we've heard that story before). However, there were so many calls asking for just one more loan that eventually the agent ran out of patience – and nearly ran out of money. The player called again, asking for some money to put on a horse that was a racing certainty . . . that then lost. What he wanted to do was to back against the horse which was a hot favourite. Now, you might've thought that there would be alarm bells ringing for the agent, but not a bit of it. The agent got the name of the horse, told the player he'd get back to him and then promptly got a friend to place the bet the player had wanted to make, but this time for his own benefit.

The horse duly lost, and even before the agent could count his winnings the Jockey Club was on his case with an investigation into illegal betting using inside information that, in effect, the race was fixed. The agent ignored the Jockey Club, they warned him off in his absence, and what he didn't realise was that the effect of a ban by one sporting body meant that he automatically lost his licence with another, namely the FA.

The player moved on to yet another agent, caring not a jot for the fate of his erstwhile agent, and got another lucrative playing deal while the agent lost his business.

It didn't end happily for the player though. My grandmother always said you never meet a poor bookie and that is so true. He carried on gambling and then drinking and then drugs and the combination of the money he shed and the weight he gained meant the end of any long term meaningful career. Last I heard, he was picking up the pieces in the lower divisions whilst earning peanuts, but still looking for the rainbow at the end of the betting slip.

It just goes to show that it's not always the agents leading the players astray; it can often be quite the reverse. We're just a bunch of angelic choirboys, really. But then it's always a matter of comparison.

TWENTY-FOUR

SPECULATE TO ACCUMULATE

NOWADAYS, WHEN IT comes to getting clients on board, a slush fund not only helps but is a real necessity. There is so much competition to sign up players that, generally speaking, you need that little edge, and when it comes to players and their families that 'little edge' comes in the shape of a crisp fifty-pound note. If there was a hundred pound note that would be even better.

Inducements are more endemic when it comes to young players, particularly really young ones, but the older ones aren't slow to come forward when they hear the inviting rustle of folding paper. With them it's not need, it's greed.

After nearly four years of building up my business and my connections I was forced (OK, I wasn't really forced, I did it for the money not because a gun was being held to my head) into a deal with one of my more experienced clients where I had to give him back half of any fee (in cash, of course). Talk about half a loaf being better than none. Never truer than in my world. I learned from R that you always need to be on the lookout for deals with fellow agents, whether licensed or not, and it's often from the deals you do with the unlicensed guys that you're able to generate the cash to spread around. Sometimes I think I should just buy myself a pipe (musical variety) and skip through the woods scattering notes of the paper variety in front of talented young kids while tootling the other kind of notes. Yep, the Pied Piper of the Premier League. That's me.

You can share more with your player when he hasn't signed a representation contract with you, and you can represent the club in the deal when he makes his move. It's a high-risk strategy because the player, or one or both of his parents, can shaft you at the last minute either by bringing in somebody else (who might up the ante of the fifty per cent) or (and this is not unknown) going to the club direct, telling them you're no longer involved, and asking for all of what would've been your fee to be added to his contract. Really nice behaviour, but you come not to expect better.

Anyhow, if you do act for the club and it pays you your huge wedge, there can be advantages for everybody (er, except HMRC). The agent negotiates a fee with the club, which can be whatever he can get the club to agree to as he's not bound by the relatively small percentage of the player's guaranteed income (as would be the case if he had a standard rep contract with the player). As I mentioned earlier, the player pays no tax or VAT, and the club can pay back the VAT it pays on the agent's invoice.

Clubs are by no means innocent babes in the wood when it comes to payments to get hold of a decent young player. In fact, when it comes to anything, clubs are not innocent. They just pretend to be holier than thou when it suits them. They're quite prepared to get down and dirty when dirty is what it takes to acquire a player they want. Or rather they are quite happy to pay for an agent to get down and get dirty.

Some of the Premier League clubs can be absolutely ruthless when it comes to acquiring or poaching (the two often go hand in hand) the best youngsters, and often use an agent to get them exactly who they want. I went to see a club chairman (who should've known better) who told me he'd just seen a couple of agents who had guaranteed they'd get him three of the best under-14s in the country if he was prepared to pay them a hundred grand a player. He said he'd told them to get lost, but I got the feeling he'd just turned down the offer because he didn't trust them. So I offered him the same opportunity and he negotiated me down to fifty grand a player. He was one of the toughest negotiators in the business. What else could I have done? I had no connection whatsoever with these kids, and I suspect the agents who had offered them up didn't either. Now I had the chance to try and fit the two ends together.

I thought fifty grand a player was a decent budget and would leave me quids in, but that wasn't the case. The parents sensed blood and not knowing me from Adam didn't help. They wanted cash in hand and up front at that. These weren't cosy meetings in front of a hearth like I might have had when I was signing players. These were truly horrible, as dads and, in one case, a mum and in another an older brother, simply horse-traded the kids' future. The conversations went something along these lines.

'Listen, I know your son is at X Academy but I've got something better for him.'

'We've had lots of people saying the same thing and why are you different?'

'Because I genuinely act for the club who wants him and they want me to look after you to make it happen.'

'X Club wants to look after me too. What are you offering that's more attractive than what has already been put on the table in front of me?'

At least once they'd said that I knew I was in the game.

Eventually I managed to nick one of the kids I'd targeted, but it cost me nearly the whole of the fifty grand I'd been given as a budget, so for a very small reward I put my whole career on the line, which probably didn't make a lot of sense. Although it did prove that I could deliver, that I could be trusted and that I could be used again when the need arose. I just had to make sure that there was a need.

I lost one really promising kid when another wealthier agency bought a house and ensconced the parents in it and then put the brother on their payroll at thirty grand a year to do nothing more than go to watch his brother play (which he did anyway). Nice work if you can get it. And if you've got a son or a kid brother who can play football really well then there is always someone around to give it to you.

Just in case it all goes pear-shaped, clubs can hide behind agents and then, if anybody gets accused of tapping up minors, deny all knowledge and leave the agent out there, spinning on the end of a rope. This chairman I just mentioned did have a proposition for me though. I'd gained a bit of a reputation for getting things done and he wanted me to get him a fourteen-year-old from a much smaller club where he knew I had some contacts. It was going to be a high-risk exercise because I was fucked if I was found out and if the smaller club discovered it was me who had winkled out this little diamond from its mine then I was fucked with them as well. Not to mention the fact that I might get myself reported to the FA along with the club who were paying me. If that were to happen, no second guesses as to which of us would go down the heavier.

The target kid had a single mum, and they were both living on a council estate. So far, so good. They looked like easy pickings, but I know some of these mums are absurdly loyal to the club which gave their little Tommy his chance and they can also be very protective and genuinely believe that where he's at now is the best place for him. Silly them. I know the right place for him. It's where I'm going to earn the most money. Do I really believe that? Have I changed that much since I started out? You know, I'm not even sure that by this time in my career I can rely on myself to answer that question honestly. Time flies, and I'm worried I may not have fastened my seatbelt yet for take-off.

The little kid (actually not so little as he was already hitting six feet) had been with the club since he was eight years old and was now part of the academy while, of course, still being at school. Clubs have real problems with securing players at that age as they're a little too young to become EPPP (Elite Player Performance Programme) players and certainly not old enough to be offered a professional contract. Mind you, some of the clubs do get those signed and then leave them undated until the relevant time, the silence of the player and his parent or parents guaranteed by a huge payment, or the purchase of an even huger house, or a scouting job offer for the dad, or an administrative job offer for the mum. I could've made that sentence and those alternatives even longer as there are certainly more ways than one to skin that particular cat.

Any compensation payable to the unfortunate club which is about to lose its promising and emerging star is tiny compared to what a club will make available to the agent who is putting the theft (yep, let's be honest for once) together for them. The FA, the Premier League and the Football League (or at least the bigger clubs in that) have all bought into the new EPPP which is actually a charter to ensure that the big boys snaffle up all the talent in return for a few crumbs from the rich men's table for the smaller clubs. That suits me fine. More for me to play with, to ensure I deliver.

This kid was one of those 'talking players' I mentioned at the beginning of the book, and with half a dozen interested parties after him the mother had realised she had a valuable asset on her hands. She knew if she played it right she might never have to work again. I went to watch the kid a few times. Nobody thought anything about me being there, because I was in with the club.

I found an excuse to talk to the mother. She was pretty, and I spoke to her initially about everything but her son. Showed an interest in her and the rest of her family. Even learned a bit about the absentee dad – always useful in case he comes back when he scents a bit of money (that happens for sure and it is amazing how a boy can suddenly reject a mother who has ferried him to matches, worked all hours to buy him boots and fed and clothed him for years in favour of a ne'er do well who strolls into town and uses his alleged superior knowledge of football to pick up where he abandoned the family years before. But in this case, the dad wasn't around and the mum started to trust me. Even asked my advice about some of the agents who were waiting to pounce. But then she made a big mistake by telling me the sort of sums that were being offered by other clubs either directly or through third parties. So now that I knew the price, I just had to work out a way to get into the bidding.

Patience was the name of the game, and, if I say so myself, I played it to perfection. Almost apologetically I told her that I'd heard a certain club was interested, that they'd outbid anybody else, that she'd be able to move to a nice detached home near their training ground, and that they had a reputation for bringing their young players through into the first team after some sensible loan arrangements.

And the kid, even at his age, would be guaranteed the offer of a pro contract when he was seventeen and I was sure I could negotiate the terms of that now, get some of the anticipated signing-on fee paid to me as part of my deal and siphon that through to her, all on top of the usual housing benefit and travel allowance that club often pay to families.

She fell into my lap like a perfectly ripe apple when she asked me if I could help the family to make it happen. Of course, I replied, and it won't cost you a penny. I'd be prepared to earn nothing because I trusted her and her son to do the right thing when he was sixteen and able to sign with me. It was that easy. The lad left, the mum moved and the acquiring club paid me a huge finder's fee dressed up as a scouting contract because they couldn't be seen to be paying anything to get a kid that age. I did what I said I would do and gave the mother the sort of money she wouldn't have expected to earn in a lifetime from her cleaning job.

And the real plus was that the kid's original club never knew that I'd been involved. I even told them I'd tried to persuade the lad to stay when I found out what was going on. Brownie points all round. Dib, dib and all that. Did I find it hard to look in a mirror after that little deal? Did I fuck. I was too busy working out how to spend the money I'd just earned – if and when I ever found the time to get off the treadmill and have some time to myself.

The frustration for me was that the player turned out to be a real good 'un, but by the time I could have openly developed his career and my income I was off the list at the FA and the mother had succumbed to the entreaties of another agent who told her it would not be a great advantage to have anything to do with the likes of me. Guess part of the price I had to pay for my own stupidity, but you live and you learn, you learn and you live.

In fact, deciding what to do with the money didn't take long because now I had the dough to get players like the one I'd just delivered. It's money that oils the wheels, money that makes the world of football go round, and by now I wasn't just on the gravy train. I was practically driving it.

TWENTY-FIVE

INVESTMENTS

PLAYERS LIKE TO spend money on themselves. They like to make money and think they're being clever in the process, even if it is their agent who is doing the thinking for them. They're super-suspicious when they first meet an agent but once they get to know him, once he's done a good deal for them (and it only takes one) then they tend to trust him. Until they find out otherwise.

Now, please don't confuse trust with loyalty. I've already made it clear that commodity is rare when it comes to player–agent relationships. But while the relationship exists, and as it develops, then there is some trust – at least until something or someone better comes along.

That means there are all sorts of service options for the agent to provide either directly or indirectly. Depending on the honesty of the agent, or those he's dealing with, they can benefit both parties or just the agent. Generally speaking, they won't benefit the player alone. Altruism is not a trait that most of us have deeply ingrained in our souls. If we had it when we started out, we tend to lose it rather swiftly.

I quickly realised that if you control a player's money then you have a better than average chance of controlling him, particularly if you appoint somebody to handle it who appears to do well with it. The challenge is to stay in the loop. You don't want your player dealing directly with the Independent Financial Adviser because he might then eventually rely more upon him than upon you. And the IFA may get some fancy ideas as to how he can also be an agent and just nick all the players you've sent him. It happens.

What the player doesn't need to know about are the commissions you get by putting the business the way of the IFA. They can be quite tasty, although the commissions are in inverse proportion to the risk of the investment. Consequently, you do have an incentive to persuade the IFA to go upmarket when it comes to risk. Sometimes that works out for the player. Sometimes not.

There has recently been a lot of publicity about investments in film schemes for the tax breaks. Now, I've always steered clear of them, which is just personal. If something looks too good to be true then it generally is and these looked amazing. You wrote out a cheque and those nice people at the Inland Revenue wrote you a cheque back by way of a tax rebate. It never felt right to me and as it transpired it never felt right to the Revenue either, because they decided they needed to close the whole scheme down.

Now, I'm not pointing fingers, but for sure there were decent commissions to be earned and some of those found their way to agents; and without claiming to be a financial genius myself, maybe some of them, and their advisers, were just prepared to take risks that I wasn't. In any event the fallout has been horrendous and whereas it may end happily, a lot of lawyers' fees are going to pass under the bridge before then.

You've all seen the headlines. It's a bonanza for journalists as headlines scream about millions lost and bankruptcies pending. Not just players, but managers too, and in many cases individuals whose best earning days behind them, which makes it very hard. Not that anybody is really doling out any sympathy because that's not how it works. All the media does is select a pantomime villain, and here it has been the financial advisers and the agents who dealt with them. It's a drama playing out as I write and all I can say for once is that it's not a drama in which I've got any involvement.

When investments don't work out, you still have a Plan B (as long as what you've done doesn't make banner headlines). Players often don't understand the sort of reports and statements that investment companies issue. I must admit I don't necessarily understand them myself most of the time. What you have going for you is that nobody on that side of the business, whether it be the large insurance company, the fund managers or the IFA ever want to admit that they're not only failing to beat the market but are actually losing money for their clients. So, in those statements and reports, the bottom line can become a bit blurry, and you can blur it further by saying that it's a long-term investment and that historically the fund has proven to have done well over five-year periods. So the player has to be patient and look to a five-year growth and income pattern with blips, particularly at the start. Best not to mention that everybody has had a bite out of the investment at the start by way of fees and commissions which the IFA has had to disclose to his client (at least, now he does, but I am just old enough to remember the days when he didn't). Only you are there when he tells the client and it isn't difficult to ensure that the player has no idea what the IFA is earning and what he's sharing with you. Yes, the IFA will put it all in writing, but will the player read it? What do you think? It isn't the *Sun* or a motoring magazine and it doesn't have any pictures so it's highly unlikely.

By the time any bad investment has proved to be irretrievably bad, either you or the player has moved on, and while he may moan a bit to whoever is acting for him then the chances of him taking any action are pretty slim. Well, that was certainly the case until the recent scandal. I suspect that a fair number of players (or at least their wives) may have wised up a bit.

Now, don't get me wrong. As you will have gathered, unlike some agents I'm not totally reckless. I've already told you I work really hard to get a player to sign with me so I'm not looking to lose him down the road because he's lost money thanks to some duff advice from somebody I introduced him to. However, even with a relatively conservative investment strategy it's not a bad little earner and if the investments do well (as most of mine have done so far) then it's a nice little earner. There are IFAs and IFAs, and what you want is not somebody so dodgy that they invest in wind farms in Patagonia, but somebody who understands that you have put a decent client their way and that you need to be rewarded for that.

Then there are cars. I've given you the feel for that already and, as you know if you've been following carefully, footballers, like most red-blooded youthful millionaires (what? You don't know any?) have a weakness for cars. The bigger, the better. The more expensive, the better. Provided you can convince them that your man is competitive and that the car will come with every extra of which you can possibly conceive, then the likelihood is that you're on to a very remunerative and, as I've explained before, more than regular income stream. There are many agents from whom you wouldn't buy a second-hand car, and there are quite a few car dealers from whom you wouldn't want to buy any car at all (or certainly take any advice on a football contract, though a few of them have now come into the game as intermediaries, together with estate agents, so in terms of quality the FA intermediaries have really pushed out the boundaries of true class).

One agent in particular caught a real cold when he teamed up with a guy who claimed he could supply cars at real bargain prices. For a while players bought into the idea, and when he told them they were saving several thousand pounds on each car, why would they not believe him? In fact it transpired that they weren't actually being sold the models they thought they were buying and even if they'd been buying the real thing without some of the accessories that normally came with the cars they were substantially overpaying. The car dealer was doing well and so was the agent on his split of the profit, but they pushed their luck too far. The dealer started taking deposits for cars he didn't have and couldn't deliver, and eventually he did a runner to the Middle East, leaving the agent to fend off not only his own angry clients (soon to be angry ex-clients) but players who he didn't even represent who had also been conned. It was a dangerous strategy. Footballers tend to come from rough backgrounds and often it is only the fact that they have a particular talent in kicking a ball that has, unlike a few of their contemporaries, kept them out of jail. Anyway, the point I am making is that they have a few heavies to fall back on and a few of these called upon the dodgy car agent, and he found himself bundled into the boot of a car. When the lid opened he did not like what he saw and liked even less what he heard.

'Our mate is upset with you.'

'Mate? Which mate? I don't know you,' the agent spluttered.

The strong arm men named the player and the agent paled visibly as he realised what this was all about.

'Now, this is what's going to happen. We are going to let you go and you are going to find the car our mate ordered, with whistles and bells on it, and you are going to deliver it to him within forty-eight hours.'

The agent tried to reason with them. 'But that's impossible,' he said.

'Make it possible or else we put you back in the trunk and we put the car in the river. Forty-eight hours.'

Just because they were acting like gangsters from a bad movie didn't make the threat any less chilling and the agent moved heaven and earth to do what they wanted – and managed to deliver. Fortunately for him, his other disenchanted clients just took their business elsewhere, but his reputation was ruined and he simply drifted out of the business and the last I heard of him he was flogging timeshares to the unwary.

Then there's jewellery and watches. Footballers and Rolexes go together like love and marriage. Or perhaps not, when it comes to footballers' wives. However, it remains an incontrovertible truth that footballers do like expensive watches. Not just one, tons of them. I mean, just how many watches can you wear for fuck's sake? I know of one player with a couple of dozen watches, each of which had cost upwards of five grand, but he only wore one because that was, as he said, 'the one I like'. You may wonder why he bought the others. I'm about to tell you. Because just as with investments, just as with cars, there are loads of agents out there who have a thing going with jewellers. Now, I don't mean the sort of thing going that leads to an engagement ring. I mean . . . well, by now I'm thinking that you know exactly what I mean. You have a ready and willing, not to mention gullible, buyer, so get your friendly neighbourhood jeweller to sell him whatever he (and you) can at inflated prices and cream off as much as you can by way of a commission from the jeweller.

As you can imagine, like so much I've related in this book, it just doesn't end happily. One player bought and bought. A nice player, this one, just buying for his wife, and not a girlfriend or a mistress or even a hooker. No, these were birthday and Christmas and anniversary presents, all selected with love with the help of his agent who was carefully noting the prices to see how much he was going to get out of it at the end of the day. The answer was a lot, because rather than negotiating the prices down he was, in fact, fixing them with the jeweller beforehand

and then seeming to get him to give large discounts to prove what a good agent and friend he really was.

This all worked well for a long while, and indeed the jeweller was recommended to loads of other players to whom he sold jewellery and watches. Sometimes their own agent got involved and also asked for a kickback (nobody ever wants to be left out in the world of agents where there's money to be earned), and sometimes he just sold directly to players, not even bothering to tell the original agent in case he asked for commission on those indirect sales as well. Where it didn't go so well was when the nice responsible player decided, after a spate of break-ins to other players' homes, that he really should get all his wife's expensive jewellery insured. The insurance company asked for valuations, and as luck would have it – or bad luck as it transpired – the dodgy jeweller was away on holiday (well, by now he could afford a few of those a year) and couldn't supply the valuations himself. The nice player wandered into an equally nice local high-street jeweller to get the whole lot valued, only to find what he'd thought to be a hundred grand's worth of expensive necklaces, rings, bracelets and watches was only worth about thirty.

His first port of call was his agent who, to be fair, hadn't realised the extent of the jeweller's dishonesty, although to be equally fair hadn't delved too deeply into the valuations placed on the purchases either. The conversation between agent and jeweller on said jeweller's return from holiday was fruity to say the least, and the whole thing ended up as a court case. The jeweller made an offer to settle, and the footballer, not wanting to look totally stupid in the public eye, actually accepted it. Yet, with the instant jungle tom-tom of football gossip it didn't take long for the jeweller to become a pariah who didn't dare even set foot near a footballer for the preservation of his own legs. Even as their agent I never lose sight of the fact that if these guys didn't have an exceptional talent in their feet they'd probably be serving time at Her Majesty's pleasure, and even if they were not going to seek revenge then they'd know somebody who could do a pretty good job on their behalf. There are some agents who can look after themselves in a scrap, but a footballer wronged is a footballer wronged, and I've known at least one agent end up in casualty (probably preferable to the boot of a car in a river) when he refused to return something a player thought was properly due.

Property investment is another popular winner on the agent's money-making charts and, believe me, this can go *really* wrong. Getting players to invest in UK-based buy-to-let schemes can be remunerative for all parties concerned. Except when the player, at the agent's instigation, through an estate agent or property adviser introduced by the agent, has bought a property (or a dozen, which is more likely) and found that they aren't that easy to let. And when they're let, the letting agent takes a commission, and when things go wrong at the property there are more hidden charges, and then suddenly the property market has flatlined and a deal that looked to be better than his pension, that was actually going to be his pension, is in fact a total dud.

If that's happening in England then the disaster as far as the player (and the agent if he's an innocent party) is concerned is sort of controllable. Lawyers can do wonderful things, at a price, and at the end of the day properties are truly worth more at the end of a five-year cycle than they were when they were bought.

However, if the property is overseas, in some country whose name you only ever come across when its only contestant at the Olympics is in the spoon-bending events and has to carry the flag into the arena on his own, then there are almost guaranteed to be problems.

The brochures for these foreign property investments always

look wonderful. I get so many of them sent to me that I could tear off the covers and open my own travel agency with them. However, when an agent and a developer are working hand in hand, and the agent loses all perspective and caution for his client because of what he's about to make, then there's likely to be trouble in Paradise with a capital T to add to the capital P. One agent told everybody that he had the best deal in the world in the Middle East but could only share it with a select number of his clients. He omitted to tell them that he was in fact the selling agent for this development (no self-regarding agent is ever going to risk his own money, particularly on some properties thousands of miles away in a country ruled by a cabal who could nationalise all foreign assets in a heartbeat).

The money poured in, a big hole was dug (it was an oil-rich country so they were good at digging holes), although sadly, as things turned out, they were nowhere near as good at building tower blocks of luxury apartments. They actually did not have the money to do it and had been hoping to sell properties off the plans, but as only this agent's players were contracted to buy anything (some twenty apartments out of a hundred) that scheme, like the apartments themselves, was never going to get off the ground. The company went into liquidation, the players saw not a penny back of their investment and the nearest they ever came to seeing the apartments were the lovely pictures on the front of the gorgeous brochure.

Needless to say, the agent lost all his players, having lost a fair old chunk of their money. For the Middle East read the Caribbean, odd tax havens, Central America, remote islands and, every time with the encouragement of the agent, the players fall for it. And most times, because they don't want their teammates to know just how dumb they've been, they just take it on the chin and move on.

I did a better deal for my clients and, you won't be surprised to learn by now, for me too. I found a lovely development in Portugal and told my players it was so good that I was buying there myself. It looked great and the prices were fair. Again, as you may have noticed I become a bit of a salesman when I believe in something. And sometimes when I don't believe in something as well.

The players flocked to the scheme. I was going to say like lambs to the slaughter, but I really wasn't selling them a pig in a poke. Amazingly, players do like to be around fellow players and go where their contemporaries have gone before. You visit one footballer's house and it's very much like another. One buys and fits his house out, and then another visits, likes what he sees and copies it all. Imagination and footballers do not go hand in hand off the pitch. Players like to spend holidays together. They speak the same language, relax in the same way and their wives generally come from the same background.

My development had a super golf course nearby, a spa, tennis courts, an Olympic-sized swimming pool and an even bigger cocktail bar. My lads – and even more so, their wives – were delighted with their purchases, particularly in comparison to the disastrous investments some of their fellow professionals had made. I was delighted too. You see, I'd told a little white lie. I hadn't really bought a unit myself although I had acquired one, so that was kind of close. The developers had given me my property for nothing in return for all the introductions. Nobody got hurt and nobody lost out. My conscience was totally clean, at least the small part that remained intact. My properties actually existed, actually held their value and the buyers were pleased with them. It wasn't like buying in the States where the market totally crashed and all that was to be shown for the money invested was a neglected tower block of unlet apartments or an empty, shuttered shopping mall in Lonesome, Wyoming, that all the tax breaks in the world couldn't turn into something profitable.

Yet another popular scam is the closed investment fund available only to a chosen few; so few that it doesn't fall within the requirement to be regulated. This is, say 100k per investor, with the investors just being 'friends and family'. For 'friends and family' read 'mugs and clients'. The agents just need ten of them to have a million quid to play with and then invests, maybe, 900k in real investments and just creams off the odd hundred for himself. As long as a return is made that's fine because the player never bothers to ask if the return could have been bigger if the whole of the fund had been invested. The assets in the fund are cloaked in smoke and mirrors. Start-up companies (usually belonging to pals of the agent), more properties abroad like student accommodation in Florida, even planes and boats and even West End theatrical productions. As long as the original investment doesn't vanish nobody stops to ask. Why should they when the investment might be equivalent to just a week's salary? Footballers and their money are soon parted.

There is a kind of moral lesson to be learned here. Honestly. There is a common theme to all the above examples of agents' greed linked to third-party dishonesty and player naivety. The theme is that whether it's property, cars, investments or obscenely expensive watches, although an agent may make money in the short term in the long run he'll always lose the client, not to mention risking a law suit or two – or even jail.

So me, I'm going to keep playing the long game (at the end of the day I found an easier way of nearly going to jail). I know by now when to stick and when to twist, when to bet and when to burn, when to bluff and when to hold. This whole business is one massive never-ending card game and if you sit at the table long enough then maybe, just maybe, you're going to get so lucky that you'll beat the house or even break the bank. Unless, of course, the house breaks you first.

TWENTY-SIX

SOCIAL MEDIA

YOUNG PEOPLE LOVE Twitter, and Facebook and Whatsapp and Facetime and Snapchat and Periscope. Or rather they loved them because, even as I talk, they're finding new ways to communicate instantly which makes all of those totally yesterday's news. I say instant communication, but what seems to be demanded now is communication before you even know you want to, or need to, communicate. Some form of telepathic social media can only be a mere thought away.

Most footballers use social media, which can be an asset and a liability for an agent. It's a plus because it opens all sorts of doors for actually getting to players. According to all the rules and regulations, you can't approach (or tap up) a player who is contracted to another licensed agent; I mean the poor sod of an agent/intermediary (forgive me if I still lump them together as 'agents' as it takes less time to type and is easier to spell) who has probably done everything right. He's legitimately targeted the player, worked hard to get him to agree that he can be represented, he's finally got him to put pen to paper and commit for the next two years, and he's put the representation contract in an envelope to the FA (or uploaded it to his FA page as you do now to help the FA do even less than they did before and charge for the privilege) with a goofy love-struck grin on his face so that they can register it. From then on he can hold himself up as the exclusive representative of the player for all his playing and (usually) his commercial contracts. The FA used to take a lifetime to formally register and send it back, but that's a sideshow. He was in business once the envelope went through the slot of the pillar box and now as he uploads. In fact, under the old system, the FA would actually check to see if the player already had signed a contract with another agent and if so send the second one back. Now it seems perfectly possible for different agents to have uploaded contracts with the same player and having to slug it out when a deal is to be done. Ah, technological advancements . . .

Yet, the minute his player-client ventures out into the wild and wacky world of social media his exclusivity is at risk and, in reality, his contract gives him little or no protection from wily predators. I know because I've tried it myself.

I found a player I liked who seemed to be switched on; he had accounts with Twitter, Facebook and LinkedIn. I started to follow him on Twitter and invited him to be a Facebook friend. Most players seem to be unable to resist accepting such invitations as they obviously think there may be something in it for them. Or perhaps they just want to boast about the number of followers or notional friends they have. I've given up trying to understand the logic.

To be honest, his posts and tweets were as boring as shit. Running commentary during a match if he wasn't playing, telling his followers how glad he was that his team had won if he was, a hard workout at the gym, exchanges about reality television programmes: pretty much nothing to get your teeth into, until he started mentioning a band or two. Now, I like music. If I had to do anything else but be a football agent I wouldn't have minded managing a band or two. I used to play drums when I was at school and I still find that having music on both in the car and when I'm working helps me to relax *and* concentrate.

I often though about moving into artist management. A fair number of agents have their roots in the music industry and it's a good grounding because if you've been able to look after a prima donna of a singer then you should be able to handle the most difficult of players. At least they don't ask for all the red smarties to be removed from the packs left in the dressing room.

Anyway, I responded to his music tweet, and we had a bit of an exchange about the virtues of this band. At that stage I didn't even mention I was an agent. I waited a short while and then asked to be his Facebook friend, and he accepted. So now I could see his more personal posts. I noted he had a fiancée and a small child (footballers do tend to do the whole engagement–marriage–child sequence in reverse) and I could also see the sort of holidays he liked, where he liked to eat, the films he saw (all pretty predictable) and even his favourite tattoo parlour.

On reflection, it all sounds a bit like stalking or grooming, and I suppose it is in a way. You, the stalker-agent are looking for some kind of consummation of the relationship while avoiding being the creepy follower who becomes a bunny-boiler. When I saw he was looking for a ticket to one of the big summer music festivals I told him I could arrange it, and you know what? He was really pleased. So I assumed that his agent had either not got the contacts or was so complacent that he couldn't be bothered. A personal handover of the tickets – which could oh so easily have been posted – was worth the trip, even though the lad didn't exactly live on my doorstep.

I got the tickets, which cost me an arm and a leg despite pulling in some favours from a friend, duly met the lad for a coffee, did the handover and we got on really well. It kind of came out in conversation that I was a football agent (I tried to steer away from the subject, I really did, I swear it), but then it also came out that he wasn't too happy with his agent. That agency represented over a hundred players, and he reckoned he was way down on their list although he felt (and I encouraged this thought, I admit it) that he ought to be way up it. Which was how he came to ask me to have a look at his representation contract, which was how I came to show it to my lawyer who found a couple of issues with it. Again, I didn't ask, but when the player asked if I could help him get out of it I sprang for the legal fees and, although the agent didn't want to roll over, I got the feeling that he wasn't looking for a public fight either.

There's always a way, and when I suggested to the player that he offer the agent a third of his commission on the next deal if he agreed to tear up the contract, and when I – by now the player's new best mate – offered to indemnify him against anything he had to pay, I'd got the whole plan over the line. The player signed for me as soon as he could, I did his next deal, told him what to pay his old agent and true to my word I coughed up with the loot. Job done, and thank you, social media.

However, it's not so great when your player goes off on one on Twitter or the like. For some reason people don't like being slagged off or threatened in the public arena. For such a brutal business as the football industry it does contain some delicate flowers. It never ceases to astonish me how a player who is an absolute beast on the pitch can be upset by comments aimed at him on social media. Or how quickly they can threaten to turn to the law to maximise profit from any alleged damage.

I've seen all sorts of comments, some of which have involved my intervention. I've had to bully players into apologising for the most inane things: questioning another player's commitment, his manhood, his ability, his integrity; suggesting that he may be putting his own interest before that of his teammates; and calling him by all sorts of fancy and/or derogatory names, some of which are funnier than others.

Sometimes they get sorted out between the protagonists themselves but sometimes they can get so heated that I have to call the other player's agent or lawyer and broker a deal to avoid a major lawsuit. It's then that the non-social media can get busy and criticise the player's agent as well as the player. I've seen the names of agents in the columns of journalists who should know better blaming them for their client's behaviour. You've earned a fortune from a player, so in their somewhat perverted and conveniently sensational view you can be held responsible for everything they do. One agent was even blamed for his client's shortcomings a couple of years after he stopped looking after him. But, hey, if it makes a headline why bother about accuracy?

As I've found out, people looking into the industry from the outside assume that you're a lot closer to your clients than you really are. Sometimes that's a perception you've deliberately created to boost your own reputation or to warn off competitors with the message that there's such a bond of steel and undying loyalty between you and your player that they'd be wasting their time even thinking of making an approach. As you'll have gathered by now, in reality that's a pretty delusional notion.

The fact of the matter is that players will do exactly what they want to do, no matter how much time you spend with them. They really don't think ahead and rarely think of the consequences of their actions, and it's a brave, not to mention foolhardy, agent, who claims to control his players. Quite literally I've come off the phone to a player having told him not to engage in the likes of Twitter when the next exchange starts off. Basically, to get on as an agent you have to learn how to fight fires, and however often you warn your clients about smoking in dry woodland they're still just as likely to toss away a cigarette butt without a second thought.

Unfortunately, that holds good for everything, not just for social media. I was in the middle of a delicate contract negotiation for a player and made the mistake of telling him why his manager didn't think he was as good as he thought he was, which was why we weren't getting the deal we wanted. I told him this before telling him that it was in confidence and to keep it to himself. That was a really stupid thing to do when it came to a footballer, and like all the other mistakes I've made as I work my way up the ladder, it wasn't one I was going to repeat. Ever.

Anyway, I told him to leave it to me, and his interpretation of that was to rampage into the manager's office without any warning and call him a cunt. The manager promptly reciprocated and told him the offer was withdrawn and that if he thought he was worth what he thought he was worth he could fuck off and get it elsewhere.

It was a real challenge to piece that one back together, particularly as I knew I wouldn't get a better deal elsewhere, but I did it eventually. Not that the player was grateful. They never are. My players, and I suspect everybody else's, just assume I'll sort out their media fuck-ups, and if I don't it will reflect badly on me and not on them.

They may well be right. I've had managers and chairmen cut off diplomatic relations with me because they've not been able to distinguish between what I say and the crap that so often comes out of my players' mouths. I used to dread waking up to the morning sports columns. What was Charlie Sale going to say about my players or me in his column? Who had let their guard down in public or in a bar or nightclub? Not any longer. They and their like are no longer my concern. What I truly dread is a social media storm that has blown up overnight to the point that my player is trending, or worse still that I'm trending.

As I said, players rejoice in the number of their followers. Normally they're not in their millions unless they've got something interesting or controversial to say like Joey Barton who is a free spirit and law unto himself. But even a few hundred can present serious problems if you upset just one of them. He retweets, and somebody who has even more followers retweets again, and all of a sudden a player is aggrieved about the kind of trivial issues I mentioned before.

Social media moves so much faster and yet seems to leave a longer impression than traditional news media. Once your client has called another player 'hopeless' or worse, and that's got to the eyes of a good few thousand followers of people you'll never meet or even know, then the genie is pretty much out of the bottle. It can get really nasty when the players meet up on the pitch and try to sort matters out behind the backs of the officials. I can think of several recent bookings which had their roots in social media.

It's just another headache for agents, and the only positive when it goes wrong for one of your players out there in cyberspace is that you can be pretty sure he's a player worth representing. However, clubs aren't stupid, and although they all have clauses in their playing contracts ensuring responsible use of social media and commitments not to say anything that brings the club into disrepute, I'm starting to get them to insist on specific clauses, in cases where my client is well known, for making controversial public utterances.

Just when you think you have a nice secure pipeline of income, having negotiated a four-year contract with your fees paid every year (and rising when the player's salary rises), it only needs one moment of madness for the club to impose a penalty on your player (and you need to foot the bill for any appeal because it's always your responsibility when it comes to paying out), or even worse they terminate the contract and bang goes your money. Yes, there's probably another deal to be done out there, but this time you're negotiating for slightly damaged goods, and buying clubs are not slow to make some mileage out of that and push the salary (and consequently your fee) down.

The public like lippy players. Clubs less so. But try telling your player to button up and he'll soon be looking for somebody to represent him who is more prone to admiration than criticism. Damned if you do and fucked if you don't. It's bad enough trying to keep a player when things are in your control. It's just impossible when they're not.

There's another kind of indiscretion now which can get into the public domain and that arose from something which should never have seen the light of day or reached the ears of anybody other than the two people having the conversation. I only had two clients who were hacked and at the time neither of them, or me, could figure out how something that only my player and I knew had hit the headlines. One of the players thought it was me who had breached a confidence about a girl in his life who wasn't his wife and the other got into terrible trouble with his club because a rumour about a move got reported from a reliable source.

The player who left me made a killing over his action against the paper in question and never even bothered to apologise to me even though it became blatantly obvious that the leak was nothing to do with me. The other one and I were in the middle of an action when all my problems (to be revealed in detail later) reared their ugly heads and my lawyer told me to settle for far less than I should have rather than see my credibility and reputation further shredded in open court. The player carried on though and did fine. That gave me cause to reflect that at the end of most days they usually do. The same can't be said for agents because somehow or other things seem to catch up with us. Certainly so in my case.

TWENTY-SEVEN

COMMERCIAL EXPLOITATION

A S I'VE JUST noted, the public like a player who speaks his mind. If a player is truly great then he doesn't need to be controversial to be marketable and, indeed, the bigger companies tend to steer away from anybody they think may implode in public. We've seen in other sports such as athletics or golf how a little thing like a very public extramarital affair can reduce the value of the sportsperson in the branding department. And a very large thing like a positive drug test or the manslaughter of a loved one (or even an unloved one) can reduce the brand value to less than zero. And the sponsor can ask for its money back.

Branding. That's what it's all about now. Brand Beckham set the benchmark. Brands Best and Gazza started off fine until both superstars became so unpredictable and so unreliable as to become unmarketable. As an agent you have to understand that the great British public likes nothing more than a sporting hero until it comes to knocking down that very same idol they've worshipped.

Every agent is looking for a Becks, of course, but we may not find him again in my lifetime so we have to work with what we've got. Just because you represent an England international doesn't necessarily mean that you have control of a licence to print money. Indeed, being part of Team England isn't always helpful when the agent is going out to maximise the commercial aspects of a player's career.

The player can be so associated with the brands linked to England that other companies hesitate as to whether or not he'll be able to maximise their brands sufficiently to justify what people like me want for their services. Mind you, all the companies love a bit of what they call 'ambush marketing', so you have to demonstrate that your player is up for it.

The sort of thing I'm thinking of is wearing boots that aren't made by the shirt sponsor, coming off the pitch pulling off (and waving around) shin pads made by another rival, turning up in all sorts of magazines and TV programmes wearing the player's personalised products. Sometimes it's the agent who gets the flak when it's a pretty blatant breach of FA regulations relating to international obligations, but who is going to drop a star player?

The problem is always getting the player to comply with the mega commercial contract you've negotiated for him. It doesn't help when a player who has a sponsorship with an aftershave or deodorant says at a launch that he never uses them because he's allergic. It doesn't help if, despite your plonking a branded cap on his head for an interview and a photo shoot, he wears totally different head gear because one of his mates has set up a company designing and selling baseball caps and has asked him to wear one as a favour.

It happens. You wouldn't believe what can and does happen when you have a player for whom big companies are prepared to pay big bucks to have him endorse their wares. Not everybody is a Gary Lineker whose campaign for Walkers crisps seems to be never-ending, mainly because he has the brains to know which side his bread is buttered on.

It's not easy getting sponsorship or broadcasting deals for players nowadays, but I like to try, not only because I can charge twenty per cent of what they get, but also because it gets me out there among the movers and shakers. When you've negotiated a deal for one of your players to be a pundit at a televised game (and they get a mere pittance for it and even an appearance on *Question of Sport* produces peanuts) then you can push on with that when it comes to bigger matches or even international tournaments. You get to know who to speak to and the broadcasters get to know you as somebody who delivers. So when they come looking for a 'talking head' on something that affects agents you may well become their first port of call. That's always good for business. Players are instantly recognisable. Less so, most agents.

I've been pleasantly surprised by the number of players who say that they've seen me on the telly or heard me on the radio and who've liked what I've said. You can even play that to your advantage a bit by praising a player in an interview, even if he isn't yours, and saying that he's the sort of player who could and should be playing at a higher level. You make plans to ensure your paths cross and hope he remembers – and if he doesn't then you remind him of what you said. When I started out I thought it was a big advantage to keep under the radar, to avoid publicity like the plague. But after four years and with a stable of about fifty decent clients, I admit that I rather like the exposure. Maybe it appeals to my ego, and if that should concern me then I don't let it concern me for too long. I even get peeved when I see other agents (who I know aren't real players in the game) showing off on the box just because they look OK and can string a few sentences together. Then I used to comfort myself in the knowledge that I was making much more money than they were so they could talk all they wanted and leave me to bank the cash.

It's all about probing the soft underbelly of the relationship between the player and his current agent. Once you do that you can find it can be very soft indeed.

It doesn't hurt to do a few favours for the regular TV

broadcasters themselves. They're always looking for a few quid to supplement their incomes and they can also be in a position to recommend your services as an agent. It's occurred to me to try and get one or more of them on my payroll as unofficial ambassadors, and I've heard whispers that other agents have tried it on too. But for the moment I'm leaving it on the 'I'll scratch your back if you scratch mine' basis. You never know where any particular road might lead, and that's one of the things I love about my job – the unpredictability.

I went into a TV studio for a show and found myself in the green room talking to a player I'd always fancied representing. He'd been with the same agent for donkey's years, and I doubt many people thought they had a chance of prising him away. We got on well, we went on air, and I did a fair job of buttering him up. Afterwards we went for a drink and he asked me what he thought I could do for him that his current agent couldn't.

Now, this agent had done a decent job for years. I knew I wasn't going to reinvent the wheel with the lad but on the other hand I was thirty years or so younger than his current bloke so I decided to play the youth-and-energy cards against the experience-and-complacency ones. It transpired that the agent had trusted him so much that he'd never had a contract with him that covered commercial matters, although he'd had to have one in place for his club transfers. I suggested he give me a chance to see what I could get for him and that meanwhile perhaps I could review what he did have in place. It was crap for his status in the game and showed me that the agent had relaxed. He'd made fortunes out of some deals and he could've ensured that the commercial stuff was the icing on the cake both for himself and the player. Getting great deals at a club that wants the player to play for them isn't rocket science but creating a brand for a player really is.

I blagged him a bit and told him we were bringing in a new brand manager to work on our high-profile players. I'm not quite sure how high the profile of many of my players was at that stage, and certainly the brand manager was a figment of my somewhat overactive imagination, but he bought into it all. I found him a boot deal that was about fifty per cent better than the one he had. I've got a note in my diary for when his rep contract runs out and I've got my fingers firmly crossed. Mind you, he's shown a distinct lack of loyalty to the guy who's been with him for years, so who's to say that he wouldn't do exactly the same to me. I've got accustomed to lowering my expectations. It helps to soften the blow. The good thing is that the two year limit on representation contracts doesn't apply to commercial deals, so you can get a player to sign with you for that alone for five or even ten years. Sometimes agents don't even bother with a contract for the football stuff, believing that the long term contract for the commercial element gives them enough of a hold on the player to stop them signing with anybody else.

Commercial deals don't come along every day and certainly not for every player. So when you get one you're not too pleased if the player screws up. And you won't be surprised to learn that they do and generally when they do then they do it big time.

Just not turning up is as good as it gets when it comes to bad. You can always make an excuse. Family emergency, traffic, car broke down, cat got stuck up a tree, kid swallowed a spoon. A sponsor may believe that once, but after that you've run out of road.

Bad, really bad, can take several forms. The sponsor has spent a fortune on renting a specific location and your player finds something better to do. Or you cover for him only to find he's all over Twitter about where he actually is. That's *really* bad.

Disastrously bad is when a player is discovered shagging one of the models for the shoot at the back of the set, and to avoid her embarrassment she claims she wasn't a willing partner. Go ask any sponsor what they feel a sexual assault when filming their ad will do for the family target audience. On the other hand, don't bother.

I know agents who have had their players turn up drunk for a sponsorship event, dressed in their competitor's clothing, slag off the product within earshot of a mike or a mobile phone and even on one memorable occasion, and this qualifies as disaster beyond disaster, have the shoot reduced to a brawl when another player involved appears and who turns out to have been shagging the player's wife.

You may wonder why you haven't heard about some of this, why it rarely makes the papers, even in the more sensational tabloids who are not averse to flashing the cash around to get stories just like that. The fact is that the sponsor generally flashes its cash around first and quietly puts the situation back in its box while at the same time either terminating what could've been a highly remunerative deal or simply not renewing.

So what happens to the payments to the players under that contract? The affronted or disappointed company wants anything it's paid back. That of course includes our twenty per cents. I confess that on the one occasion it happened to me I just made the player pay it all back and kept my commission. He was earning so much money he didn't even notice, and anyway my conscience was clear because I'd delivered on the contract after all.

Getting them to write a book may seem to be remunerative, but sometimes it turns out to be anything but. You either negotiate the deal yourself with a publisher or, better still, actually get a literary agent to do it for you (not forgetting to ask for half of his commission while still charging your own). You get a great deal and a good advance but then the problems really start because you also need to find someone to write it given that in 99.99 per cent of the cases the player is incapable of writing anything more complex than a nursery rhyme.

So, you or the publisher or the literary agent puts forward the name of a reputable ghost writer and then he either wants more money than the player is prepared to give up, or the player doesn't like him, or even more importantly the player's wife doesn't like him and doesn't want her husband to work with him.

You finally nail a writer at a knock-down price (which means his heart isn't really in it because he can earn more writing about the turbulent life and career of a sixteen year old pop star) and then he has the problem of pinning the player, his family and acquaintances down to write the fascinating story of the life and loves of the football star. Only they won't open up and under pressure from his missus the player doesn't want to tell it like it is. So you end up with either a sanitised boring version that nobody over the age of eighteen would want to read and has the publisher reaching for the vodka in despair or else you get a really racy warts and all version that the player won't agree to be published. That's why the rare volumes that surmount all those problems sell so well.

If a stalemate is reached the publisher may demand the return of the advance or there's a fight with the ghost writer as to whether he should be paid for re-writes or indeed whether or not he should be dumped from the team altogether.

The whole situation can end in tears, through not fault of yours, when the publisher decides it's all become far too much trouble and asks for his money back. Now, you've had twenty per cent of the advance, the literary agent may have had ten percent so it can be hard persuading the player to return a hundred per cent when he's only had seventy per cent and out of that has paid the ghost writer as well.

It's easie when the player is earning so much money that you can handle it all and he doesn't notice. It is much harder when you have a player who can add up and sometimes the agent has to bite the bullet and give up his commission, even though he's worked very hard to get the player to a position where he can, and does, fuck it all up.

You should never steal from your clients just because they won't miss whatever you take. However, in the example above I didn't think keeping my commission and making the player pay back money he had never received was stealing. I was just making sure I got back for my work. Trust me – and most of my players do – other agents don't have such a principled approach to life as me. If they've got access to a client's money and they've convinced themselves he won't miss it then why not just pocket it? Why not? Well, because it's wrong, but that doesn't seem to trouble some of my contemporaries.

I like to take the moral high ground sometimes. You can't do it all the time in this business so you have to grab every opportunity you can.

Sometimes, an agent can get really lucky and create a brand for a player, or the player effectively creates a brand for himself. Gazza was like that in the nineties before he imploded and had a lawyer and an accountant handling his affairs. I read once that after the 1990 World Cup semi-final when he famously cried that his entourage felt like they were handling the Beatles so great was the commercial interest. Nowadays I think it would be easier to market a beetle than poor Gazza which reflects how quickly things change in our business.

Brand Beckham was totally more reliable and more professionally marketed with a whole team of expertise behind him. To a lesser extent Brand Rooney (less good-looking and more unpredictable) was handled in the same way. The trick for the agent, if he gets that lucky, is to bring in the right people before his client realises that his agent just can't cope and brings in people himself who put the agent's own position at risk.

R would've laughed if I'd mentioned PR and marketing to him when it came to players. 'Just let them kick the fucking ball and you do the rest,' he once said to me.

Only now, that's not enough. The world has moved on. There are still dinosaurs amongst us agents, but I don't intend to be one of them and become extinct. I know agents who don't even know how to send an email let alone work a computer and have to have it all done for them. Twitter to them is strictly for the birds. Facebook is standing in front of the shelves in a library and choosing something to read. Periscopes are on submarines. Websites are just for spiders. Believe me, I've met the guys in question and they don't even use calculators. Everything is written down on whatever scrap of paper they happen to have with them and they usually have to borrow a pen.

Meanwhile, for the rest of us, football, like everything else, is constantly developing, and you have to move along with it. If your player is talented – maybe even hugely talented at that – it goes along well. If he's also good-looking with a great personality then you're almost home and dry. You just need to know how to exploit it and somewhere along the way you may need to give up a bit of that twenty per cent you're charging him for commercial matters.

I know one agent who took all that and then sent his client an invoice every month for all the other costs he'd incurred: public relations, marketing, website design, even a stylist. Players are notorious for only looking at how much is in their bank account, not necessarily what comes off before it gets there, but this one did, and he went crazy when he realised, having taken some independent advice, that with all the bits and pieces on top he was giving away about forty per cent of what he earned. When he did a search of the company that had been set up to market his image he also found that his agent had put himself and a few others on the payroll, not to mention taking twenty per cent of the whole company. So he took his twenty per cent commission off the top and then actually owned twenty per cent of the remaining eighty per cent, which meant that, if my arithmetic is correct, he was getting thirty-six per cent of every commercial deal. There was some heated legal correspondence and the agent hastily left the arena.

I've figured out that it doesn't do to be too greedy. You may think I am, but you need to look at everybody else in the industry to make the comparison and then decided. It's just that I feel that if you're lucky enough to get a golden goose then why kill it? And if you try, then the likelihood is that it may kill you.

TWENTY-EIGHT

TRAVEL AGENT

I'VE FOCUSED ON representing players and clubs, but there's another way. There's always another way, and as long as there is, agents are going to try and make money out of it. FIFA used to issue special licences to agents to enable them to arrange matches. They might have considered a licence to fix matches as well, but I doubt those who would want to do that would be seeking consent (I've told you of that experience and how I actually survived it). No, this is when you bring over a foreign team to play an English side pre-season or during a break. Or arrange matches between two foreign countries on English soil when both countries have enough of their nationals here to give you hope of a decent crowd.

Sometimes it goes further. An agent puts together a whole pre-season tour abroad for a club and arranges everything: flights, transportation, hotels and the opposition. A word of advice. Don't. I got involved when I was with R and it's the biggest nightmare you can imagine.

Let's look at the tour first. R was never going to sign up for something unless he was fairly sure he was going to make something worthwhile out of it so he'd always try and cover all the bases. He'd get a kickback from the travel agents for arranging the flights. He'd ensure that he also got something from the hotels. He'd make deals with local restaurants in return for him ensuring the travelling party were going to eat there.

If it was the Far East he'd have tailors going in to measure up the players for suits and clothes that would be ready for them before they departed. Local jewellers would arrive with bargains galore. Then he'd have 'arrangements' with the clubs who were going to be the opposition. Cash from gate receipts, a share of any television deal, merchandising, even takings from the drinks and food at the stadium. He had it all down to a fine art . . . but it could still go wrong.

The agent who takes a football team abroad needs the experience and guile of a tour guide on an Under-20s holiday to Magaluf. I arranged a trip to Spain and lost, yes, *lost* two of the players and one of the club's directors, only to find they were down at a local police station having 'allegedly' failed to pay the three girls with whom they were having an educational night out on the town. They hadn't realised that the girls had a deal going with the local police who were not best pleased that their cut of the night's takings was under threat. The only upside to all of it was that the director was never going to risk crossing me in the future and I got both the players to sign with me rather than risk me tell their wives. As if I would. You'll see I've even kept this book anonymous, although if anyone I know buys it then they'll have no problem recognising themselves. As long as the wives don't recognise them too then I've kept my part of the bargain.

It has to be said that the players are the least of the agent's problems on such a tour. The directors act as if they're on a stag weekend (or week, as the case may be) and as they've usually left their wives at home they're not as easy to control as the players, who have to answer to a gimlet-eyed manager who does hourly inspections of their rooms at night and fixes them with a stare that can shatter crystal at 500 metres. That's not to say that some of the managers aren't averse to finding some new friends with benefits.

The players also become totally indiscreet, particularly when they're out on the lash. I had a player at a club and decided to combine a holiday with seeing him play in a pre-season friendly (that's how sad I've become). I was sitting in the hotel bar when a group of four men came in, already fairly well refreshed, who began to order cocktails like there was no tomorrow. Not unsurprisingly they were soon joined by four girls young enough to be their daughters, or nieces, but from the way these middle-aged guys were all over them it did not need a genius to work out that the only relations that might come into the situation would be sexual ones.

The men's voices rose in direct proportion to the alcohol consumed (although my guess was that anything else was going to have a hard time rising that night), and I was able to discover that the manager of their club was walking a tightrope and that he was only in the job anyway because the owner had something on him which had enabled the club to get him cheap for the job.

I also learned the names of a couple of players they wanted at the club and a couple they wanted out. I wasn't slow to contact all four. Not too tricky when two of them were, of course, in the same hotel, but a bit more of a challenge when the other two weren't even on the same continent.

When I told the two who were about to be shown the door that they were unloved and unwanted by the club and pointed out that their own agent should've known this, I had a couple of potential clients who, as luck would have it, were both coming to the end of their current representation contracts. They both signed with me, recommended by my existing player at the club, and as far as I was concerned it was a good evening's work for the price of a couple of drinks.

It transpired to be a somewhat less positive evening for the club officials. A journalist had also been listening, he'd summoned a photographer, and they all woke up on Sunday morning to see themselves and their young female friends plastered over a tabloid. So did their wives, and I suspect that cost them a lot more than their not inconsiderable bar tab. Obviously they didn't have agents or PR companies to clean up after them.

R always sussed out the local talent before he embarked on any tour. If he controlled the girls indirectly then at least he could be fairly safe there would be no accusations of sexual assault or any souvenirs from the trip in the shape of STDs for the players. But if the girls were prepared to go for four overweight and balding officials (albeit, I suspect, with a bit of a financial inducement) then there was no holding them back when it came to virile, fit young men who looked like Greek gods, except for the tattoos.

Although he didn't hold with it himself, R also told me of an agent who always had a local drug dealer on hand whenever he had a tour abroad. Although players are routinely tested, there's far less chance of being subjected to a drug test in a friendly in a foreign country. This agent had all the bases covered because he also used to pay whoever was doing the tests, if there were to be any, to ensure that he knew the result beforehand.

There are a few druggie agents out there to my knowledge, mainly the younger ones. They tend to be the guys who drive themselves insane to get to matches, to be on the phone to players, to arrange a dozen meetings a day (or night) to ensure that some of them come to fruition. They can only cope with sleep deprivation if they are high and wired and the ones I know, somehow or other, seem to cope. As I say, not for me. I can't see myself going home to see my parents with a joint in my hand. My mother still complains if she smells other people's cigarette smoke on me.

However, in respect to pre-season friendlies, generally speaking, it's money rather than drugs that's always a problem for the agents. I know of an agent who, naively, had signed off on the contract for an Eastern European club, and when the club went missing when it came to paying the visiting English club, then the agent received a letter from the English club's lawyer demanding payment as he'd been the signatory to the contract.

It's not much easier when the agent brings the foreign team over. Normally he has to get them to agree to bring their first team, including such international stars as they might have. The problem is that there's a very strong possibility that the said stars will have been on international duty somewhere in the world when their domestic season has ended and will have buggered off on a late holiday, missing the pre-season matches. That does not please the English clubs. It's hard enough to get their fans to pay for meaningless friendlies when there's now so much top-class football on TV for free. When the star attractions go walkabout then it becomes even harder.

If a club is making a loss on a match, then they'll look for somebody to blame, and it's usually the poor old agent who finds himself in the firing line. The bombardment can get much worse when the visiting club wants cash up front, irrespective of what the contract may say, and the home club refuses to pay anything until it satisfies itself that the opposition the agent has lined up is both genuine and credible and not a bunch of academy kids. You can have the contract drawn up by the best lawyer in town, make it as tight as possible, but when you have to start suing abroad you know you are on a hiding to nothing.

The risk for the agent is not just financial. One European club was effectively mafia-owned and made it quite clear to the agent what, not just might, but what would happen if they were not paid up front. The agent's pleas to the English club fell on deaf ears and he was forced to borrow some money from individuals who proved to be every bit as unpleasant as those who had threatened him.

The numbers in the visiting party are also up for debate. The club brings its players and its manager, which is fair enough. Players share rooms, so a squad of, say eighteen, will only need nine rooms with a couple more for the coaching staff. However, a visit to England is quite often appealing to directors and their wives and various hangers-on passing themselves off as security and medical staff, which is yet another challenge to the agent to get close to making any pre-season or international break tours anything like profitable.

As R said when he'd completed what he swore was going to be his last operational tour – in the commercial rather than the military sense – 'There are easier ways to make a quid or two. I'm done.'

An agent has just so much time to develop his business, and although there's always a chance that you might pick up a contact or a player or two when you bring in a foreign club, the only certain thing that you'll pick up is a headache and believe me, any agent has more than enough of those.

You have to balance what will make you money and what won't. I know of one agent who specialises in bringing over groups of kids from wealthy families in the likes of India, China and the Middle East. They've not got a clue about value and he overcharges for everything. Hotels, tours, coaching sessions, even the tickets to the matches he takes them to see. It's a licence to print money and, amazingly, he wasn't interested in taking players to those countries – which opened a new world for me.

I soon realised that you can't do business in China without a partner on the ground. When I eventually found one I discovered that he was both honest and incorruptible. I wasn't bothered. It made a refreshing change. The Middle East and India were other stories altogether. They'd made corruption a way of life for thousands of years and I was to learn a fair bit from them.

They had it down to an art form and it seemed that you had to bribe everybody from the guy who met you off the plane to avoid going through customs right up to the relevant head honcho whose house was really a palace and had obviously built up immense wealth by doing what he did best. Being corrupt.

I have to say I never felt totally comfortable with what was going on and for me to say that it had to be bad. I won't say it was dangerous but it just seemed that I was walking not just a tight-rope but on a knife edge. At that stage I had never done any business in Russia and when I finally did I soon learned exactly what fear was and kind of held my breath from the minute I landed until my plane was in the air heading home.

I'll deal with foreign travel and how it broadens your mind and fattens your wallet in the next chapter.

How was I to know that the real danger, when it came, would be domestic and would come from within?

TWENTY-NINE

FOREIGN ADVENTURES

THEY DO SAY that travel broadens the mind, and I've found that to be the case, only not in a good way. Don't get me wrong. I'm not racist or xenophobic, like so many people in football. What? I hear you say. If there is xenophobia in football then how come there are so many foreigners playing here? Well, signing them and paying them doesn't mean you have to like them, and I know for a fact that most agents (apart from the money from foreign deals) would prefer to represent English players, and most managers (apart from the fact that most of them aren't as good as the foreign imports) would prefer to have home-grown talent – players who know what it means to wear the shirt and who, when they kiss the badge, don't merely do it because it pleases the fans.

Sometimes you just have to make your players travel to satisfy their financial needs. Actually 'needs' isn't quite the right word. In the real world one hundred grand a year would be enough to satisfy anyone's most basic needs. However, what you quickly learn as an agent is that your client's perceived needs are based upon what his contemporaries are getting. That's why every effort by the leagues to impose some kind of informal cap on salaries by an unwritten and tacit agreement between their clubs has failed miserably. Player power always wins in the end, and player power means agent power, which is why the clubs and the authorities hate us so much.

I've never really understood it myself. Does Hollywood hate Tom Cruise's agent because he demands trillions for his client to make a movie? Was Brian Epstein reviled because he tried to do his best for the Beatles? And what about the literary agent I mentioned before taking his ten per cent? Or the guys repping tennis and golf stars with their twenty per cent cuts? The answer is a resounding no, which is why I'm always asking, why us? Anyway, we do our best to make our clients happy and if you can't get the guy a deal here that does just that, then you look abroad.

Now, not every player is good enough to play in the top foreign leagues like La Liga in Spain, Serie A in Italy or Germany's Bundesliga. What I have learned is that, for example in Spain, apart from the top clubs like Real Madrid or Barcelona, Spanish players can earn more playing in the Championship here than they can back home. So, to move a player into a smaller club in Europe or a lower division isn't going to set the pulses racing or the bank balance soaring.

No, the places to earn the money are in the likes of China, Russia, Turkey, and any of the Middle East countries like Dubai or Qatar. Even some of the big Greek clubs pay serious money. Or do they? This is the problem that faces the agent. It's all very well doing the deal and getting your client a huge net salary in a country where the quantity of the pay cheque far outweighs the quality of the football. However, having a contract, having an agreement for the club to pay you, the agent, a six-figure sum, is no guarantee that you're ever going to bank those sums.

I once took a player to an Asian club because they offered five times the best I could get for the player here. The only snag was that the player wanted to see for himself what he was letting himself in for before he signed. The club agreed to pay for his flight out there, and I let him go on his own as this particular city wasn't on my bucket list.

In fact, as it transpired, a bucket was a sort of luxury there. The minute he arrived, the player found himself deprived of his passport (allegedly for immigration and security reasons) and was then taken to stay, not in the five-star hotel which had been promised, but an Eastern bloc-type high-rise where the television reception was non-existent, his phone didn't work and the plumbing was so basic that a bucket would've been well and truly welcome.

The club's facilities were not much better. He was asked to train on a pitch that was so uneven, cracked and bereft of grass that he feared for his personal safety. He should've been more concerned about the security of his belongings; on the first day, his expensive watch and a few hundred dollars that he'd been advised to take as a preference to the local currency just disappeared.

He called me and told me that he wanted out and wanted out that day. Not so easy. The club said they'd brought him over in good faith, liked what they'd seen from his brief training session and wanted to sign him. They had his passport and they were going to keep it until he did sign. Discussions ensued. I felt more like a hostage negotiator than a football agent, as it was quite obvious that the player was being held to ransom.

Eventually, it was agreed that the airfares and 'accommodation expenses' would be reimbursed and that a 'compensation' fee would be paid. I had to fork it out – very noble I felt as I gritted my teeth. I'm sure some agents would've just left their client there until he came up with the dosh himself. It wasn't an entirely altruistic gesture. I already had another club lined up for the player that would reimburse me and more so.

You learn from experience. I've sent players off to exotic places for what seemed like really good deals, for them and for me. One lad turned up in the Middle East and was delighted. A plush suite in a luxury hotel, a private car to collect him and take him to training every day, all his food paid for and the fact that the hotel was dry was no problem when he was invited to regular 'tea' parties at the compounds in which many other ex-pats were living.

The problems started on the second month when his salary didn't hit his bank account. He tried to find someone to talk to at the club, but everybody who had been so friendly and helpful on his arrival was now unavailable. So he called me. I'd done the deal through a local agent with whom I was to share my fee. That also had not yet been paid, or if it had then my local partner hadn't bothered to tell me about it. He made some sympathetic noises, but then made it clear that this was by no means an unusual occurrence as far as this club was concerned and they'd sort it out in the end. I asked him when and although I couldn't see him I could feel the shrug all the way down the telephone line. This wasn't good.

The player and I agreed to give it another month, but there was still no money forthcoming. My local guy wasn't taking my calls, and I felt I had to get tough so I found myself a local lawyer who was recommended to my own English lawyer and who, we were told, unlike most of his compatriots was incorruptible. He may well have been but he was also bloody expensive and insisted I transferred ten thousand dollars to him before he'd even look at it. This whole deal, my first in the area, was not going well. Instead of making money I was well out of pocket because the travel agent with whom I'd arranged the flights (first class, at the club's insistence) now told me they'd also not been paid and were having to look to me as their regular client.

We got the money to the lawyer, the lawyer threatened the club, and when the player got back to his hotel he found that his room had been emptied and all of his belongings had

234

been thrown into his suitcases which were waiting for him at reception.

We had two choices: hang around and hope that things would improve; or terminate the contract because of the non-payment and get out of Dodge. We decided to take the latter course. Even then, the officials at the airport detained him long enough to ensure he missed his plane, and we then had to begin the long and what at times seemed endless action through FIFA against the club. We won in the end and, very reluctantly, when they were subjected to a transfer embargo, they paid up. A nightmare for me and my player – and a nightmare that did not end well because the player got the hump with me because I had not taken the first plane out to be with him when the problem first arose. There are some players with whom you just can't win, no matter how many times you roll the dice.

What I did after that when I took a player abroad to non-EU countries was to try to insist that the club deposited the whole value of the contract in a bank account, including my commission. I tried that on in China too, and they were most offended. It was as if I'd insulted their national integrity. When I asked in Russia I was threatened. When I suggested it in Greece (and yes, I know Greece is in the EU) they laughed.

The thing to do is to avoid the temptation of the quick and what seems to be the easy buck. I try to tell myself that. But it's hard. If I don't find a club for a player then there will be a dozen other agents whispering in his ear to tell him that they can. That's the pressure. That's why, eventually, you have to pack away your caution with your conscience and go for it. Those are the rules of the game. You either play by them or you fold. Me, I decided to draw another card and take the risk of going bust. I wouldn't have done that when I'd first started out, but I was a different person with four years in the industry under my belt.

Not better, just different, and there were times when I woke up in the middle of the night and simply could not get back to sleep as I wrestled with that fact. Previously, I'd slept like a log, gone right off as soon as my head hit the pillow. Those days were gone, and, as I counted pounds rather than sheep, I wondered if perhaps, just perhaps, I might have got it all wrong. But agents can't work with doubts. They can't work with greys. Black and white certainties are what it is all about: certainty in your own ability, certainty that whatever you were doing was absolutely right. There is no other way.

I comforted myself with the though that I wasn't the worst. I guess the Nazi foot soldiers did the same after the war. And I wasn't. I got to act for one player after his agent pulled a real stroke. The lad had found himself playing abroad – in a proper European country and a proper top league. To be honest, I've no idea how he got there because he really wasn't good enough and certainly didn't merit the salary that he was being paid. All credit to his agent so far, although I suspect he'd had to grease a few palms (and have his own greased back along the way) to make the deal happen.

But then the club changed managers and the new manager wanted the player out and offered to pay up his contract. The agent then found the player a club back in England but at a much lower salary; the player said that he could live with that if he was getting money from his foreign club which he'd also been assured was tax free. The agent got the player to sign for his new club but no matter how often he asked, the money from the old club was not forthcoming.

'I think they've shafted us,' the agent said.

'What can we do about it?' the player asked, having had to adjust (and get his wife and family to adjust) to a more frugal lifestyle back home.

'I'm doing all I can,' the agent assured him

'Can't we sue them?' the player asked.

'Well, we could, but it would take a while and be expensive.'

'Shouldn't you pay?' the player asked.

Now, normally I would make some sarcastic comment about how players hate to spend money, but in this instance the player was spot on in asking the question.

You see, what the agent had done is to cut a very private deal with the foreign club. The sum they were to pay to make up the shortfall between their contract and the English club contract was a massive 800k. The agent had told them he could get the player out of their hair for 400k. The foreign club snapped his hand off and transferred the funds to his off shore account. And there they stayed. The agent earned his commission on the deal with the English club which was another six figure sum and then spent the next few months spinning the player a line until, as was so often the case, the player simply gave up not wanting the aggravation of either suing his own club or even taking action against the agent. Unbelievably, by telling the player that he was about to sue the old club at his own expense the agent even got the player to sign with him again and did his move when he left the English club, and therefore managed banked another substantial commission. Totally fraudulent, yes, but par for the course when it came to a dishonest agent and a gullible player.

*

THIRTY

CHAIRMAN K

YOU NEVER KNOW just how bent club officials are until you test them out. You can hear all the rumours about this or that manager, CEO and chairman, but nobody is going to broadcast the truth to the world at large. There is always the suspicion these days that you may have done a deal with a newspaper or a television programme and been recorded.

There are clues that a prudent agent can follow. I once took a player to a club, and the chairman seemed really interested, telling me they'd been following the player for a while, hadn't known who represented him and had even spoken to the player directly. Quite innocently, of course.

I raised my eyebrows. The chairman couldn't see that because we were on the phone. My player hadn't mentioned the conversation, and that in itself was a cause for concern. I was guessing they'd slagged me off and said it would be simpler if I wasn't involved in the deal at all. So, my call to the club had been timely to say the least.

The chairman said he'd get back to me but he didn't. In fact Agent L called me and told me frankly that if I wanted to do a deal with this particular club then I'd have to do it through him because he represented them exclusively. I pointed out that the chairman hadn't mentioned that, to which he suggested that I try and call the chairman again, although on second thoughts not to bother, because he wouldn't be taking my calls. I needed to face up to the reality. If I wanted the club to take my player then I needed to tell L what he wanted and not to bother about what I wanted because that was going to come down to what he was prepared to give me. And I could fucking well forget about five per cent because there simply wasn't going to be that amount left in the deal after everybody else was kept happy.

I thought about what to do next. I could try and find my player another club, although I knew he had his heart set on this one and I had little doubt that he'd already been told by L (who I assumed had been the one to have spoken with him) that this was a done deal and if it didn't happen then I'd be the one who had fucked it up.

I could get on to the FA and tell them. But tell them what? I knew that both the chairman and L would deny everything, and anyway this wouldn't get my player his move and would certainly mean the end of our relationship. So, I decided to go along with it. I took the few grand I could from the deal, which amounted to about two and a half per cent, and as soon as my rep contract with the player expired he promptly signed with L along with the other half a dozen players he already had at the club.

I didn't like any of it, and my reaction when I don't like something that has been done to me is to see how I can get myself into a position where I can do it to others. I know that isn't the sensible thing to do, but by now I'd kind of gone past sensible. That's what this industry does to you. It moves so fast it sweeps you up in a tidal rush and you just get carried away. You've no time to stop and think about repercussions – only the money you're making at that particular moment.

There was one club where I'd done a few deals (both in and out), and I got on well with the chairman who was a bit of a Jack the Lad and had sold out his business in an industry where cash was king. I reckoned he wouldn't be averse to doing a deal with me. I wasn't wrong. We'll call him Chairman K.

The FA have a bee in their bonnet about third-party ownership. What that basically means is that they don't want to have anybody other than the club to which the player is contracted having any control over the player or his sale. They seem to think that owning a part of a player means you have influence and that influence can affect the outcome of . . . well, practically anything, I guess.

This all blew up over the Carlos Tevez deal and ended with Sheffield United claiming damages against West Ham who had got the advantage of Tevez, even though it was revealed that certain individuals were benefiting from an interest in his transfer fee. That has reduced a very complicated issue to a few lines, but all I really need to make clear is that an agent can be paid for introducing a player to a club. He can be paid by the club and the player if he acted for the player. He can be paid a higher fee if the club stays up, but what he can't receive is any share of anything the club gets paid for the player in the future.

I need to explain that one too. If a club sells a player for, say, a hundred grand to another club (usually a bigger club), then to ensure they get an upside if the players kicks on (excuse the pun) with his career, they seek, and often get, a sell-on. Which means that if the buying club sells him for a million and they have a ten per cent sell-on clause, they'll get another ninety grand when he's sold, based on the buying club's profit.

The FA won't register any kind of agreement with an agent that contains a clause like that, but as with most things in football there are more ways than one to get to where you want to be – or to circumvent the rules in this case. Although all payments to agents in relation to player transactions have to go through the FA, that doesn't apply to retainer or bonus payments, and unless the FA comes in to go through the club's books (which will only happen if the club is in trouble or under suspicion) or unless it asked to look at my accounts (again unlikely as I strive to keep below the radar), I reckoned this might be a good way to earn some extra money in the middle to long term.

It doesn't always work. One agent struck a deal to get an uplift on future sales of a player and had it documented in a series of emails with the chairman of the club. Unfortunately for him, the club got sold and the new chairman simply refused to pay, claiming, quite correctly, that if he did he'd be in breach of the rules. It might have ended there but the agent was a persistent sort of fellow and decided to call the new chairman.

The conversation began in a friendly enough manner.

'Hi, I'm (let's call him Agent D) D. I'm the one who got that player (let's call him Smith) sold for you. I didn't take any money at the time because the club was skint . . .'

'Yes,' said the new chairman, 'that's why I bought it. Been a fan for years and wanted to help them out.'

D liked the sound of that. Most fans who bought the club they supported tended to be financial fools once they'd acquired it.

'Well,' said D turning on the charm, 'I wish you well with that and if there's anything I can do to help, happy to do so. Be good to meet up some time. I had a really good relationship with your predecessor.'

'Yes, I heard that, and I've seen some of the paperwork and your emails.'

D walked right into it. He wasn't a man renowned for his subtlety.

'Then you know you owe me some money on Smith's transfer.

I mean you made over a million there because of me,' D claimed.

'I don't think so,' the new chairman said. 'I've had words with our club secretary and he accepts that kind of arrangement should never have been entered into. So let's just leave it and see what we can do in the future together.'

If D had been a more prudent man he would have left it there but he wasn't and he didn't.

'If you think I am waiting for the fucking future for my fucking money then you've got another fucking thought coming. I'll go public on this whole thing and get your club relegated. And sue the arse off the lot of you. And make sure there's not an agent alive who won't know you don't keep to your end of the bargain.'

The new chairman was an experienced businessman, but was, as yet unused to the jargon of the football agent and the empty threats that are often made out of sheer anger and frustration but which would normally be forgotten in the morning. So he made sure they wouldn't be forgotten in the morning – or at all.

'Thanks, Mr D. I now know exactly where I stand. And by the way, I've recorded this call and even though it may get my club into trouble, this isn't the way I do business or intend to do it in the future so I'll be sending all this with a formal complaint to the FA.'

'Well,' said D, 'I'm also reporting your fucking club to the FA.'

As you can imagine, when the FA heard about what had gone on they rubbed their hands with glee and charged both D and the club with various misdemeanours. The club just got warned and handed a small fine – as well as a little pat on the back to the new chairman for toeing the line. D, however, found himself suspended and issued with a huge fine for his troubles, leaving the club to keep the profit from Smith without having to pay a penny to D or any other agent. I guess you know where my sympathies lie on this transaction. It always seems to be the clubs that the FA protects and never uthe agents. But at least we know where we stand.

Anyway, the approach I made to Chairman K (who was a very different animal from the new chairman who locked horns with D) was simple: I'd find him players from whom I reckoned he could make money when he developed them and sold them on. K and I got on well. He was a big, bluff guy from up north, always in braces and long-sleeved shirts whatever the weather. He seemed to be permanently cold and even at the height of summer had the central heating stoked up, maybe to ensure that visitors were glad to get away.

I wasn't asking for a fortune but I did reckon that if they sold a player for a hundred grand and then earned another ninety grand because I'd negotiated the sale for them, then it wasn't unreasonable to pay me twenty per cent of the whole shooting match. I started at twenty, knowing they'd offer ten and with a view to settling at fifteen. As you can imagine, I love bartering. I'm a nightmare when I visit markets abroad and I've left stallholders on the brink of suicide because of the prices I've got them down to. I just can't help myself. My mother is exactly the same. If it wasn't for the fact that she hates football she would've made a great football agent.

K and I agreed that he'd produce some documentation by way of a consultancy agreement to cover what I was going to get, and it seemed a perfect arrangement. Everybody would gain, and quite frankly neither of us thought it was any of the FA's business that we'd be making a buck or two.

As far as I was concerned, it also led to another interesting discussion where I offered the chairman what was, essentially, a kickback: whereby the club paid me a fee for any deals I did either for players I was bringing in, players I was taking out or even contracts I was renegotiating. I admit I hesitated here. This was really crossing the line as far I was concerned. I'd bent the rules before – we all did – but this was smashing them into smithereens, and I was worried that I might get seriously hurt by a sliver.

K was a minority shareholder, so he didn't really control the club and was grateful for anything extra he could make on the side. Just my sort of guy. A pragmatist.

A helpful one too, because now that he was effectively on my payroll he was also trying to push players my way. I've known managers do that but here I had a real live chairman, the man who held the purse strings, the man who made the final decision on contracts and who was able to tell players that either he didn't like their agent, or that their agent was no good, or, best of all, that I was the agent who did the most lucrative deals for his clients.

I actually had to rein him in, so enthusiastic did he become, because players might have grown suspicious and thought that we were hand in glove. As if. Yet, even with him proceeding with caution and even with me being choosy about which players I wanted to represent (I mean, if you don't have some standards then you have no respect), we still had a nice thing going. Yes, quite a nice little thing indeed.

It got to the stage where I was fast becoming the gatekeeper for this particular club. Other agents would come to me if they had a player they wanted to place there, and I was always happy to oblige for an entry fee which was, in this case, a slice of the action. OK, I had to share it with Chairman K but as I've said so many times, a little is better than nothing and a lot of littles add up to quite a lot.

As you can imagine, I wasn't earning a lot of friends along the way. K and I had another chat and decided that it might be wiser if I wasn't paid directly by the club. The idea was for him to cream off enough from the club by inventive invoicing to pay into the account of another company, which would ostensibly be providing a whole raft of marketing, public relations and IT services to the club, and then that company would pay a service company of mine. In that way, if the FA ever got suspicious after a complaint by another agent they'd have the devil's own job to prove anything.

I know what you're thinking. This was, in essence, a total fraud. The second company was one huge slush fund, a kind of money-laundering exercise, but K and I didn't think of it like that at the time. Truth to tell, we didn't really think about anything other than the amount of money we were both making.

That's the problem when it all comes so easy. You get complacent, you get careless, and looking back I admit I got more than a little up myself. Whereas I'd always had time for agents even younger than myself, to meet them for a coffee and give them some free advice, now I just ignored their emails and didn't return their calls. Time was money, and money was everything.

THIRTY-ONE

FOREIGN TRAVAILS

I MAY HAVE painted a Hogarthian picture of some of my fellow agents in this country but they can't hold a candle to the guys I now encounter in some of the more volatile countries in the world.

I heard about a Russian agent who went to meet his player in a hotel only to be met by a hail of bullets instead, because he'd refused to share his business with the local mafia. Everything there depends on who you know, who you have paid off, and your ability to keep in with not just the ruling party but also the billionaires who make the machinery go round by greasing the wheels.

Russian agents and, indeed, Russian players are laws unto themselves, largely because they're often armed. They're not individuals you want to cross, either singly or as a group. Things are what they say they are there, and facts become facts simply because they're voiced. It's all about 'protectzia': protection. I'm guessing this attitude is, in part, due to their Communist upbringing and in part because they're a tough, miserable bunch of bastards.

Ukraine and Serbia are not much better. I once got to act for a Ukrainian player and asked him what had happened to his previous agent.

'He was shot,' he replied, 'so now I have English agent. You. Think it safer for me and my family.'

'But was it safer for me?' I thought. But it didn't stop me acting for him because I knew there was a remunerative deal to be done and by then I was getting both increasingly careless and reckless. As for Serbia, well everything you see or read about it is true. Belgrade must be the most threatening city of earth and when I went there to meet a Serbian international that K wanted for his club I really doubted if I was every going to get home. The player was a decent footballer, that was for sure, but his family were not decent people, that was another equal certainty; I have never seen so many tattoos and piercings in my life and it was only later that I realised that they weren't decorative. They meant something. And what they meant was that I was dealing with one of the most feared gangland families in the whole of Eastern Europe, let alone Serbia.

It was when they told me that they wanted to get into the football agency business (presumably as a sideline to sex trafficking and arms and drug smuggling) that I decided to lie to K and tell him that I couldn't get the player interested and beat it out of Dodge just as fast as I could.

In fact the player did sign for another British club and I heard that the agent involved had got some new business partners. Rather him than me.

Given the level of crime involved in sport in Eastern Europe it should come as no surprise that tax liability is a concept unknown to the normal Eastern European player, hence their agents, when they ask guys like me to help them place a player, are always talking 'net' when it comes to salaries. As the figures they want are pretty high to start off with and are virtually doubled when they add the tax on, they become a pretty hard sell.

I once tried to move a black player to a club in Russia and was shocked by the racism, which they regarded as quite normal. They told me it would be unkind for me to sell him there because he'd be subjected to monkey noises for the entire match. I acted for an Israeli player in Europe, and he had the crowd making gas-chamber hissing noises and waving the Palestinian flag. Once you get exposed to the fans then the players actually seem quite nice.

Dealing in Turkey is an experience as well. I got quite excited when a South American agent assured me he 'owned' a player and gave me an exclusive mandate for a few countries, including Turkey. I got Turkey because I'd talked up (well, lied about actually) the strength of my connections there. I did actually know somebody who had done a fair amount of work in Turkey and so I decided to cut a deal with them to help me place the player.

It took a little over twenty-four hours for my guy to call me back and tell me that so far he'd come across half a dozen other agents who also claimed to have the exclusive right to market this particular player.

Not that getting a player into Turkey is such a big deal. The odds are that whatever attractive package you may get him and whatever chunky fee you may negotiate for yourself, that's just the beginning and by no means the end. Because so many clubs simply don't pay.

Well, eventually they might pay the player, but that will be for purely selfish reasons, usually to avoid some kind of universal embargo being put in place to stop them buying players. There's no such penalty when it comes to not paying agents. We're not what are called 'Football Creditors'. We have no leverage whatsoever to encourage clubs to pay our fees. When it comes to the UK we can't even sue a club in a court (some think that may have changed under the intermediaries rules but as intermediaries are 'participants' as well as clubs I am not sure that is right), which is what any other creditor can do when they've been owed money for months (or even years) for a job well done. All we can do is bring an action under an FA system called Rule K, whereby we have to start off a claim, pay a fee, choose an arbitrator, pay a fee, receive directions, pay more fees, and then if we're lucky finally get a hearing and a judgment. But that is useless anyway, as we have to take it to the High Court to turn it into a proper judgment and then, and only then, can we try to get the player or the club to pay us.

By then clubs usually will cough up, as they don't want to be wound up, but with players it can take so long that they may not even be playing in this country by then, which leaves you even more out of pocket and trying to track them down in the wilds of Uzbekistan and the like.

When you're working abroad then it's even more difficult. You can bring a complaint to FIFA, but given their track record you might only have a chance if you can find someone to bribe. Otherwise you end up in a tangled Kafkaesque process where you pay an awful lot of money and indulge in endless correspondence in a form of broken English that leaves you wondering if they even want to understand what your claim is all about.

You can't even do what you can do here when a claim is absolutely clear-cut, that is, go for a summary judgment, a statutory demand, bankruptcy, or a winding up. However spurious the defence of a foreign club or player or agent, he'll be allowed to buy time with it, and I can just imagine how many agents must give up on the process because they've run out of patience or, more likely, money.

Even when you have some kind of enforceable judgment you still have to enforce it. I've recently gone all the way with a foreign player who'd made his home permanently in England and married an English girl. He owed me money and I did it reluctantly, for all the good reasons I've explained before, but

I just couldn't let this one go because the two fingers he was sticking up in my face were so belligerent and cocky that I felt he needed to be taught a lesson.

I had got this player a contract worth five grand a week. The club, unusually in this instance, hadn't paid my fees, but I'd got them to give him a signing-on fee of fifteen grand a year which, after tax, netted down to what I'd agreed he'd pay me. He'd just banked it and then spent it, because when I came to try and enforce my judgment he was able to show the court that after all the bare essentials of life he needed to pay – a mortgage, support for his estranged wife and kids, the cost of his new live-in partner and her kid, trade essentials like travel, a car and equipment – all he could offer me was a hundred pounds a week, because he was no longer on the same contract I'd secured for him and had moved to a smaller club with less money (a deal I'd been denied doing even though he was still, just about, under contract to me).

I could've brought another action against him for the fees on that one, but he'd just worn me down and I couldn't be bothered. My lawyer helped me to get an attachment of earnings order where his club deducted what he owed me monthly and paid me direct, but it was going to be a long hard path and I'd wasted six months of my life that I was never going to see again.

I know I've drifted off the subject of working abroad (well the player concerned was foreign, though that doesn't mean to say a domestic player wouldn't have shafted me in exactly the same way) but I suppose I want to show that there are times when this business isn't all it's cracked up to be – and it certainly isn't when you get sucked into deals in the Middle East.

Like everybody else in football, we agents read about the Qatar World Cup bid and the FIFA corruption, but all I did was shrug my shoulders and think, what's new? Every deal I've ever known of in the Middle East has been rotten from the ground up.

The first problem is that you can never get to the clubs direct like you can here. There's always some middleman or middlemen who'll assure you that if you want to bring your player over they can make it happen, albeit at a price. In other countries your contacts are prepared to bide their time for their share of the deals, but in the Middle East there are times when it's made clear that you have to make an up-front payment.

Even if you do that, there is no guarantee that you've paid the right man or that he can actually do what he says he can. The fact that he may be a sheik himself means absolutely nothing. Being a sheik in Saudi, for example is a bit like being 'Mr' here and the only people I've met who aren't sheiks are the immigrants who work for the sheiks doing secretarial and administrative work and the like. It's a bit better if he's a member of the relevant royal family, but even that isn't necessarily the biz as the families are so huge and extended. There's no point in talking to the coaches either, because they tend to take what they're given, and if the owner of the club has a child who supports a particular club or idolises an individual player then they may be the ones responsible for any signings.

I've managed to complete one deal out there without even visiting, and if I'd needed to go, then I would've done so reluctantly, and not just because I've got Israeli stamps in my passport. I do have a second passport anyway for dealing deals in countries who don't like the fact that you've visited the Holy Land. I know of one agent who was detained so long at immigration over his entry papers (he'd obviously not paid off the right people) that he missed the deal completely. They let the player who accompanied him through and did the terms directly. He had signed without any provision for agent's fees before the agent had been put on a plane back to England with a warning that if he decided to visit again he might not be so lucky.

The player got his first month's wages but not the second, and then had the gall to call the agent who had gone with him to seek help in getting paid.

I could go on forever about the countries where deals are to be done without any guarantee of payment: Greece, all the old components of the Soviet Union, South America, some parts of Eastern Europe and even countries like Italy, where every club seems to be walking a financial tightrope and agents are the first to suffer when it comes to making the economics work.

As I've mentioned, there are new markets opening in India and China now as well, but I think a lot of agents have decided to stick to what they know and, like careful financial advisors, ignore the emerging markets.

The fact of the matter is that we're the whipping boys when it comes to getting paid for what we do. People may say we get paid too much but not to be paid anything at all just isn't right. Maybe that's why we get tempted to cross the line into criminal behaviour. Can you really blame us?

THIRTY-TWO

SWITCHES, SHADOWS
AND SCHEISTERS

THERE ARE SOME agents who are frightened to death by the FA. But then there are also some agents who are scared of their own shadows. They tend to be the same agents. The regulations for agents were a bit like regulations about paying tax and those for intermediaries are not that much different. Everybody would avoid them if they could. If you're rich and pay for proper advice they call it tax avoidance. If you just don't pay then it's tax evasion.

The fact of the matter is that intermediaries pay a lot of money to the FA to register, the FA collects fortunes from them in fines and what does the FA give back in return? Fuck all. It is hardly a surprise that the new breed are pushing for self-regulation. I mean who better to regulate agents/intermediaries than agents/intermediaries? At least they know what's going on rather than that bunch of chinless twats at the FA HQ who haven't got a clue as to what makes the football carousel go round. As much as they try to jump on board to drag the odd miscreant off and spank his bottom it just goes faster and faster so that the expert riders always elude their clutches. And good luck to them. I'm not sure self-regulation will solve all the problems, but it will eradicate the bitterness of being regulated by the enemy.

R told me about the good old days before licensing. He reckoned that there were only about a dozen agents and players who would actually ask to be represented rather than having to be virtually bribed. One player who eventually became a regular England international actually invited him to his house for tea and had his wife bake a vast array of cakes as if he were an honoured guest.

'Can't see that ever happening again,' he'd said wistfully, shaking his head.

Too right, I thought. Now you'd be lucky to get past the driveway, and even then you'd be stumbling over all the other agents queuing up to get in.

Fathers would phone to see if R would look after little Johnny, and all this would be done on a handshake with R even sometimes charging the player rather than the club.

Then word got out, and individuals flocked to become agents in the same way as they rushed to California to find gold or Kimberley in South Africa to seek diamonds. Some were good, some were professional, but few had any idea of what was expected of them and simply learned on the job. But learn they did and, as I discovered, nothing in this business can replace experience at the end of the day. You can come into the profession with a barrow load of money and throw it around as if every day was Christmas, but if you don't know what you are doing you will soon be found out.

The FA watched the whole drama unfold and then, it would appear, decided that as everybody representing the players was earning barrow-loads more money than they were they had to try to put a stop to it. So they decided in their wisdom – not a word commonly heard or used when the FA is mentioned – to regulate. This wasn't a Magna Carta or Declaration of Independence moment. This was them saying that anybody who had experience was now regarded as a Licensed Agent, but that anybody who wanted to get into the industry afterwards had to pass an exam. And I've already pointed out what a farce that is.

Then, when all the agents had worked out how to work around the regulations (and some had even found a way to cheat themselves through the exam), the FA spent a fortune bringing in a whole raft of even more complicated and challenging regulations. It was a hard battle, R explained, but by then all the leading agents had formed their own association and clubbed together to buy expensive legal advice, which saw the FA back down and try again, this time with a bit of consultation. 'They treated us like schoolkids, only when we turned on the teachers, they ran away.'

To those of us trying to operate now it doesn't seem that they ran away because, after 2007, it became a bit of a challenge to evade them. But I reckon we've not done too badly. At first they said we couldn't act for both parties, so all the tax burden of the fees fell on the player. The agents just went into the clubs and told them they needed to pay more, so whatever extra they gave the player netted down to pay the fees. That was when the big clubs, who it hit the hardest and who'd been the biggest opponents of duality (acting for both sides), backed down, and it was reinstated.

Then they banned what they called 'switching'. This meant acting for a club when they bought a player and then changing sides and acting for the player when he moved on. The FA said that there had to be a clear two-transfer-window gap before we could do that.

I once asked somebody from the FA who'd turned up at an agents' meeting what the reasoning behind that was, and he wouldn't tell me, so I told him I reckoned it was just to make life more difficult for us, and he wouldn't comment on that either.

Then they banned 'shadowing'. By now they were making the words up as they went along, and I reckoned a ban on 'breathing' was just around the corner. Anyway, what they meant by 'shadowing' was that you acted for a club when a player joined. Then, when they sold him, you acted for another club. However, they reckoned that all the time the agent was really acting for the player.

That may not have been the best for HMRC. No players are registered for VAT (and they can't contract through a company either), so they wouldn't have been able to claim back the VAT they paid to theiragents on top of the fees if the agent had been acting for them. Clubs of course can reclaim back the VAT. I know this is getting a bit dull, but I just want to illustrate what a bunch of spoilsports the FA really can be and demonstrate that representing footballers is not all fun and frolics, clubbing and show biz parties and running off to the bank with ill-gotten gains.

These restrictions were so easy to get around it was laughable. I just made deals with some acquaintances whom I kind of trusted (well, as much as you can trust other sharks when you swim in shark-infested waters) so that when I couldn't act – because it would've been a breach of the switching or the shadowing (or the breathing) regulations – I'd put one of these friendly sharks in to front it and then give him a small percentage of the fees for the favour. And then he'd return the favour when the boot was on the other foot. The clubs were willing accessories to the scam as well. They knew full well that whoever they were dealing with, whoever was signing it off, was merely a front; but they didn't give a toss as long as they got the player they wanted. Football is just a matter of expediency.

The agents' business was a cartel back then and amongst the Premier League of football agents it still is. For five years I was at the heart of it all and one of the real players. Or at least I liked to think so. It's a different ball game now with about a thousand intermediaries registered, not to mention people like me who are forced (or choose) for one reason or another to operate in the shadows.

The FA knock off a few small-fry agents or intermediaries now just for appearance's sake, but the big boys are generally too clever for them and remain beyond their reach. If they had any real brains they'd be out there with us agents making a bob or two, rather than being pen-pushing footballing civil servants trying to apply rules that simply aren't worth the candle. I was quite amused to see that a former member of their regulatory team left the FA to join an up and coming agency. Talk about gamekeeper turned poacher. I'm sure that some of the things he'll see in our world will open his eyes and see just how closed they were (blindfolded even) during his days in regulation.

From time to time the FA team does catch a big fish and thump their corporate chests whilst holding him upside down for all the world to see and making sure that the papers make headlines out of it by leaking the story. But the fact of the matter is that these are mere pin pricks, minor annoyances to guys who can still make a million quid out of a deal even while they are temporarily sidelined.

By the time I appeared on the scene and joined up with R there had to be an agreement with the player, and it had to be in a form that the FA approved and it couldn't be for more than two years and it couldn't be automatically renewable. There were lots of things it couldn't be, but the one thing it most certainly could be was crap.

Most of us have worked out ways to get round it all, of course. I'd get my players to sign two contracts, date one and lodge it with the FA. Then, when it was coming to the end I'd date the second and lodge that. I was so canny I even got the player to use different pens to sign the contracts, so they looked different.

I tried to hedge my bets and generally have the sort of

relationship with my players that enabled me to do so. I got a player to sign and not lodge or date the contract (they were supposed to be sent to the FA within five days of signing in those days before uploading). Then, when a transaction loomed, I could see if I could act for a club who would pay more than the commission per centage I had in the representation contract with the player. If so, I would switch and just keep the contract for the future.

As I've said, for some that could be a risky strategy if the player turned rogue and signed with somebody else, but it didn't seem to happen to me. Either my players loved me to bits, warts and all, or else it might have been that over a time I came to know a secret about each and every one of them that kept them close to my bosom. I never really found out which it was, though the proof of the pudding was in the fact that most of the players I represented above the radar are still represented by me in one way or another even though my name can only be spoken in hushed whispers.

The FA also decided to play bankers. All for transparency, they said, but given the time they took to pass monies on to us from the clubs, I reckon they were all taking holidays in Barbados on the interest. One brave agent took them on and challenged their right to hold deposits, and although it didn't enamour him to the powers that be, and although he was probably right, they just kept (and even under the new Intermediary stuff) keep right on doing it.

A favourite trick is to launch an investigation into any transaction that seems to them to be dodgy – haven't they realised that most of them are dodgy? – and delay payment until they're satisfied all is well. One poor bastard was totally reliant on money from a deal and nearly went to the wall when a substantial sum he was due got locked into the FA's bank account because (as it transpired quite unjustifiably) they didn't like the smell of a transaction.

They play all sorts of games, like claiming that the money that arrives from a club can't be identified as it's part of a bulk payment, so they've had to send it back. I had a deal where I'd done the player a favour and charged him less than the commission rate in my contract, and they even queried that. They must have thought I'd taken the balance in cash. I hadn't on that occasion, but there were other times when I felt I'd done a really good job for the player (which wasn't reflected in a five per cent commission that I was getting, and that spread over the three years of the contract) and asked him for a bit more on the side – and he was happy to pay it.

R did it as a matter of course, and then stashed the cash away for his holidays and such like. Did I mention that R had a penchant for young, pretty women? The cash also helped to buy the jewellery they'd wear by the side of the pool, jewellery more often than not a hell of a lot chunkier than the bikinis they wore.

So much for the FA as a governing body. Nobody had elected them to govern us. Nobody ever asked us what we thought or felt about it. Nobody at the top, or the middle – or even the bottom, if it came to it – gave a flying fuck. So why should we care that we make fools of them? That was how I thought about it then, and it was to contribute to my downfall. I seriously underestimated them and overestimated myself.

THIRTY-THREE

EXPANSION

YOU CAN SEE by now I'm a bit of a loner. All my parents' fault for making me an only child. I once heard another agent in my situation say that once you've created perfection why would you need to carry on? I made that my own personal mantra – which didn't really endear me to people. But you don't have to be liked to make money which is proven by the fact that so many of the more successful agents are so damn unlikeable.

OK, I'm not the sort of lone wolf you read about in the papers who buys half a dozen AK-47s and goes on a shooting spree; I'm just somebody who prefers his own company and finds it hard to trust anybody else. Mainly because I've seen so many people let down by others. Everybody lets you down in the end so you reduce the risk by reducing the number of people that you know. It's a simple policy.

For all those reasons I'd decided that a full-blown partnership was simply not for me. I'd seen too many of them go horribly wrong. One agent went to use his debit card and found it rejected, even though he knew he had several hundred thousand pounds in the account having just been paid for a profitable deal. He went back to the office he shared with his partner only to find that his partner had removed his personal effects along with everything else of value they had in the office.

When he called his partner and heard the ringtone that tells you for sure that the recipient of the call is abroad, then he knew he had a problem. And it got worse. The partner had assumed responsibility for all the administration and the finance, while the other guy had been the rainmaker when it came to getting in clients and doing the deals. In the partner's desk – he hadn't bothered to remove that as, like all the other office equipment, it was leased – he found a huge pile of unpaid bills, lawyers' letters and correspondence from various debt collectors, some quite clearly more reputable than others, but no less demanding if a little less threatening. I've used debt collectors to try and get money in from the odd player and let me tell you that without my delving too deep into their exact methods they can clearly be very persuasive. Anyway, everything this poor sod had worked for during the five years of being together with somebody he'd thought to be a friend had been destroyed.

He called the police. But given that the erstwhile partner was sunning himself on a beach in South America after marrying a very attractive local girl and given that the partner was a full signatory on all the accounts and had unrestricted use of all the company cards, there wasn't a lot of interest shown in the agent's plight. He instructed lawyers but was in such a financial mire he found it difficult to fund their efforts; something that the errant partner had obviously worked out for himself before he'd embarked upon his asset-stripping spree.

The partner had convinced his gullible associate that he was building up a nice base of young South American players and was actually buying the rights to them. In fact all the money that had been transferred abroad simply went into his bank account and feathered his nest for his early retirement.

Just when it seemed that things couldn't get any worse, the naughty partner's players started to complain that they'd not heard from him and then initiated an orchestrated series of letters (obviously drafted by a lawyer or a sharp rival agent) saying that they were giving notice to terminate their contracts.

The standard representation contract provides for a period of notice to be given to remedy any breach, but given that the agent was several thousand miles away and, as the hapless guy left behind thought, unlikely to be contacting the players very soon, there appeared to be little or no chance of any remedy in the immediate future.

The agent tried his best to persuade the players to re-sign with him but, although he thought it a bit odd at the time (he knew some of them quite well), not a single one agreed to do so. It was only some time later that he discovered that they'd, virtually to a man, signed for a rival agent. Eventually he figured out that his former partner had orchestrated the whole thing and done a deal with the new agent, so that he continued to benefit from the players' deals to the exclusion of the man he'd left behind.

Just when he thought it really could not get any worse, the pipeline income upon which he'd been relying to bail himself out and build himself up again, suddenly dried up. Every agreement that triggered off that income from deals his partner had done contained a clause that if the agent ceased to hold a valid licence then all bets were off. The partner who had fled had decided that not only did he no longer need a licence when he could use equally unscrupulous individuals to front for him, but that by advising the FA that he was surrendering it he also had the advantage of removing himself from their disciplinary process, as he was no longer a participant and subject to their rules and regulations. In any event the monies were to be paid to him personally as the FA (and FIFA) simply don't recognise companies (unless in FIFA's case they're offshore for stashing away their ill-gotten gains), only individuals. To add insult to injury, in a couple of cases where he'd been close to certain clubs, he'd got them to agree to pay him a discounted amount by way of early payment by convincing them they were actually saving money.

Talk about being fucked every which way but loose by somebody he thought he's known for years. It is amazing what people will do to further their own ambitions. And looking back I am still a little gob-smacked by what I did myself.

You can see why taking on a partner did not seem a very attractive option to me, particularly when I was doing so well all by myself. Having somebody work for me though was becoming more of a necessity than an option because I was signing up so many players that I simply couldn't get to watch them all on the regular basis that had been my practice. One player I signed told me he'd dumped his former agent because he never came to watch him play and that had always stuck in my mind as a warning. Although quite how turning up at Blackburn or the like on a wet and cold February night makes you a better agent I could never understand. But I toed the party line because if that was what it took, if a bout of pneumonia was the price to pay for a profitable deal, then I would pay it. A few hundred grand will buy you an awful lot of anti-biotics.

I was a reluctant employer though, I must say. Apart from the drag of setting up a PAYE system and having employment contracts, I'd seen what employees could do and what some employers do to them. There was one poor guy who had mystifyingly been persuaded to take a second-hand car in return for commission that was properly due to him. Nothing appeared on the books, so our old friends at HMRC were the losers again on the grand stage of football agents. That was the employee's choice, of course, but things went awry when he left. The employer demanded his car back, alternatively requesting payment for it and virtually accusing the guy of theft. The employed agent's problem was a lack of paperwork, not to mention a lack of money to fight off any claim. I gather that particular dispute did have a happy ending with David beating Goliath, but it was just another example of how things can go wrong when you try to operate outside your own private bubble.

Another warning was given to me every time I looked in the mirror. I knew what I'd done to R and I wasn't proud of it. What I also knew was that I didn't want it done to me. So many agents had told me (not realising the irony) of how they'd trained up a young agent and given him every opportunity, only to find that the minute he found himself with a potential star player on his hands he headed off for greener pastures, even if he didn't, like me, set up his own business. It is the worst feeling in the world to read of the multi-million pound transfer of a player you have lovingly nurtured, for whom you have worked day and night to get and keep, for whom you have sold your soul dealing with while schmoozing his unlikeable greedy parents, and who you have then lost to some young traitor you brought into your business to help service him. The younger agent will have gone clubbing with him, pulled birds with him, had threesomes with him and all behind your back, leaving you feeling like a husband who had no idea of his wife's affairs.

It was so dog-eat-dog that the idea of inviting a hungry dog into my kennel wasn't an attractive one, much as I like dogs. I kept meaning to buy one for company but then I was never sure when I would find the time to take it for walks. Apart from that I was not sure I wanted to get much bigger as an agency when one of my selling points was that I was not like the big agencies. I know what goes on out there with agents scrapping over the driest of bones. A player signs for one of the agents at an agency. Everybody knows that. Maybe he's gone with a younger guy at the bottom of the food chain. Then the player starts to do it on the pitch, and the big hitters at the agency get interested. They don't hesitate to try and steal the player away from the lad who brought him in and then not only try to claim the credit but try to do the kid out of his slice of the action.

There's pressure on them to deliver big deals, but they've already won their seat at the table. The poor sod who watched him play on freezing-cold winter afternoons up north, who invested time, effort and money on persuading him to sign, is now left to start all over again because the pressure is back on him to perform. And if he doesn't repeat the miracle, if this time around the players don't kick on, then he'll get a kick up the arse while being shown the door. The bigger the company, the more ruthless they can be. Maybe you've come to the conclusion that I'm not the nicest of individuals either, and there are times when I'd have to agree with you, but I still don't think I would, or could, do something like that. Mind you, there are quite a few things that I didn't think I'd do when I set out on this career path, so who knows? At my age there's still a fair old way to go until I get to the end of the road – unless I burn out before then.

I've noticed lately that a few of the old-time agents, men I admired when I was first thinking about this business, are giving up on player representation. They've moved on to media consultancies, entertainment, music, even other sports. Nothing compares to the stress of the rat race of this particular profession. It's becoming a bit like football itself – a young man's game.

I'd had my eye on one young up-and-coming agent, J, for a while. I'd seen him when I'd been watching one or two of my young kids playing and I quite liked his style. He got on well with the parents, the mothers in particular, although that could be a double-edged sword . . . You can flirt with them a bit because they like that, but you don't want to offend them by turning down their advances and you certainly don't want to sleep with them unless you don't want to represent their offspring. Yet another example of the delicate balance that faces us.

I noticed him chatting up the mum of one of my players and decided that if I could persuade him that he couldn't beat me, then he might well want to join me. And that's what transpired. I had my first paid employee. Like a lot of the younger agents J had played a bit himself. He had the brain to realise fairly early on that he wasn't ever going to be good enough to earn the sort of money that could persuade him not to bother with a degree and a career. He'd seen how the agents had hit on the fourteen-year-olds who had trained with him and, as he put it, some of them were so desperate just to get numbers on their books rather than quality they even hit on him.

He knew how the kids thought, knew what their parents wanted from them, and how, for so many working-class parents, the talented footballing child represented a meal ticket for life. He'd worked as an intern in a large agency during his university holidays so he knew how they operated, and he'd shown enough foresight to gather a handy collection of phone numbers and contacts while he'd been there.

He also had the talent for being invisible at times, so he knew which of the agents at the large agency had players who could be targeted, and once he'd identified the weak links he was ruthless in trying to close a deal. Because he'd never had a contract he had no restrictive covenant stopping him from poaching clients.

It always amazes me how lax agents are with their paperwork. Maybe they're so busy running after the next big deal they don't have time to attend to the little details, but those oversights can cost them more than they make from the big deals themselves.

Even when they do have a proper contract, so many agents are too mean to use a proper employment lawyer or cobble something together themselves from stuff they've seen or been subject to.

That's a formula for disaster, and it's not a trap into which I'm ever going to fall. I told you, I have a good lawyer, and anything I spend with him is money well spent. It's an investment as far as I'm concerned, and having approached J and his having taken to the idea of joining forces with me, I was going to ensure that his agreement was as watertight as it could be.

The challenge with contracts in our industry is that I'm told you can't actually stop the guy working in it after he's left you. Yes, you can put something in it to stop him approaching your clients or nicking your staff, but the fact is that as long as he's out there working then everything is at risk. I thought very carefully about it before I put pen to paper with him, but then I thought, 'Fuck it. No pain, no gain.' I wanted to move forward, I needed to move forward. I feel frustrated when I sense I'm standing still. Call it what you want. Greed. Ambition. To be honest, there are times when this whole thing goes beyond the money. I want to act for the best there is. I want to find the best young talent and water them and see them grow. Now, for better or worse, I had somebody to help me achieve that.

My final interview with him was short and to the point.

'So,' I said, 'I've told you how I work, how I want to grow and how I think you'll fit in. And if it all works out then I promise you I will gradually cut you into other deals, even when you're not involved. Are you in or are you out?'

It was when he nodded and simply said, 'Show me the money,' that the red warning flags should have gone up and if I'd known how it was going to pan out, believe me, I would've stayed exactly as I was.

THIRTY-FOUR

RUNNING TO STAND STILL

I'VE NEVER REALLY wanted to have a whole bunch of footballers as my best friends. I mean, footballers themselves don't necessarily have their teammates as their best friends and tend to stick to their old mates. But some kind of personal touch is not only necessary but makes a welcome change for players whose previous agents would just pop up out of their boxes when a deal was in the offing – for which they appeared to have some kind of sixth sense.

Players like to have tickets for major events. If there's a big boxing match on, then you can be sure the ringside seats will be filled by footballers and their mates. Tickets for those don't come cheap, but I've managed to set up an arrangement with a promoter whereby we exchange tickets – big matches for big fights.

It's the same with music festivals. I sometimes wonder if I'm running a football agency or a ticket agency, but it's just one of those things that has to be done. And it's not just for the players themselves. It's for brothers and sisters and cousins and even parents. I've organised tickets for bands from One Direction to Status Quo, from Glastonbury to the O2, from Neil Diamond to up and coming bands of which I had never heard and never wish to hear again.

The other thing that has to be done is to keep up with your rivals when it comes to doling out gifts or providing services.

One agent waits until the end of the season and then, depending on the achievements of his players, buys them presents. If a player has been an essential part of the title-winning side they might even get a car; a promotion justifies a Rolex; and international caps get a player the best and latest electronic gizmo.

Although it's difficult to get players together at the end of the season, when they leave as swiftly as swallows in the winter for warmer climes, another agency always rents a luxury boat for their end-of-term party and fills it with fine food, finer champagne and hand-picked lovelies to make the voyage a memorable one.

There are a lot of other 'presents'. A day at the races with 'free' bets afforded to your player-guests. That can be expensive, as I found out at Cheltenham one year. Tickets for Wimbledon, grands prix and even FA Cup finals: you'd be surprised how difficult players find getting tickets for themselves, particularly when they generally can't be arsed to ask and certainly aren't prepared to pay. It's much easier, not to mention cheaper, to get their agent to do their shopping for them.

I've just started taking over a whole nightclub for one night. I've called in a few favours, got a few B-list celebrities along from the TV reality programmes they all seem to watch, and hired, at no little expense, a band whose music gets played in a fair number of dressing rooms around the country. Not that there's any great consistency about that sort of music as one (usually self-elected) player tends to be in charge. So, you can get hip-hop at one club, indie at another, blaring rock at a third and rap at a fourth. The band I chose were all big football fans, and the players, for the most part, liked them too. When they all sat around at the end of the set like lifelong mates, girls draped around them in various stages of intimacy, then I reckoned I'd got myself quite a few Brownie points with all my players who had come, and made the ones who hadn't feel as if they'd genuinely missed something.

Christmas is an expensive time for agents. Players talk to each other, and not just the players you represent. So if one agency is sending out five hundred quid hampers from Harrods and you're relying on John Lewis to deliver a hundred pounds worth of goodies to your players then you can bet you bottom dollar your players will find out. Even spending according to what you've earned out of a player doesn't work. You've done a deal for a player in the previous transfer window so you feel generous towards him and spend more than you do on a client whose pipeline income is running down. That may well mean you'll miss his new deal because he'll take umbrage that another player in your stable got a bigger Yuletide gift than he did. It really is like dealing with a bunch of schoolkids.

But it's not just at celebratory times that an agent has to be there for his players. One of mine has just broken up with his wife. She came home unexpectedly and found him in bed with the kids' nanny. Nanny and player were promptly dismissed. Nanny went back to Poland, but player was faced with the choice of a hotel or my spare bedroom and chose the latter.

I could've put up with his drinking and whining, and even the womanising, but when his wife found out where he was and decided to use my little home for the re-run of the *Gunfight at the O.K. Corral*, I came close to throwing him out myself. She arrived shortly after midnight, pretty well tanked up herself. Trust me, hell hath no fury like a wronged footballer's wife. She leaned on the front-doorbell until my neighbours screamed complaints, and when I decided that the choice lay between calling the police and creating an ugly newspaper story, or letting her in, I made the wrong choice and opened the door.

She went for him like a wild animal, nails extended and,

strong athlete though he was, she managed to draw first blood. I couldn't let him beat the living daylights out of her, so I tried to hold him back while I reasoned with her. She just took that as an invitation to go for his eyes, and rather than have a player blinded on my premises, I let him go. He flattened her with a perfect (or as he said later in court 'defensive') right hook.

I promised myself never again to get so involved in a matrimonial issue. Now, I introduce the player to a good divorce lawyer (with whom I also have an arrangement for an introductory commission and a share of his fees) and then restrict myself to saying yes and no during interminable phone calls from the player where he uses me as a sounding board for everything that has gone wrong with his life.

Yes, I've stood by players at funerals sobbing their hearts out for their mums or dads. Say what you will of professional footballers, I've never known one of them abandon his parents, however awful they've been to him as a child. And some of them have had pretty rotten upbringings. Yet, there's this sentimental streak in most players when it comes to their parents that makes them forget all that and go the extra mile. Which means that you, the agent, have to travel that road with them too even when they can see that the family are draining the player dry. Ours not to reason why when it comes to family. Just to do and lie.

I've even had to spend Christmas Day with one player's family because he'd broken up with his girlfriend in the run-up to the holiday and didn't want to turn up at his parents' on his own because he was too scared to tell them that they wouldn't be seeing their grandchildren that year.

But I had J with whom to share the burden and he was the most willing of sharers. Volunteering to babysit players on nights out, to take them out for an evening when I thought I had better things to do, even to cover the odd family occasion for me when

I decided that I simply could not spend another couple of hours in the purgatory of cheap wine, stale perfume, unclean houses and predatory women. J never complained. He did everything that was asked of him. And more.

And meanwhile I did my best. I spent to earn. I accepted that most of what I did was taken for granted by players, because it's what they expected – largely because they're a selfish bunch of tossers, but also because it's what others would do for them if I didn't . I was on this treadmill and I could not get off. I had to ensure that deal after deal would arrive to refill my wallet which kept on emptying as I pursued the pot of gold at the end of football's rainbow. But I was beginning to realise that I couldn't run forever. My legs and my heart were telling me that the end of the race was near and that I was not going to win. There were others out there faster and more determined than me and that was the thought that was beginning to keep me awake at night. If I was awake at night then I was struggling the stay awake during the day and that, in football parlance, was when I took my eye off the ball.

THIRTY-FIVE

THE GOOD GUYS

G IVEN THAT I'VE frequently called players a bunch of tossers, and given my experiences throughout my career so far, you may be surprised when I say that there are some really good guys amongst them.

It often works out in football that like attracts like. Good managers get good players because they know how to inspire loyalty. Players may have a great ability on the pitch but that doesn't necessarily make them nice people. But when you get the combination of a talented player who is also a really warm-hearted and loyal person then you really have struck pay dirt.

I've not being doing this long enough to have represented players from cradle to grave (well, not literally but certainly from their first to their last playing contracts), but I do have a few players who are on to their third contracts with me so I must be doing something right.

The dream player involves you in everything he does. He confides in you, seeks your advice and, most important of all, actually takes it. I've got this little group of players now who do just that. When another agent phones them they call me at once, having told the invasive agent that they're with me, they're happy with me and that if he has anything for them then he needs to speak to me.

Sometimes, they go the extra mile. I had one player who got called by a club for which he had always wanted to play. I knew it because I'd tried to put him in there and been rebuffed. Then, suddenly, the club calls him direct and say they've agreed terms with his current club and can he get there as soon as possible for a medical.

There are some players – quite a few actually – who would've done just that and been pelting down the motorway to put pen to paper before you could say David Beckham. This lad hadn't done that. He'd fought my corner and told them he was with me.

'That's a problem,' the manager had told him. 'You see, we've had some bad experiences with your man and we won't deal with him.'

This was totally untrue. In fact the only experience they'd had with me was when I called them (politely) about my player and they told me (impolitely) that he wasn't for them.

'So, who's going to negotiate my deal?' my player asked.

'Don't worry about that. We've an agent we deal with all the time. He's very good and he'll fight for you to get every last penny. And best of all is that we'll say he acted for us, so it won't cost you any tax and what we pay him won't come out of your deal. Now, when can you get here? We've got some other irons in the fire and if we can't get this signed off today then we need to move on to other targets. But you're number one on our list so we'd really like to get this done, if we can.'

Even though my player knew it was going to cost him the move of his career he had the guts to call me and relay it to me word for word.

I was in a quandary. He'd been good as gold, and I knew an angry call from me to the club and another call to report them to the FA would put the kybosh on the whole deal. So I gritted my teeth, told him to do what they'd asked and let him know what the deal should be worth for him. Which was fortunate, because when he got there and was introduced to the sleazebag who the club had introduced he was told, 'I've got you a great deal. You just need to sign off and do your medical.'

'Er, can we go through it first?' my player asked.

'Are you not trusting me, son?' the agent replied aggressively, and with some reluctance set out the terms which were about half of what I knew he could get and were not much better than what he was on.

My player got in his car and drove home, and then even came with me to my lawyer to give a statement so that I could have a letter before action written to the manager and the club for defamation.

Ultimately, it all worked out well and the player and I were rewarded. The club's chairman called me when the legal letter landed on his desk and apologised (doubtless because he didn't want a scandal), and then invited us back to negotiate a proper deal. The manager was less than happy, and I was really worried about how my player would be treated at the club, but as it transpired what came around, went around. With his card well and truly marked, and some dire results at the start of the season the manager got his marching orders. I went on to develop a great relationship with the club and even helped to recruit his replacement. And my player got the move of his dreams.

Other long-standing players of mine go out of their way to talent-scout for me. They tip me off about youngsters at their clubs and put in a good word. They don't want anything back in return, and it's their way of saying thank you for the great deals I've achieved for them. As I say, what goes around, comes around.

I've got one particular player who regularly phones up for a chat, and when I ask him what he wants (in a nice way, of course) he just says that he hasn't heard from me for a while and just wanted to check that I was OK. In fact, all my players hear from me every week. If I don't call or make contact through Facebook, then I text. It gives a small agency like mine an edge over the bigger boys who have 600-plus clients and can't possibly preserve the personal touch.

I'm not one for showing a lot of emotion (or even feeling it, if truth be told), but when one of my players asked me to be the godchild for his son I did feel a few tears welling up. Mind you, when I went to the christening and the little bugger weed all over me I felt a different kind of dampness.

There's always a warm glow when a player calls me and tells me he wants to speak to me in confidence. It isn't always good news. He might have broken up with his girlfriend or left his wife (or she's left him), or there might be a child who's ill or a parent diagnosed with a terminal illness, but the fact is, it's me that he trusts with the secret and it makes me want to try even harder for him.

Of course you can't like all your clients, and so many footballers just aren't likeable. Yet, it makes it much easier to act for somebody if you're really fond of them, although that in itself brings another kind of problem. The fear of failure, of letting the person down who has placed his blind trust in you. You've always found him a club, so he assumes you always will. However, there are episodes in all players' careers when they simply run out of road, and try as you may there are no clubs for them. Or at least no club that will pay him the sort of money you feel he deserves. Honestly, it doesn't bother me when I let somebody down at the end of the day who has just taken, taken, taken from me, but when it's somebody who's given his all to stick with me, then I'll move heaven and earth to stick by him.

I've used all my contacts and powers of persuasion to get a player I like into a club even when, in my heart of hearts, I fear they may be punching above their weight. It's not often that my heart rules my head, and I'm well aware of the dangers of lying to a club about a player's ability or fitness, but sometimes I just feel the need to go that extra mile even if I may end up with egg on my face.

Once, I had a player in desperate straits. His marriage had broken down, he was drinking too much and although he'd had enough skill in the past to earn himself (and me) some decent money, there wasn't a club in the country who would touch him despite all my efforts. So, I found him something abroad through a local agent, waived my fee just to make it happen and paid for his fare out there myself so that he could have a trial. It must have happened on one of his better days (it was a Muslim country and he couldn't drink) and he was offered what was a really lucrative contract given his age and physical condition.

A week later, a DHL package arrived at my door. Somehow or other he'd managed to get hold of a Rolex watch in Duty Free and then get it out of the country for me. He'd even had it engraved: 'To the best agent in the world'.

Gestures like that make this stressful industry bearable. For a while . . .

THIRTY-SIX

LEGAL EAGLES

THE PROBLEM WITH lawyers is that they're fine when they act as lawyers, but not so great when they think they can do anything better than anybody else – including being an agent.

For a long time they were exempt from registering with the FA. They could act for players because they could treat them as clients and they felt that it wasn't for another regulatory body to regulate them when they already had the Law Society and then the Solicitors Regulatory Authority (SRA) regulating them to high heaven. However, so many unlicensed agents were using a lawyer to front for them on transactions, paying them an hourly rate and keeping the bulk of the fee for themselves, that the FA finally managed to persuade the SRA to allow them to be brought into the tent. This they did by creating a new class of agents called Registered Lawyers. All the lawyer had to do was register with the FA, and that was that as far as his right to represent footballers in contractual transactions was concerned.

I understood what the FA were trying to do. Until then, lawyers could put two fingers up to them as they weren't participants, so they had no need to co-operate on any investigation. The FA could turn spiteful from time to time and report a non-co-operative lawyer to his own regulatory body, but unless there was a clear breach of his professional code they never got terribly excited about things that had the FA jumping up and down with frustration.

I was never quite sure how lawyers put through the monies they received and paid out through their books. I understood that there were all sorts of rules about not sharing professional fees with others who were not lawyers, but I'm sure they found a way around it. Where there's money then there's both the will and a way when it comes to lawyers.

I've been to see players who are 'interviewing' a few agents. That's quite often the way it works nowadays, particularly if there's a greedy parent involved. They might say it's to see who they feel is the best qualified to represent their kid but more often it's to see who offers them the most. I saw one young player and his parents recently. I knew they'd already seen one of the big agencies, a local guy who had been watching the boy since he was tiny, and a registered lawyer who seemed to be running his agency in parallel to his law practice rather than through it.

It was all so well rehearsed. We had a chat, the dad said nothing but still managed to consume three pints, and then the mum said she had to go, leaving me and the dad to our 'men's talk'. I knew what was coming. Within minutes he told me the big agency had already offered to help them financially as well as offering him a job, but I was taken aback when he told me the 'reputable lawyer' had offered them a house near the club to which he'd virtually guaranteed them a move, as well as half the fee he'd be earning.

I did some quick mental calculations, went through the motions as to why they'd be better off coming with me – knowing I was wasting my breath – and then called it a day. I just couldn't understand why a lawyer would risk losing his professional status for what would, at the end of the day, be scant reward after he'd given so much away. So much for the integrity of that profession.

I know of one lawyer who continued to specialise in fronting transactions for unlicensed individuals who could not sign off on deals themselves, even after he'd become accountable to the FA. It was really simple. The individual did all the work, recruited the player, spoke to clubs who were happy to talk to him (despite it being a blatant breach of the regulations), actually went in with the player to discuss and negotiate the terms, and then, when all was done, finally and belatedly brought in the lawyer to 'check' the contract and sign off on it. He charged a basic ten per cent, so I suppose he was acting as an agent for all the flotsam and jetsam who still managed to thrive in football.

Lawyers sell themselves to players as a cut above the rest of us. They claim to be professional – like none of the rest of us – and say that a football contract is a complicated document that needs a legal brain to make sense of it. Players' families in particular seem to fall for this line, especially when the lawyer persuades them that a club won't raise the same objections when a player says he has a legal adviser to when he says he has an agent.

I'm not sure it matters a toss to the club. They'd rather have the player without any representation at all so they can rip him off. One lawyer was really taken down a peg or two when he rolled up at a club with his player only to be told by the secretary that the manager had a thing about young players having any advisers at all and that he would see the player on his own, although the lawyer was welcome to wait in the car park and give advice if and when the player sought it.

There ensued a bizarre series of events with the player shuttling to and fro between the manager's office and the car park, bringing offers from the club and then returning with a counter-proposal from the lawyer. When they finally got to the point where the terms were agreed, the lawyer asked about his fees and the player brought back a message from the manager saying that he (the player) was his (the lawyer's) client and he could fucking well pay him. End of.

I've had clubs refuse to speak to me as well, but nothing quite like that. The fact of the matter is that when a player signs with an agent, and the agent registers the contract with the FA, then the club is obliged to speak to the agent. However, I've yet to meet an agent brave enough to complain to the FA about a club refusing to do so. They know it would get the player into trouble with the club and the club would make sure that the player knew his problems had been triggered off by the agent's complaint. Which would mean that the relationship between the player and the agent wasn't likely to be one for life.

Don't get me wrong. As I've said, I've got a good lawyer myself. But I don't let him loose on my clients. I'm not saying he'd try to nick them away from me but I've seen it done so why tempt fate? Personally, I try to use them for what they're good at, like getting my clients off speeding offences. I even took the rap for one myself when the player was on nine points. The photo we requested didn't show definitively who was at the wheel but it did reveal two blokes in the front seats. There are times when you just have to go the extra mile for your clients, although I was a bit shocked when the Huhnes went to jail for precisely what I'd done. I won't be repeating the favour, that's for sure.

Divorces, drunken punch-ups in bars or the street, paternity claims, plain ordinary conveyancing, tax planning, wills: it's all good stuff and I don't mind paying for it. Somehow or other my players never quite get around to writing out the cheques, but as long as the fees I get for their transfers more than compensate me then I'm not one to complain. I try to make a merit out of it all, but, generally speaking, they just take it for granted. I suspect they take me for granted too. If something happens to me then there will be another agent close behind to mop up my clients. And even if nothing does happen, the likelihood is that eventually they'll get bored. What I don't want though is a lawyer stepping in who knows all my business and is able to tell them exactly where I've gone wrong.

I had to smile when the FA decided to give lawyers no favours as intermediaries. They have to register alongside everybody else, get CRB checked if they are dealing with minors and best of all have to pay the same fee. Bet they don't like that. But, lawyers being lawyers, they want to get value for money so they seem to be cropping up more and more in transactions, one firm even getting a retainer from a club, I've heard. Some of them are still delusional and think that hooking up with an agent is going to see quality work streaming through their doors. Only it doesn't work like that. Very few players have enough serious legal or commercial work to justify the involvement of a lawyer and they don't even get the purchase of players' houses as the one thing footballers do all seem to have is a solicitor who has bought houses for them from day one – and if they don't, the club is happy to direct the work to their own lawyer who will do it far more cheaply and save the club money as there is a tax-free eight grand allowance that they can give a player to relocate when he joins a club.

I know of one player who got a bit suspicious of some of the investments his agent wanted him to make. He thought the agent might have a vested interest in a couple of the businesses or was getting too high a kickback. So he went behind the agent's back and consulted the lawyer to whom he'd been introduced by that very agent.

You might have thought that the lawyer would feel conflicted or, even if he didn't, would've felt obliged to mention it to the agent who'd regularly sent him work. Not a bit of it. He was in like a monk who'd just given up his vows of celibacy. Muddying the water, only too keen to show exactly what the agent had done wrong. To be fair, the agent had pulled a fast one in some respects, but it still didn't seem right to me. Anyway, the end result was that the player dumped the agent and used the lawyer from then on, who in turn used him as his calling card to develop a very nice sports law practice with an agency tucked neatly into it. So much for professional standards.

Just made me even more careful. Trust nobody except yourself and even then keep looking in the mirror. Although I was beginning to trust J. Big mistake.

THIRTY-SEVEN

HUBRIS

ONE OF THE great benefits of having J on the payroll was that I could use him to help deliver the bespoke service I promised every player I signed. I encouraged J to get out there with the younger lads and make them feel as if he was one of them. I gave him a budget. I prefer to call it a budget rather than a slush fund, but if it means keeping the players happy, in every sense of the word, then I'm good with that.

J's much more of a techie than me and he set up a database which detailed every piece of information we could possibly want on the players: family birthdays, wedding anniversaries if they were married, clothing sizes for freebies, personal likes and dislikes for presents; even a rating as to how much we might make out of them so that I could estimate how much to spend to keep them happy. I've always understood the need to balance investments against reward.

I took J to meetings with me, and he learned at my knee just as I had with R. As fate would have it, one day we ended up at the same Midlands club where I'd received my slight from the CEO. And fuck me, if he didn't do it again to J.

'Can you get your lad to pour us a coffee?' he said, pointing to the pot on a side-table. 'And I'll have a couple of biscuits as well.'

Not even a please. I stopped J in his tracks before we considered a 'thank you'. 'He's here to learn how to be a football agent, not to be a tea-lady,' I said sharply.

J poised in mid-air, having risen from his seat to do as the CEO asked. I nodded to him to sit down, and he did, knowing on which side his bread was buttered.

The CEO wasn't going to admit defeat. He just lifted the phone to his secretary who was seated outside and asked her in to serve the drinks. I was seriously tempted to tell her not to bother and that the CEO would be doing it for himself, but I resisted. I didn't want to screw up the deal we were negotiating.

J thanked me when we went out, said he'd learned a lot and was grateful to me for sticking up for him, but somehow I didn't get the feeling that he was as grateful as I'd been to R in the same situation.

Gradually I realised I should've stayed on my own. J proved to be good at getting players, but he had his own methods, some more orthodox than others and a few of them not just outside the FA regulations but beyond anything they could conceivably have envisaged. Within months of J joining he had the signature of some really good players on undated representation contracts. The reason they were undated was because the players who had signed already had contracts with other agents, but J knew when they expired and was ready to shoot the contract off to the FA to register it for the very next day.

Some of the agents were so taken by surprise they didn't even know they'd lost the player until he stopped taking their calls and they read about a new deal in the papers. Of course I got the blame for all this, and with a few agents I knew I even went to the length of offering them a bit of the next deal to appease them. I kept telling them the kid was just enthusiastic but I could see that he was as driven as I'd been when I first started out. Just how driven he was I didn't realise until it was too late.

My relationship with Chairman K was still useful, as his club had recently got itself into Europe. This meant that they had a fair amount of money to spend, which in turn meant that they were the first port of call for some of the players I was acquiring through my little helper. That was another mistake. I should've kept him out of it, because when we did a deal at the club I had to tell J his commission was going to be based on the net figure after I'd paid off K.

I thought he'd accepted it and could see that the relationship was going to be good for us all, but I guess I underestimated his ambition, which had clearly taken on the heights of a Shakespearean tragedy. The only problem here was that I was going to be playing the title role, and we all know what happened to Hamlet.

It all came to a head when K's club indicated that they wanted to sign one of the players J had brought in. There were other clubs interested too, but I encouraged the player to sign where I wanted him to play rather than at a club where he might have earned more money and certainly where the commission wouldn't have been tainted by a kickback.

I could tell J wasn't happy but I thought he'd get over it. I told him I was so pleased with him that I was upping his basic salary and increasing his commission by five per cent. Surely he'd be pleased and grateful given that he hadn't had to come to me to ask for anything? How wrong can you be . . .

It started with a letter from the player's lawyer – not the tame one who I used – putting me on notice that he was terminating my representation contract because I'd breached all my obligations of acting in good faith. Oh, and by the way he'd also be coming after me for damages because I hadn't told him about the better deal on offer.

I didn't even have time to think about how he could've known about the better deal before I got a letter from J telling me that he was resigning with immediate effect because he 'didn't like my business practices'.

I was disappointed but consoled myself thinking what a little shit he was and how I was just grateful that all the players were signed to me, and how his departure wouldn't have that much impact. I was confident that I could get all the players he'd recruited to stay with me, even when their contracts ran out, by schmoozing them and convincing them that I was the one with the ability to do the deals while J had just been a boy doing my bidding.

All that optimism evaporated with the next post. I got a letter from the FA informing me that they were launching an investigation into the transfer to K's club and, as a participant, I was invited to come in and sit down with their nice regulatory people to assist with the inquiry.

I reckoned that the second company and the club's separate bank account were not going to be easy to discover, so I still wasn't too concerned. However, this complacency was a huge mistake. By the time I got to the FA for my interview, my lawyer, whom I thought it wise to involve now, had received a huge bundle of papers, which included a statement from my erstwhile assistant (now a totally ungrateful little cunt rather than merely a little shit) telling them what he knew about my relationship with K and his club, and how I'd carved up the player on the transfer.

I could've bluffed that one – they had no proof, and I could've just said that J was trying to destroy my business so that he could steal it himself – but they had a silver bullet. They'd done what the Americans call a plea bargain with K. In return for his blowing the whistle on his entire under-the-radar operation (which to my surprise extended to a couple of other agents I knew and a few unlicensed guys as well) they'd said they would take his co-operation into consideration.

What could I do? I've always liked a fight, but this wasn't one I was going to win. My lawyer told me that all I'd do by pleading not guilty would be to piss them off even more. Come the day of the hearing, I put on my best suit and tie, sat alongside my lawyer and the eye-wateringly expensive barrister we'd engaged to lodge a plea in mitigation, and felt like a murderer waiting for the judge to put on his black cap and sentence me to hang.

They read out what they were doing to everybody else first – just to extend the agony. The club was fined a hundred grand and had twenty points deducted, of which ten were suspended to acknowledge their assistance. My old partner in crime had already resigned as chairman and director, and had even got rid of his shares to show that the club, at least, was starting afresh. One of the agents received a twenty-grand fine and a year's suspension of his licence; the other got ten grand and a year as well, but with six months suspended.

And what happened to the last man standing? They threw the book at me. Said that I'd concocted the whole thing and brought good people down, that K had been in the industry with a totally blameless record until he'd met me, that the whole accounting structure had been my idea, that a player had found himself funnelled into a club (which was now likely to be relegated because of the points deduction) just to satisfy my relentless financial greed, and that they had to set an example. The sacrifice on the altar of high moral standards was going to be yours truly. I was hit with a five-year ban from any involvement in football whatsoever, a fine of £150,000 and an order to pay costs which, with the fees of my own legal team, were likely to be in the region of about another £50,000.

And to compound matters, it wasn't as if this was going to be the best-kept secret in football either. They issued a press statement, posted it on their website, and even posted the whole hearing word for word for all to read. Overnight I'd become a pariah in the sport I loved.

So that was it. All my contracts with my players were terminated.

So were all my deals with clubs, including a ton of pipeline income they would've had to pay over the next couple of years. I reckoned that the cost to me in actual terms was about two million. And that didn't take into account the money I would've earned over the next five years. It was, basically, a case of what goes around comes around. R had taken me on as his apprentice and I'd fucked him to set up on my own; I'd taken J on and he'd now done the same, but with more devastating effect.

A few people called me to say how sorry they were. When you'd been as ruthless as I'd been in building up a business, even those few were a miracle and I was really touched. Amazingly, R was one of them, and I really appreciated the gesture. I'd acted badly towards him when he'd given me the chance in the first place, and he'd no reason to feel any regret for my demise within the business.

He asked me to meet him for a drink which I gratefully accepted. My lawyers had gone back to their offices and chambers to gird their loins and don their gowns for the next case. To them it was just business. To me it was my life; R understood that.

I got calls from some of my players to say that they, at least, appreciated all I'd done for them, wanted to know if we could find a way so that I could still look after them, and one of them even asked if I needed any financial help. That really touched me, as I'd put them all in the same box when I'd been in business.

When I arrived at the bar, R had already ordered me a large whisky. He'd remembered that I didn't drink a lot but I did have a weakness when it came to expensive Scotch, and as it slid smoothly and numbingly over my palate I knew it was probably the most expensive the bar had to offer.

'It's not the end,' he said. 'If you play it properly then the game is never over.'

THIRTY-EIGHT

FULL TIME

THE GAME IS never over. R's words never left me and R never abandoned me as he was quite entitled to do. We agreed that he and I would go back to where we started off. I'd find him the deals and he'd front for me. It was a risky strategy, because it only needed one player or club to tip off the FA that I was back in the game and they'd be down on me like a ton of bricks. Though what they could do to me that was any worse, I wasn't quite sure. It was really R who was taking all the risks.

I think he'd become just a little devil-may-care, because we all knew by then that FIFA had decided that all licences had to be handed in in April 2015. The irony wasn't lost on me. Hundreds of good guys who had obeyed the rules, played it by the book, and missed out on all the opportunities that I'd seized upon were now in exactly the same position as me. Licenceless. (If there's such a word and my spellcheck seems to be telling me there isn't.)

FIFA had finally thrown in the towel. They couldn't cope, they couldn't administer and they'd kind of lost the will to regulate. I mean, there's obviously a lot more to be earned by taking backhanders to dole out the largesse of World Cups and sell the tickets for the tournament on the black market, than there is in drafting and supervising incomprehensible, vindictive and, as it transpired, meaningless regulations for agents. Perhaps the AFA (the agents' trade union) should have had a whip-round to pay FIFA off like everybody else seems to do, but they didn't, so goodbye it was to the licensing system. Goodbye agents, and hello intermediaries.

At that time I clung to the hope that at some time in the future even somebody like me who'd been banned could rise from the dead and register as an intermediary, and in fact that certainly happened with other guys who'd been ground down by the FA and disciplined by them. But fate hadn't finished with me yet, so it was going to prove a false hope.

At the time I still felt mildly optimistic despite the massive financial and career destroying blows that had been meted out to me. April 2015 seemed a while away and there were a whole two transfer windows stretching ahead for R and me to make hay. He'd struck a hard deal: all I got from everything I generated was twenty per cent, but as you'll have gathered by now, anything you get is better than the zero you have, so I didn't even try to negotiate on that.

R raised an eyebrow when I just accepted what he offered. 'I hope you haven't lost your old skills, and gone soft on me,' he said.

'Watch me,' I replied.

And I hadn't. The players were as good as gold, and I had to eat my words about their loyalty to me. I knew I'd done well for them, and they didn't seem to hold it against me that the FA had found me guilty regarding the player who had gone to Chairman K's club. He was known as a moaner in the game anyway, and the deal he'd got had hardly put him on the poverty line.

We were doing fine, R and me. He was still the best in the business, and after a week or two I kept asking myself why I'd left him in the first place. I answered myself by saying that I was younger then, more impatient and that I'd just not understood the game. The fact of the matter was that it wasn't football itself that was the game. It was being involved. What I did, what R did, what all the people I'd met along the way did off the pitch, that was our game. Not the beautiful one that the likes of Brazil and Spain play, but a brutal one, an unforgiving one, where losers tend not to get a second chance. Maybe in some way I had lost, but I couldn't admit defeat to myself. That was why I'd needed to get back into the game, where the regulators think they lay down the rules but where, in reality, there's only one rule: to make as much money as you can in the shortest time possible.

Did I still believe that? Was I still so arrogant as to make that my mantra? I really didn't know and with what happened next I doubted if I would have the time to find out.

At five a.m. one morning there was a knock at my door. I looked out the window and my stomach fell with the heaving sensation I used to get on seaside rollercoasters or the day before I had to go back to school after the summer holidays. It was the police, and they weren't the friendly neighbourhood type. They explained, politely, that they had a warrant for my arrest and a search warrant permitting them to remove my computer and any other papers or equipment they deemed necessary. Deep down inside I'd felt this might be coming. The Bribery Act had caught up with me. And that was what I was charged under, for all the payments I'd made for favours.

It was like my whole life flashing in front of me, as they say in the movies. Managers I'd accommodated, sports manufacturers, players' relations and last but by no means least, my old friend Chairman K.

Somehow, none of it had seemed wrong at the time. If what I'd done was criminal, then where were the victims lining up to accuse me? Where were those who had been defrauded or lost money? Already, in my mind, I was preparing my defence just as I was contemplating how to explain it all to my parents when my face was plastered across tomorrow's papers.

I just wanted to be rich – not famous and certainly not infamous. I wanted what they never had. Was that such a crime?

R came through again and bailed me out, even though there was a chance he'd now be in trouble if the FA saw anything on my computers they didn't like. I'd tried to be careful in my dealings with him, but had I been careful enough?

Fortunately, as far as R was concerned, I had been.

For a while I slumped into a depression, even thought of getting myself checked into the sort of clinics I had found for a few of my players in the past. I still had the phone numbers and knew the directors personally. There was one night where I tossed and turned for hours that I even thought about ending it all. But that was the nadir in my fortunes. I got my act together, I got myself a great lawyer, one who I had favoured during all the problems that beset my players and to be fair to him, he did it all for me at a knock down price. .

I had to be positive. The basic essential of any good agent is optimism and I'd always had it in spades. I was still alive, and as far as I was aware there wasn't a death penalty in the UK for the offences of which I'd been accused. I would work through this and find the solution. There always was one.

EPILOGUE

THANKFULLY, MY LAWYER was brilliant. I came across as more sinned against that sinning. A babe in the wood caught in a nightmare world of greedy monsters who had seized on the opportunity to use me for their evil, calculating ends.

I played the role to perfection – thanks to my barrister, who had rehearsed me in the part so well. As I stood in the dock at the end of my trial, I had managed to retain my self-confidence and, despite everything, my dignity. I was going to walk out of there and face the world.

I listened to my sentence respectfully. Yes, a jail sentence, but only twelve months and suspended; yes, community service, but only two hundred hours and that was during the day, so I could still work at nights; and yes, a fine, but R had promised to cover that from commissions that he would still pay me.

R took me for a coffee afterwards and he was obviously relieved that he had got out of the mess unscathed – unlike some of my other associates, who had also received similar sentences to me and were finished, at least for the moment, in the world of football. I realised that I couldn't carry on with R and this time we shook hands as we parted and he wished me luck.

I couldn't really afford it, but I decided to take a break. I couldn't recall the last holiday I'd had and one of my long-standing players had a holiday home in Spain and told me to stay there for as long as I wanted. I chilled out for the first month and then a plan began to form in my mind. I followed what was happening in what had been my world, who was in and who was out, who was up-and-coming and who was finished – both in terms of agents and players. I watched as the managerial merry-go-round went on its crazy way and then I decided to create a few targets and return to England.

It was much easier than I had expected. I wasn't going to steal any players from R this time but my loyal bunch soon found me a few likely lads who needed proper representation. Of course, I couldn't be seen to be doing it myself, but a couple of decent young agents, very un-J like, could see the advantages of fronting for me, particularly when I told them I only wanted forty per cent and they could have the rest.

So it was that within a few months I had a business again; although not one I could tell anybody about. I was doing what I had always done, looking after players, developing their careers, making money for them, myself and those around me. It felt good. And this did feel, at times, like something from a spy movie; because, after all, what was I but a secret agent?